W9-ANK-238

THE
CHEROKEE
NATION

The Seal of the Cherokee Nation. The seven pointed star in the center represents the seven Cherokee clans. It is surrounded by oak leaves. Oak was used in keeping the sacred fire in the townhouse. The Cherokee symbols following the words, "Seal of the Cherokee Nation," are pronounced "jalagihi ahyeli," and are translated, "The Cherokee Nation." The date, September 6, 1839, is the date of the adoption of the constitution of the Cherokee Nation at its new home in the west following the Trail of Tears. The seal was adopted by the Cherokee National Council and approved by Chief Lewis Downing on December 11, 1871. Courtesy of the Cherokee Nation.

THE
CHEROKEE
NATION
A HISTORY

ROBERT J. CONLEY

University of New Mexico Press
Albuquerque

09 08 07 06 05   1 2 3 4 5

Library of Congress Cataloging-in-Publication Data

Conley, Robert J.
  The Cherokee Nation : a history / Robert J. Conley.
      p. cm.
  Includes bibliographical references and index.
  ISBN 0-8263-3234-X (cloth : alk. paper)
  1. Cherokee Nation—History. 2. Cherokee Indians—History.
  3. Cherokee Indians—Government relations. 4. Cherokee Indians—
Social life and customs. I. Title.

  E99.C5C716 2005
  975.004'97557—dc22

                        2005006822

Book design and composition by Damien Shay
Body type is Utopia 9.5/13.
Display is Aquitaine Initials and Impact.

CHEROKEE HISTORICAL NOVELS
by Robert J. Conley

The Way of the Priests

The Dark Way

The White Path

The Way South

The Long Way Home

The Dark Island

The War Trail North

The Peace Chief

War Woman

Cherokee Dragon

Spanish Jack

Sequoyah

Captain Dutch

Mountain Windsong

Nickajack

Zeke Proctor: Cherokee Outlaw

Ned Christie's War

CONTENTS

ACKNOWLEDGMENTS   xiii

CHAPTER ONE   1
Theories and Legends
Source List and Suggestions for Further Reading   12
Glossary   13

CHAPTER TWO   17
Early Invasions
Source List and Suggestions for Further Reading   22
Glossary   23

CHAPTER THREE   25
Beginnings of Central Government
Source List and Suggestions for Further Reading   30
Glossary   30

CHAPTER FOUR   33
Visits Back and Forth
Glossary   37

CHAPTER FIVE   39
"What Nation or People Am I Afraid Of?"
Source List and Suggestions for Further Reading   42
Glossary   42

CHAPTER SIX   45
"Let Him be Wary."
Source List and Suggestions for Further Reading   50
Glossary   50

CHAPTER SEVEN 51
"President of the Nation"
 Source List and Suggestions for Further Reading 55
 Glossary 56

CHAPTER EIGHT 57
"I Have My Young Warriors around Me"
 Source List and Suggestions for Further Reading 61
 Glossary 61

CHAPTER NINE 63
"Our Cry Is All for Peace."
 Source List and Suggestions for Further Reading 70
 Glossary 70

CHAPTER TEN 73
"A Pipe and a Little Tobacco"
 Source List and Suggestions for Further Reading 79

CHAPTER ELEVEN 81
"Perpetual Friendship"
 Source List and Suggestions for Further Reading 85
 Glossary 86

CHAPTER TWELVE 87
Tecumseh and Red Eagle
 Source List and Suggestions for Further Reading 93
 Glossary 93

CHAPTER THIRTEEN 95
Five Treaties in Three Years
 Source List and Suggestions for Further Reading 100
 Glossary 101

CHAPTER FOURTEEN 103
Many Changes Taking Place
 Source List and Suggestions for Further Reading 106
 Glossary 107

CONTENTS

PHOTOS AND ILLUSTRATIONS   109

         Maps   109

         Chiefs   111

     Historical Plates   119

CHAPTER FIFTEEN   131

"The Cherokee are Not Foreigners"

     Source List and Suggestions for Further Reading   135

     Glossary   136

CHAPTER SIXTEEN   137

The Treaty of New Echota

     Source List and Suggestions for Further Reading   143

     Glossary   144

CHAPTER SEVENTEEN   145

"Living upon the Roots and Sap of Trees"

     Source List and Suggestions for Further Reading   151

     Glossary   152

CHAPTER EIGHTEEN   153

Hundreds of Babies Died

     Source List and Suggestions for Further Reading   157

     Glossary   157

CHAPTER NINETEEN   159

Killings on Both Sides

     Source List and Suggestions for Further Reading   165

     Glossary   165

CHAPTER TWENTY   167

The Golden Age

     Source List and Suggestions for Further Reading   170

     Glossary   171

CHAPTER TWENTY-ONE   173

Confederates and Pins

     Source List and Suggestions for Further Reading   177

     Glossary   177

CHAPTER TWENTY-TWO 179
Indian Territory
Source List and Suggestions for Further Reading 182
Glossary 182

CHAPTER TWENTY-THREE 183
Jurisdictional Confusion
Source List and Suggestions for Further Reading 190
Glossary 191

CHAPTER TWENTY-FOUR 193
The Dawes Commission and Redbird Smith
Source List and Suggestions for Further Reading 199
Glossary 199

CHAPTER TWENTY-FIVE 201
Oklahoma
Source List and Suggestions for Further Reading 205
Glossary 205

CHAPTER TWENTY-SIX 207
World War II
Source List and Suggestions for Further Reading 211
Glossary 211

CHAPTER TWENTY-SEVEN 213
Renaissance
Source List and Suggestions for Further Reading 217
Glossary 218

CHAPTER TWENTY-EIGHT 219
Self-Determination
Source List and Suggestions for Further Reading 222
Glossary 222

CHAPTER TWENTY-NINE 223
The First Woman Chief
Source List and Suggestions for Further Reading 227
Glossary 227

CHAPTER THIRTY   229
"What Do They Want with This Old Building?"
Source List and Suggestions for Further Reading   237
Glossary   237

CHAPTER THIRTY-ONE   239
"What Greater Gift Can We Give Our Children?"
Source List and Suggestions for Further Reading   242
Glossary   242

APPENDICES
Principal Chiefs of the Cherokee Nation   243
Chiefs of the Western Cherokees   246
Chiefs of the Texas Cherokees   247
The Confederate Cherokee Nation and Chief Stand Watie   247
Chiefs of the Eastern Band of Cherokee Indians   248
Chiefs of the United Keetoowah Band of Cherokee Indians   249
Cherokee Nation Treaties   249
Western Cherokee Treaties   251

INDEX   253

ACKNOWLEDGMENTS

The following people all graciously read the manuscript and provided comments and suggestions. I am grateful to them. Ray Fogelson, Rennard Strickland, Theda Purdue, Dan Littlefield, David Scott, Richard Allen, Wyman Kirk, John Ross, Duane King.

Mike Miller and Paulette Thomas worked on logistics and in collecting and documenting the illustrations, an often thankless job, but I do thank them.

Delores Sumner and her staff at the Special Collections Room in the John Vaughan Library, Northeastern State University, were a great help and, as always, are much appreciated.

My all too rare conversations with Tom Belt on Cherokee history and culture and language are always delightful and very informative.

The book would never have been written without Principal Chief Wilma Mankiller, Principal Chief Chad Smith, and Gloria Sly. The original contract with the Cherokee Nation came under the Mankiller administration. Chad Smith was tribal prosecutor, and Gloria Sly was head of the Cherokee Nation's Education Department. These three people, together, conceived the idea and approached me with it. Chief Smith and Gloria Sly have been with me on this project from the beginning to the end, and I am very much in their debt.

A project like this could not be done alone. If I have left out anyone, I apologize for it. This has been a long process.

CHAPTER ONE

Theories and Legends

Contemporary Cherokees are the descendants of a large and power-ful American Indian tribe that has existed since prehistory, further back than anyone can really say. No one knows for sure from whence the Cherokees originated. Many scholars still insist that all peoples native to the Americas came into America from Asia by way of the Bering Strait land bridge. They say that twelve thousand years ago, during the last ice age, there were no human beings in the Americas. Therefore, they say, there are no true natives of this land, only the earliest immigrants.

These earliest immigrants, they say, came down into North America from Asia across a land bridge that had formed during the ice age, link-ing the two continents. These people, they say, were simply wandering, i.e. nomadic, big-game hunters, and they were following the game. They apparently continued to follow it until they had spread out and covered two continents, North and South America, and as their population grew and they separated into different groups and eventually settled in differ-ent areas, slowly different languages and different cultures developed. That's the theory that is still widely accepted, and at least one Cherokee migration legend might be seen to support this theory. Told originally by a Cherokee to an Englishman named Alexander Long in 1717 in Carolina, the tale was published in "A Cherokee Migration Fragment" by Corkran (and quoted in Thornton's population history), and it runs partly as fol-lows. (The spelling has been modernized here and some few words pro-vided in brackets to clarify the sense.)

For our coming here, we know nothing but what was had
from our ancestors and has brought it down from generation to generation. The way is thus. [We] belonged to another land far distant from here, and the people increased and
multiplied so fast that the land could not hold them, so that
they were forced to separate and travel to look out for another country. They traveled so far that they came to another
country that was so cold. . . . Yet going still on, they came to
mountains of snow and ice. The priests held a council to
pass these mountains, and that they believed there was
warmer weather on the other side of those mountains
because it lay near the sun setting. [It] was believed by the
whole assembly we were the first to make [snowshoes] to
put on our old and young. [We} passed on our journey and
at last found [ourselves] so far gone over these mountains till
we lost sight of the same and went through darkness for a
good space, and then [saw] the sun again, and going on we
came to a country that could be inhabited. (Thornton, p. 6)

At least one scholar, Dr. Jeffrey Goodman, in his book *American
Genesis*, takes exception to that theory. As far as the Bering Strait migration theory is concerned, Goodman maintains that just the opposite
from the standard belief probably occurred. He says that Modern Man
existed in North America, specifically in what is now Southern California,
at least fifty thousand years ago, at a time when Europe and Asia were
still populated by Neanderthal Man.

He further speculates that there is no "missing link" between
Neanderthal Man and Modern Man, because the two were never linked
in the first place. The Bering Strait migration did take place, Goodman
says, but it involved the migration of Modern Man from America as he
moved north into Asia and then into Europe to displace the
Neanderthals. That too is a theory, and like the other, it is based on a
certain amount of evidence followed by speculation. One theory is perhaps as good as the other. And more recently, some scholars have begun
to argue that there could have been several, if not many migrations into
the Americas, from Asia and from islands in the Pacific Ocean.

And Vine Deloria, Jr., in his *Red Earth, White Lies* (Scribner, 1995),
says that some of his "history colleagues were beginning their courses on
American history with a mindless recitation of the Bering Strait theory. . . . Basically they were simply repeating scholarly folklore, since there
is, to my knowledge, no good source which articulates the theory in any

reasonable format. Indeed, this 'theory' has been around so long that people no longer feel they have to explain or defend it—they can merely refer to it." Later he says "The Bering Strait exists and existed only in the minds of scientists."

But if we choose to belabor the issue of the Bering Strait, there is yet a third possibility, one not often considered. If the land bridge was, as they say, a vast plain, is it not reasonable to assume that people lived on the plain, and that when the water level rose, the people were separated, some going north into Asia, some south into North America? Probably the argument over the land bridge will never be resolved, but from a Native American perspective, it is really not all that important anyway. It certainly never entered into any of the origin tales of the Cherokees. Here is the best known, collected by James Mooney in North Carolina between 1887 and 1890 and published by the Bureau of American Ethnology in 1900.

How the World Was Made

The earth is a great island floating in a sea of water, and suspended at each of the four cardinal points by a cord hanging down from the sky vault, which is of solid rock. When the world grows old and worn out, the people will die and the cords will break and let the earth sink down into the ocean, and all will be water again. The Indians are afraid of this.

When all was water the animals were above in Galun lati, beyond the arch; but it was very much crowded, and they were wanting more room. They wondered what was below the water, and at last Dayuni si, "Beaver's Grandchild," the little Water-beetle, offered to go and see if it could learn. It darted in every direction over the surface of the water, but could find no firm place to rest. Then it dived to the bottom and came up with some soft mud, which began to grow and spread on every side until it became the island which we call the earth. It was afterward fastened to the sky with four cords, but no one remembers who did this.

At first the earth was flat and very soft and wet. The animals were anxious to get down, and sent out different birds to see if it was yet dry, but they found no place to alight and came back again to Galun lati. At last it seemed to be time, and they sent out the Buzzard and told him to go and make ready for them. This was the Great Buzzard, the father of all the buzzards we see now.

He flew all over the earth, low down near the ground, and it was still soft. When he reached the Cherokee country, he was very tired, and his wings began to flap and strike the ground, and wherever they struck the earth there was a valley, and where they turned up again there was a mountain. When the animals above saw this, they were afraid that the whole world would be mountains, so they called him back, but the Cherokee country remains full of mountains to this day.

When the earth was dry and the animals came down, it was still dark, so they got the sun and set it in a track to go every day across the island from east to west, just overhead. It was too hot this way, and Tsiska gili, the Red Crawfish, had his shell scorched a bright red, so that his meat was spoiled; and the Cherokees do not eat it. The conjurers put the sun another hand-breadth higher in the air, bit it was still too hot. They raised it another time, and another, until it was seven handbreadths high and just under the sky arch. Then it was right, and they left it so. This is why the conjurers call the highest place Gulkwa gine Di galun latiyun, "the seventh height," because it is seven hand-breadths above the earth. Every day the sun goes along under this arch, and returns at night on the upper side to the starting place.

There is another world under this, and it is like ours in everything—animals, plants, and people—save that the seasons are different. The streams that come down from the mountains are the trails by which we reach this underworld, and the springs at their heads are the doorways by which we enter it, but to do this one must fast and go to water and have one of the underground people for a guide. We know that the seasons in the underworld are different from ours, because the water in the springs is always warmer in winter and cooler in summer than the outer air.

When the animals and plants were first made—we do not know by whom—they were told to watch and keep awake for seven nights, just as young men now fast and keep awake when they pray to their medicine. They tried to do this, and nearly all were awake through the first night, but the next night several dropped off to sleep, and the third night others were asleep, and then others, until, on the seventh night, of all the animals only the owl, the panther, and one or two more were still awake. To these were given the

power to see and to go about in the dark, and to make prey
of the birds and animals which must sleep at night. Of the
trees only the cedar, the pine, the spruce, the holly, and the
laurel were awake to the end, and to them it was given to be
always green and to be greatest for medicine, but to the others it was said: "Because you have not endured to the end
you shall lose your hair every winter."

Men came after the animals and plants. At first there
were only a brother and sister until he struck her with a fish
and told her to multiply, and so it was. In seven days a child
was born to her, and thereafter every seven days another,
and they increased very fast until there was danger that the
world could not keep them. Then it was made that a woman
should have only one child in a year, and it has been so ever
since. (pp. 239 ff.)

This tale would seem to constitute a claim that the Cherokees have
always been in the old Cherokee country in what is now the southeastern part of the United States.

Cherokees speak an Iroquoian language, their nearest linguistic relatives being the Iroquoian people from around the Great Lakes: Mohawks,
Oneidas, Senecas, Onondagas, and Cayugas. The Cherokees' neighbors in
the old southeast were mostly Muskogean speakers, though there were
also some Siouan, some Tunican, some Algonquian, and others.

For that reason, and because the Lenni Lenape, also known as the
Delaware, may have an ancient tale called "The Walam Olum" in which
they describe a war between themselves and the Cherokees, whom they
called "Talligewi," scholars maintain that the Cherokees lived in the
northeast and migrated south. (It should be mentioned here that some
scholars believe "The Walam Olum" to be a hoax.)

However another tale from the oral tradition comes from the
Nighthawk Keetoowah Cherokees of Oklahoma. As told by Levi Gritts, it
was published in *The Cherokee Nation News* in 1973, and it goes something like this.

A long time ago the Cherokees lived on an island off the coast of
South America. Then a time came when they were attacked by seventy
different tribes, and they fled the island, moving to the mainland. From
there they went farther inland and then turned north. They wandered
for a long time until they finally settled in what we know today as the old
Cherokee country, the contemporary southeastern United States. It is
interesting to note in connection with the Keetoowah tale that some

scholars also believe that the Cherokees originated in South America. They cite cultural evidence, particularly the Cherokee double-weave basket-making technique, a technique, they say, that is unique in North America to the Cherokees, but is fairly common in South America.

Combining the evidence of several of these tales and theories, it seems reasonable to say that the Cherokees likely came from South America and migrated north through Central America and Mexico, eventually stopping for a time in the northeast along with the other Iroquoian-speaking tribes there. (If we take into consideration the story from 1717, we might even say they migrated as far north as what is now Alaska before turning south and east again.) Then following a long period of warfare with those people and with the Delawares, they moved southward again, settling in "the old southeast."

At best, origins are obscure. We tend to believe what we want to believe. Often, it seems, even scientific-minded individuals work very hard to "prove" what they have already decided is the "truth." Let it suffice here to say that no one of the origin stories referred to above can be proved. Some are legends. Others are theories.

The first we know of Cherokee history, Cherokees were living in what is often referred to these days as the Old South, or the Deep South, or the southeastern part of the present United States. The vast Cherokee range of the time of the arrival of the Europeans and before encompassed all or parts of the present states of North and South Carolina, Kentucky, Virginia, West Virginia, Alabama, Georgia, and Tennessee. They lived in eighty or more towns or villages, each with its own autonomous government. A typical town probably had about 200 or 250 inhabitants. It had a Peace (or White) Chief and a War (or Red) Chief, and each chief had his councilors, probably one from each of the seven clans. There were probably also women's councils representing the seven clans and wielding a significant amount of political power.

We don't know exactly how these town governments were structured and how they worked. Early European observers, however, did eventually take note of the powers of the Cherokee women (something which they, of course, did not allow their own women), and wrote comments about it, such as "Among the Cherokees the women [*sic*] rules the roost," and "The Cherokees have a petticoat government."

The Peace Chief was in charge of domestic issues and the ceremonial life of the town. The War Chief was charged with matters involving outsiders, not just war, but negotiations, alliances, trade, and other external matters. But many things that we today consider governmental matters were then matters for the clans. The clans were all important. First of all, the clan was the family. The Cherokee clan is a matrilineal clan. That means that descent is traced only through the female line. If a woman belongs to the Bird Clan, for example, then so do all of her children.

But clans were also responsible for righting any wrongs done to clan members by members of other clans. In other words, they had certain rights or responsibilities that we today would consider police or court functions. For instance, if a member of the Bird Clan killed a member of the Wolf Clan, then Wolf Clan members not only could but would be expected to kill a Bird Clan member in exchange, or to exact some other kind of retribution.

The worldview of the early Cherokees, who called themselves Ani-yunwi-ya (the Real People) or sometimes Ani-Keetuwahgi (People of Keetoowah), described three worlds. There was the world on top of the Sky Vault, and there was a world underneath the one on which we live. Both the world above and the world below were populated by powerful spiritual beings, and those two spiritual worlds were opposed to one another. The world we live on was thus seen to have been placed in a very dangerous position, and the most important thing for us to do was to maintain the proper balance between the two opposing forces above and below us.

Balance and harmony and purity were therefore all important aspects of the old religion, and there was a rich ceremonial life to help achieve those ends. An annual cycle of seven major ceremonies was performed over and over again, and there were special ceremonies performed when events called for them. For example, if a person dreamed of eagles, he was required to sponsor an eagle dance. In addition to the busy ceremonial cycle, daily life was full of little ritualistic observances that every individual had to be aware of constantly.

The early Cherokees were also farmers and hunters, and both of these activities were closely associated with the ceremonial cycle. Hunting was primarily a male activity, and the main animal hunted was the deer. There was an annual buffalo hunt (though the eastern buffalo had become scarce by 1775, according to Adair), and other, smaller, animals were also hunted and used for food and other things. A hunter was required to follow certain prescribed rituals, and to apologize to the spirit of the animal he killed. This practice is explained, along with several other things, in the following tale recorded by Mooney (1900).

Origin of Disease and Medicine
In the old days the beasts, birds, fishes, insects, and plants could all talk, and they and the people lived together in

peace and friendship. But as time went on the people
increased so rapidly that their settlements spread over the
whole earth, and the poor animals found themselves beginning to be cramped for room. This was bad enough, but to
make it worse, Man invented bows, knives, blowguns,
spears, and hooks, and began to slaughter the larger animals, birds, and fishes for their flesh or their skins, while the
smaller creatures, such as the frogs and worms, were
crushed and trodden upon without thought, out of pure
carelessness or contempt. So the animals decided to consult
upon measures for their common safety.

The Bears were the first to meet in council in their
townhouse under Kuwa'hi mountain, the "Mulberry Place,"
and the old White Bear Chief presided. After each in turn
had complained of the way in which Man killed their
friends, ate their flesh, and used their skins for his own purposes, it was decided to begin war at once against him.
Someone asked what weapons Man used to destroy them.
"Bow and arrows, of course," cried all the Bears in chorus.
"And what are they made of?" was the next question. "The
bow of wood, and the string of our entrails," replied one of
the Bears. It was then proposed that they make a bow and
some arrows and see if they could not use the same
weapons against Man himself. So one Bear got a nice piece
of locust wood and another sacrificed himself for the good
of the rest in order to furnish a piece of his entrails for the
string. But when everything was ready and the first Bear
stepped up to make the trial, it was found that in letting the
arrow fly after drawing back the bow, his long claws caught
the string and spoiled the shot. This was annoying, but
someone suggested that they might trim his claws, which
was accordingly done, and on a second trial it was found
that the arrow went straight to the mark. But here the chief,
the old White Bear, objected, saying it was necessary that
they should have long claws in order to be able to climb
trees. "One of us has already died to furnish the bowstring,
and if we now cut off our claws we must all starve together.
It is better to trust to the teeth and claws that nature gave us,
for it is plain that man's weapons were not intended for us."

No one could think of any better plan, so the old chief
dismissed the council and the Bears dispersed to the woods

and thickets without having concerted any way to prevent
the increase of the human race. Had the result of the council
been otherwise, we should now be at war with the Bears, but
as it is, the hunter does not even ask the Bear's pardon when
he kills one.

The Deer next held a council under their chief, the
Little Deer, and after some talk decided to send rheumatism
to every hunter who should kill one of them unless he took
care to ask their pardon for the offense. They sent notice of
their decision to the nearest settlement of Indians and told
them at the same time what to do when necessity forced
them to kill one of the Deer tribe. Now, whenever the hunter
shoots a Deer, the Little Deer, who is swift as the wind and
cannot be wounded, runs quickly up to the spot and, bend-
ing over the blood-stains, asks the spirit of the Deer if it has
heard the prayer of the hunter for pardon. If the reply be
"Yes," all is well, and the Little Deer goes his way; but if the
reply be "No," he follows on the trail of the hunter, guided by
the drops of blood on the ground, until he arrives at his
cabin in the settlement, when the Little Deer enters invisibly
and strikes the hunter with rheumatism, so that he becomes
at once a helpless cripple. No hunter who has regard for his
health ever fails to ask pardon of the Deer for killing it,
although some hunters who have not learned the prayer
may try to turn aside the Little Deer from his pursuit by
building a fire behind them in the trail.

Next came the Fishes and Reptiles, who had their own
complaints against Man. They held their council together
and determined to make their victims dream of snakes twin-
ing about them in slimy folds and blowing foul breath in
their faces, or to make them dream of eating raw or decaying
fish, so that they would lose appetite, sicken, and die. This is
why people dream about snakes and fish.

Finally the Birds, Insects, and smaller animals came
together for the same purpose, and the Grubworm was chief
of the council. It was decided that each in turn should give
an opinion, and then they should vote on the question as to
whether or not Man was guilty. Seven votes should be
enough to condemn him. One after another denounced
Man's cruelty and injustice toward the other animals and
voted in favor of his death. The Frog spoke first, saying:

"We must do something to check the increase of the race, or people will become so numerous that we shall be crowded from off the earth. See how they have kicked me about because I'm ugly, as they say, until my back is covered with sores;" and here he showed the spots on his skin. Next came the Bird—no one remembers now which one it was—who condemned Man "because he burns my feet off," meaning the way in which the hunter barbecues birds by impaling them on a stick set over the fire, so that their feathers and tender feet are singed off. Others followed in the same strain. The Ground-squirrel alone ventured to say a good word for Man, who seldom hurt him because he was so small, but this made the others so angry that they fell upon the Ground-squirrel and tore him with their claws, and the stripes are on his back to this day.

They began then to devise and name so many new diseases, one after another, that had not their invention at last failed them, no one of the human race would have been able to survive. The Grubworm grew constantly more pleased as the name of each was called off, until at last they reached the end of the list, when someone proposed to make menstruation sometimes fatal to women. On this he rose up in his place and cried: "Wadan! [Thanks!] I'm glad some more of them will die, for they are getting so thick that they tread on me." The thought fairly made him shake with joy, so that he fell over backward and could not get on his feet again, but had to wriggle off on his back, as the Grubworm has done ever since.

When the Plants, who were friendly to Man, heard what had been done by the animals, they determined to defeat the latters' evil designs. Each Tree, Shrub, and Herb, down even to the Grasses and Mosses, agreed to furnish a cure for some one of the diseases named, and each said: "I shall appear to help Man when he calls upon me in his need." Thus came medicine; and the plants, every one of which has its use if we only knew it, furnish the remedy to counteract the evil wrought by the revengeful animals. Even weeds were made for some good purpose, which we must find out for ourselves. When the doctor does not know what medicine to use for a sick man the spirit of the plant tells him. (pp. 250 ff.)

The women were primarily responsible for the farms and gardens, but then, they owned the farms and gardens, as well as the houses. And they grew a tremendous variety of food crops: corn, squash, pumpkins, several varieties of beans. In addition they harvested various plant foods that grew wild: berries, nuts, mushrooms, wild greens.

War was also for the most part a seasonal activity, and like other activities, it involved a great deal of ritual and ceremony. And the Cherokees were much involved with war against many of their neighboring tribes and with some who lived off quite a distance. They fought with the Creeks, the Choctaws, the Chickasaws, the Shawnees, the Delawares, and even with members of the Iroquois Confederacy (Mohawk, Seneca, Oneida, Onondaga, Cayuga) who lived far to the north, and who are, at least theoretically, their relatives.

Each Cherokee town was autonomous in those days. Each town had its own government and was not tied to the government of the other towns in any way. In other words, in those days, there was no Cherokee Nation as we know it today. There were simply many Cherokee towns. Perhaps we could say (ignoring anthropological definitions) that there was a Cherokee tribe, in that all of the Cherokee towns were populated by people who spoke the same language, followed the same ceremonial life, and shared the same seven clans, so that, in theory at least, every individual Cherokee had relatives in every Cherokee town.

According to a tale told to Mooney, and recorded in his *Myths of the Cherokee* as "The Massacre of the Ani-Kutani," there was once a time when the Cherokees did have a central government, a government of priests. These priests, called the Ani-Kutani, became all powerful and eventually began to abuse their powers. One day a hunter came home, and he could not find his wife. After he had asked around for a time, one of his neighbors at last told him that while he was out hunting, the priests had come and taken her away.

The hunter organized his friends and neighbors and convinced them that they had put up with the abusive priests for too long. They revolted and killed all of the priests. After that each town became autonomous. Each town government was democratic. There were no hereditary leaders, and there were no rulers. There was no central government (pp. 392 ff.).

We don't know when this event occurred. Some scholars even take the tale to be a dramatic illustration of changes that actually took place over an extended period of time. We do know that the Cherokees would not have a central government again until after the arrival of the Europeans, when the Cherokee Nation evolved in reaction to new circumstances and new needs.

Much has been glossed over in this introductory chapter, for this book is presented as a history, and therefore neither time nor space is devoted to detailed discussions of prehistory, ceremonial life, myths and legends, government, clan structure and other ethnological kinds of material. Interested readers are encouraged, however, to examine the combined source and further reading list that follows this chapter. Each successive chapter will conclude with such a list, adding only new titles relevant to that chapter.

SOURCE LIST AND SUGGESTIONS FOR FURTHER READING

Adair, James. 1930. *Adair's History of the American* Indians, ed. Samuel Cole Williams. Johnson City, Tenn.: The Watauga Press. Reprinted, New York: Johnson Reprint, 1969.

Brinton, Daniel G. 1885. *The Lenape and Their Legends*. Philadelphia: Library of American Aboriginal Literature, vol. 5. ("The Walam Olum or Red Score" in this book has been reprinted, among other places, in A. Grove Day, 1964, *The Sky Clears*, Lincoln: University of Nebraska Press.)

Collier, Peter. 1973. *When Shall They Rest? The Cherokees' Long Struggle with America*. New York: Holt, Rinehart and Winston.

Corkran, David H. 1952. "A Cherokee Migration Fragment." *Southern Indian Studies* 4:27–28. (Also in Thornton, below.)

Deloria, Vine, Jr. 1995. *Red Earth, White Lies*. New York: Scribners.

Feeling, Durbin. 1975. *Cherokee-English Dictionary*, ed. William Pulte. Tahlequah: The Cherokee Nation.

Fogelson, Raymond D. 1978. *The Cherokees: A Critical Bibliography*. Bloomington: Indiana University Press. (Any serious scholar will want to make use of this very thorough listing of Cherokee materials.)

Goodman, Jeffrey. 1981. *American Genesis*. New York: Summit Books.

Gritts, Levi. 1973 "The Legend of Keetoowah," quoted in John D. Gillespie, "The Organization of the Nighthawk Keetoowahs among the Cherokees." *The Cherokee Nation News*, Tahlequah, July 17.

Hudson, Charles. 1977. *The Southeastern Indians*. Knoxville: University of Tennessee Press.

Kilpatrick, Jack Frederick, and Anna Gritts Kilpatrick. 1965. *Walk in Your Soul*. Dallas: Southern Methodist University Press.

———. 1967. *Run toward the Nightland*. Dallas: Southern Methodist University Press.

Maxwell, James A., ed. 1978. *America's Fascinating Indian Heritage*.

Pleasantville, N.Y.: The Reader's Digest Association. (This book and a dozen or so similar generic American Indian "coffee table" books repeat as fact the Bering Strait migration theory.)

Mooney, James. 1891. "The Sacred Formulas of the Cherokees." Smithsonian Institution, Bureau of American Ethnology, *Seventh Annual Report, 1885-1886*, pp. 301–97, Washington, D.C.: U.S. Government Printing Office.

———. 1900. "Myths of the Cherokees." Smithsonian Institution, Bureau of American Ethnology, *Nineteenth Annual Report, 1897–98*, Part I, pp. 3–576. Washington, D.C.: U.S. Government Printing Office. (This work and the Mooney listed above have been reprinted several times by different publishers, often in one volume. One example is *Myths of the Cherokees and Sacred Formulas of the Cherokees* by James Mooney, Cherokee Heritage Books, Cherokee, N.C., 1982.)

Reid, John Phillip. 1970. *A Law of Blood: The Primitive Law of the Cherokee Nation*. New York: New York University Press.

Speck, Frank G., and Leonard Broom. 1951. *Cherokee Dance and Drama*. Berkeley: University of California Press.

Strickland, Rennard. 1975. *Fire and the Spirits: Cherokee Law from Clan to Court*. Norman: University of Oklahoma Press.

Terrell, John Upton. 1971. *American Indian Almanac*. New York: The World Publishing Company.

Thornton, Russell. 1990. *The Cherokees: A Population History*. Lincoln: University of Nebraska Press.

Woodward, Grace Steele. 1963. *The Cherokees*. Norman: University of Oklahoma Press. (This widely read book has been a standard Cherokee history since its publication. Unfortunately, its tone is set with its first sentence: "The emergence of any primitive Indian tribe or nation from dark savagery into the sunlight of civilization is a significant event.")

GLOSSARY

Algonquian. An American Indian language family. It includes the Delaware, Massachuset, Nipmuc, Wampanoag, Narragansett, Pequot, Mahican, and other languages.

Ani-Keetoowahgi (or Ani-Kituwagi). A name the Cherokees called themselves (and sometimes still do), it means Keetoowah People. "Ani" is a plural prefix. Keetoowah was an ancient town, said to be the "Mother Town" of the Cherokees. The word "Keetoowah" or "Kituwah" can no longer be translated.

Ani-Kutani. The ancient Cherokee priesthood, killed off in a rebellion. "Ani" is
the plural prefix. "Kutani" cannot be translated, but a Kutani was a priest.

Ani-yunwi-ya. The Real People. What the Cherokees used to commonly call
themselves. It has come to mean "Indians" in the contemporary
Cherokee language. "Ani" is the plural prefix. "Yunwi" is a person. "Ya" is
an intensive, usually translated "real" or "original."

Autonomous. Independent, self governing.

Ayunini. Swimmer. Literally, "he is swimming (the way a snake swims)." A well
known and influential Cherokee "Indian doctor" (or medicine man)
from the reservation in North Carolina. One of the main informants of
ethnologist James Mooney.

Bering Strait. The narrow passage of water between Alaska and Asia connect-
ing the Bering Sea and the Arctic Ocean.

Bering Strait land bridge. The vast prairie that appeared during the last ice
age, about twelve thousand years ago, when the water level in the Bering
Strait dropped. The land bridge connected Asia and North America and
made it possible to walk across from one continent to the other.

Bureau of American Ethnology. A United States government bureau that
existed from 1879 to 1965 with the purpose of recording information
about American Indian tribes. It was eventually absorbed by the
Smithsonian Institute.

Cherokee. A word that apparently was imposed on the Cherokees from outside, possibly of Choctaw origin, possibly meaning "Cave People."
Cherokees eventually came to accept it, adopting it into the Cherokee
language in the form of "Tsalagi."

Cherokee Nation News. The official newspaper of the Cherokee Nation from
1968 to 1977. The current official newspaper is *The Cherokee Phoenix*.

Chickasaw. A Muskogean-speaking southeastern Indian tribe closely related
to the Choctaws. They lived in what is now Mississippi and Alabama.

Choctaw. Muskogean speakers, closely related to the Chickasaws and living
near them.

Clan. A clan is a family unit in which the individual traces his or her descent
only through one parent. There are matrilineal clans and patrilineal
clans. Cherokee clans are matrilineal, with a child belonging to its
mother's clan and tracing descent through the female line. There are
seven Cherokee clans: Ani-waya (Wolf), Ani-kawi (Deer), Ani-tsisqua
(Bird), Ani-wodi (Paint), Ani-sahoni, Ani-gatagewi, Ani-gilohi.
Translations of the last three are somewhat controversial. Ani-sahoni is
usually translated "Blue." The Kilpatricks claim that it is actually the
name of a "large extinct feline." Ani-gatagewi has been called the "Blind
Savannah" and "Wild Potato." Mooney says that the name cannot be

translated. And Ani-gilohi is most often designated either "Twisters" or "Long Hairs." The Kilpatricks maintain that it is actually "They just became offended."

Creek. A large and powerful southeastern tribe. Their name for themselves is Muskogee or Muscogee, and that name has also been given to the language family to which their language belongs. They were also the principal member of a confederacy of southeastern tribes which included the Hitchiti, Yuchi, Okmulgee, Alabama, Koasati, Tuskegee, and others. This confederacy was known as the Creek or Muskogee Confederacy.

Dayunisi. The Cherokee name of a type of water beetle. Mooney gives "beaver's grandchild" as the translation.

Delaware. From Lord De La Warr, title of Thomas West, governor of the colony of Virginia. The people called Delaware call themselves Lenni Lenape. See below.

Galun lati. Above or on high.

Gulkwa gine Di galun latiyun. Seventh (from Gulkwagi, or seven) and a height, one of a series.

Iroquoian. An American Indian language family. It includes Cherokee, Mohawk, Seneca, Cayuga, Oneida, Onondaga, Tuscarora, and other languages.

Iroquois Confederacy. Also known as the League of Five Nations, or the Iroquois League. The confederacy was made up originally of the Mohawk, Oneida, Onondaga, Seneca, and Cayuga tribes, all speakers of Iroquoian languages. Later it was joined by the Tuscaroras and became known as the League of Six Nations. A confederacy is a loose union of nations.

Kuwa'hi. Mulberry Place, from kuwa, mulberry tree, and hi, locative. It is called Clingman's Dome in English today.

Language family. A group of related languages. They are similar enough to one another that linguists believe they all came from one original language long ago. As an example, both English and German are members of the Germanic language family.

Lenni Lenape. True Men or Real Men. The American Indian tribe commonly called Delaware. They originally lived in what is now New York and New Jersey and parts of what is now Pennsylvania and Delaware. They speak an Algonquian language.

Missing link. A hypothetical primate forming an evolutionary link between Neanderthal Man and Modern Man.

Modern Man. Man as he exists today.

Muskogean. A language family. It includes the Muskogean or Creek language, Choctaw, Chickasaw, Alabama, Cusabo, and others.

Neanderthal. A type of early man that existed in Europe and western and central Asia.

Nighthawk Keetoowah. The Keetoowah Society and the Nighthawk Keetoowah Society which developed from it are Cherokee traditionalist organizations, dedicated to Cherokee nationalism and to preserving Cherokee culture.

Prehistory. That time before anyone was writing, or before anyone was recording history.

Shawnee. A relatively small but very influential tribe of American Indians. They lived in earliest times in what is now Ohio but ranged widely throughout the midwest and the east. Their language is Algonquian.

Siouan. The name of a linguistic family. It includes the languages of the Lakota, Dakota, Nakota (Sioux) people, as well as Assiniboine, Crow, Hidatsa, Mandan, Omaha, Ponca, Kansa, Quapaw, Winnebago, and others. In the old southeast, the Catawba, Congaree, Peedee, Santee, Waccamaw, and others spoke Siouan languages.

Talligewi. A Delaware name for the Cherokees.

Tsiska gili. Large, red crawfish.

Tunican. A southeastern language family consisting of the Tunica, Koroa, and Yazoo languages. The tribes speaking these languages lived in the present states of Mississippi and Louisiana.

Wadan. More commonly, wado. Thank you.

Walam Olum. A historical account of the Delawares, written in petroglyphs on bark sheets, it was translated and printed in 1836. The Delaware words mean "printed tally" or "red score." "Walam" means "painted," particularly "painted red." "Olum" means "score" or "tally."

Worldview. A term much used by anthropologists and ethnologists, it encompasses the entire way in which a people view themselves and their place in the universe.

CHAPTER TWO

Early Invasions

When the Spaniards of the Hernando De Soto expedition went through the southeast in 1540, they reported seeing temples and mounds, and rulers they called "emperors" and "queens" who were carried around by their "subjects" on litter chairs. They also reported a densely populated region with roads that led to many towns. There is no specific description of Cherokees or of any Cherokee town in the chronicles, although the De Soto expedition seems to have visited a little in Cherokee country. But given the nature of the southeast at that time, the story of "The Massacre of the Ani-Kutani," and other tales also collected by Mooney, which make references to old Cherokee mounds, it seems reasonable to assume that the Cherokees were probably a mound-building theocracy at least into the early part of the 1500s. Then the theocracy was destroyed, as reported in the tale. (Some say the Cherokees were never Mound Builders, but instead replaced the Mound Builders when they moved into the southeast.)

With the destruction of the Ani-Kutani, the Cherokees gained a democracy and freedom from the tyranny of the priests, but in so doing, they must also have undergone a tremendous cultural change. (According to the same Cherokee who told the migration story to Alexander Long in 1717 [quoted in Chapter 1], "we are told by our ancestors that when we first came on this land that the priests and beloved men was [*sic*] writing but not on paper as you do but on white deer skins and on the shoulder bones of buffalo" [Corkran, p. 6].) Then, perhaps on the heels of this event, the Europeans began to arrive on American shores. According to Francis

Jennings, in his book *The Invasion of America*, between 1492, when Columbus's boats landed, and 1607, the date of the founding of the colony of Jamestown, 90 percent of the native population of North America died as a result of European diseases (pp. 22 ff.). Surely the Cherokees did not escape this scourge, and if they did not, then in addition to the misery of the plague and the resulting deaths, there had to have been once again a great change. Changes in culture come about in many different ways.

When our standard history books tell us about the early Spanish explorers in America, they are really talking about roving bands of ruffians, murderers, and thieves, operating with the blessing of their monarch back in Spain. De Soto was one of the worst. In 1593, he landed on the west coast of Florida with somewhere between five and seven hundred "soldiers," some mounted and some on foot, and a herd of a few hundred pigs. He began what was to become a three-year expedition into the country that is now the southeastern part of the United States. It was to be his last expedition, for he died before it was completed.

From Florida, De Soto and his men traveled through what is now Georgia, Alabama, Mississippi, Tennessee, Arkansas, Oklahoma, and then back to Mississippi, where De Soto died and his body was dumped unceremoniously into the Mississippi River. The survivors straggled through what is now Texas and finally on down into Mexico. But along the way on their relentless search for gold, the bloodthirsty Spaniards enslaved, tortured, and killed hundreds, even thousands of Indians. They would stop at a town and ask the chief for gold. If he did not give them any or did not tell them where to find it, they might kill him, or kill thirty, or kill two hundred.

Sometimes they demanded slaves from the local population, both men and women, and if their demand was not satisfied willingly, they resorted to the same tactics they employed when asking for gold. Sometimes they just grabbed the chief and held him hostage, threatening to kill him if the people refused to cooperate with them. One of their favorite methods of "punishing" an uncooperative Indian was to turn loose their big dogs to rip the person to death.

Considering the three years of devastation and horror inflicted on the southeast by De Soto and his followers, it is remarkable that the Cherokees suffered little at their hands. It seems that the Spaniards may have actually stopped at perhaps three different Cherokee towns where they were cordially received and given food, and then went on their way without causing any serious problems.

We could say that the Cherokees were lucky. We could say further that the Cherokees must have known how lucky they were, for they could not have been ignorant of the bloody trail the Spaniards had left behind them. So while the Cherokees apparently did not suffer directly at the hands of the Spaniards of the De Soto expedition, they must have been affected by it at least indirectly in profound ways, even though it would be extremely difficult to specify just what those ways might have been.

Though apparently untouched (or nearly untouched) themselves, the whole land south of them, an area in which they were used to traveling and trading and dealing with neighbor tribes, had been utterly changed from what it had been before. Cherokee lives must have been also changed by that brutal fact.

Finally, it is surely safe to say that because of the De Soto expedition, the Cherokees must have been painfully aware of the fact that there were new forces in their world, forces of which they had never before been aware, that they had not known even existed, but nevertheless, forces with which they would have to deal in the future. They had to have learned that their children and grandchildren would face dangers that they had never before even imagined. They had to have known, in other words, that the world as they had always known it had suddenly become a thing of the past.

In 1561, the Spaniards returned. They took possession of the Bay of Santa Elena on the coast of what is now South Carolina. Then came the French, and they attempted to settle the same area in 1562. As a result, the Spanish established a fort there that they named San Felipe. In 1566, Juan Pardo led an expedition out from San Felipe to explore the interior. In the country of the Sara Indians (also known as Cheraw, a Siouan-speaking tribe), in what is now North Carolina, Pardo built a fort, but because of snow in the mountains, he went no farther. Had he continued on, he would undoubtedly have gotten into the Cherokee country. Pardo left a sergeant and thirty soldiers at the fort and returned to San Felipe.

The sergeant sent letters back to San Felipe in which he claimed to have fought and won some battles with Indians with overwhelming, in fact unbelievable, odds against him. (With only fifteen soldiers, he claimed to have slaughtered one thousand Indian men.) The victories he claimed may have been against Cherokee towns, but then, the fights probably never even took place. Receiving orders back from Pardo, the sergeant led his men into the country of the Creeks, where he built another small fort and waited for Pardo, who arrived there in 1567. From there the Pardo expedition visited a number of Creek towns and possibly some Cherokee towns, apparently with no untoward incidents.

Perhaps Pardo and other Spaniards had learned a lesson from the disastrous De Soto expedition and behaved more in the way visitors should behave. If so, perhaps they got much further with friendly manners than

De Soto ever did with his brutality. According to Mooney and other chron-iclers, there is physical evidence of Spanish mining operations in the Cherokee country, although there are no written records of such activity. We can only speculate, but perhaps Pardo got on well enough with the Cherokees to have received permission to mine for gold.

We can assume, though, that during this period the Cherokees must have become familiar with the Spaniards. Perhaps they engaged in some kinds of negotiations with them. They must have done some trading, and it is therefore likely that the Cherokees first became familiar with at least some European trade goods at this time. They also learned during this time that the Spaniards were not the only strangers to come into the land, were not the only white men, for the French had also come around. And the Cherokees must have learned from either the Spanish or the French, or both, that the two different types of Europeans did not get along with one another. They may even have heard about the English during this time, although they would not actually meet any English for some time yet.

In 1607 the first permanent English colony in America was established at Jamestown, Virginia. Their immediate Indian neighbors were the mem-ber tribes of the powerful Powhatan Confederacy. The actual Powhatan tribe was small, but it was the leading member of the confederacy of thir-ty or so tribes that also bore its name. Some of the other member tribes of the confederacy were Appomattoc, Chesapeake, Chickahominy, Pamunkey, and Potomac. The Powhatans were Algonquian speakers. At first the colonists at Jamestown got along well with the Powhatans. They had to. They would never have survived their first hard winter without the friend-ly help of their Indian neighbors. One of the members of the colony, John Rolfe, even married a daughter of the chief. Her name was Pocahontas.

Over the next few years, two things happened to change the friend-ly relations between the Jamestown colonists and the Powhatans. With the help of the Powhatans, the colonists became stronger. Thanks to the Powhatans, they had learned to live in the new land, and they no longer needed to be friendly. They had also learned about tobacco from the Powhatans. They had not only learned to enjoy its use, but they had also discovered its tremendous commercial value, and they had begun culti-vating it as a cash crop for export back to England. They needed more cleared land for growing tobacco, and rather than clear woodland, they coveted the already cleared fields of the Powhatan Indians, and they pressed for that land, pushing the Powhatans back a little at a time.

In 1622, the Powhatans finally struck back and in one day killed 350 Englishmen and burned a number of settlements. The English respond-ed with an attitude of total war, and by the late 1640s had utterly destroyed the once powerful confederacy. Those tribes that remained in the area did so as subject tribes to the Jamestown colony.

In 1654, with much of Powhatan land having been vacated, six or seven hundred Cherokees established a town at the falls of the James River on the site now occupied by Richmond, Virginia. The Jamestown colonists, having but recently concluded their bloody war against the Powhatans, were alarmed and enraged. They resolved in assembly "that these new come Indians be in no sort suffered to seat themselves there, or any place near us, it having cost so much blood to expel and extirpate those perfidious and treacherous Indians which were there formerly."

They raised a force of one hundred Englishmen and called on their recently subjected Indian neighbors to add their numbers to it. The Pamunkeys sent one hundred men, and the combined force marched against the newly established Cherokee town. They were soundly defeated by the Cherokees. Most of the Pamunkeys were killed, and the English surrendered, agreeing to humiliating terms of peace. Back in Jamestown, the colonial government was furious. They removed their militia commander from his post and forced him to pay the expenses of the treaty himself. There are no further records of the Cherokee town at the falls of the James River, but the episode is the first known encounter of the Cherokees with the English (Mooney, 1900, pp. 29–30).

Details are scant for the next sixteen years, but various European traders were active in the area, so much so that Mooney says that by 1670, all the tribes in the area were in possession of firearms. That was also the year of the establishment of the first permanent English settlement in South Carolina.

Englishmen first visited Cherokee country in 1673. Abraham Wood was a trader at Fort Henry (now Petersburg), Virginia. He wanted access to the Cherokee trade goods (especially pelts, beeswax, and bears' oil) for shipment back to England. In an attempt to open up trade between the Cherokees and Virginia, Wood sent James Needham and Gabriel Arthur, accompanied by a group of Oconeechee Indians and a translator known as "Indian John," to the Cherokee town of Chota on the Little Tennessee River.

There were some Weesock Indians living at Chota with the Cherokees, and the Oconeechees and Weesocks got along well with each other. Needham and Arthur made friends with the chief of Chota, whose name was not recorded, and Needham headed back to Fort Henry, accompanied by Indian John, the Oconeechees, and a few Cherokees from Chota, to load up on trade goods. Arthur stayed behind to learn the Cherokee language. Everything seemed to be working out well.

On his return trip, loaded up with guns, axes, steel tomahawks, beads, cloth, and other trade goods, Needham was murdered along the way by

Indian John. Indian John then told the Cherokees to go back to Chota and tell the people there to kill Arthur. When the Cherokees arrived back at Chota, the chief was away. They delivered Indian John's message to the people, and the Weesocks there tied Arthur to a stake and piled dry brush and cane around him. Before they could light the fire, the chief returned. He was carrying a rifle over his shoulder.

When he saw what was about to happen, the chief ran to the stake and demanded to know who it was that intended to put fire to Gabriel Arthur. A Weesock stepped forward and said, "That am I." The chief cocked his gun and shot the Weesock dead. Then he cut Arthur loose and told him to go to his house.

Gabriel Arthur stayed at Chota for nearly a year, during which time he lived as a Cherokee and even went along with Cherokee warriors on raids. Once he was captured by Shawnees, but when they discovered that he was a white man, they released him, allowing him to return to Chota. Finally, some Cherokees from Chota made the trip back to Fort Henry with Arthur, and his long adventure was over (Woodward, pp. 27–30).

Two things of note occurred in 1690. James Moore, from the South Carolina colony, made an expedition into the mountains. According to his native guides, at one point on this trip he was within twenty miles of a place where the Spaniards were still engaged in mining gold. He never actually visited the spot. 1690 was also the year in which "Cornelius Dougherty, an Irishman from Virginia, established himself as the first trader among the Cherokee, with whom he spent the rest of his life" (Mooney, 1900, p. 31).

SOURCE LIST AND SUGGESTIONS FOR FURTHER READING

Bourne, Edward Gaylord, ed. 1904. *Narratives of the Career of Hernando de Soto*. 2 vols. New York.

Hoig, Stanley W. 1998. *The Cherokees and Their Chiefs in the Wake of Empire*. Fayetteville: The University of Arkansas Press.

Jennings, Francis. 1975. *The Invasion of America*. University of North Carolina Press. Reprinted, New York: W. W. Norton Co., 1976.

GLOSSARY

Jamestown. The first permanent English settlement in North America, established in east Virginia in 1607.

Mounds. Manmade elevations of earth. Mounds were constructed by American Indians for a variety of reasons. There are temple mounds, which seem to exist only to raise the elevation of the temples that were built on top of them. There are burial mounds, and there are effigy mounds, such as the so-called Great Serpent Mound in Ohio, which are thought to have some religious significance.

Mound Builders. For a long time, scholars believed in a race of "Mound Builders" who had mysteriously disappeared. Indians knew better all along, and the scholars are now beginning to understand that many American Indian tribes once built mounds, but most of them had abandoned the practice by historic times. For example, the Cherokees, under the rule of the Ani-Kutani, almost certainly built mounds, and they probably abandoned the practice after the rule of the Ani-Kutani was overthrown.

Oconeechee. A Siouan-speaking tribe located in Virginia. According to Terrell, their remnants may have been absorbed by the Saponi and Tutelo tribes.

Pamunkey. At one time a member tribe of the Algonquian-speaking Powhatan Confederacy.

Powhatan. The name of a small Indian tribe and of the confederacy of which it was the dominant member. It was also apparently the name of the town in which the chief of the confederacy lived. His name was Wahunsonacock, but the Jamestown colonists apparently despaired of pronouncing it. They called him Powhatan, and many of our history books have followed the same practice. He was the father of Pocahontas.

Powhatan Confederacy. Thirty or so small Algonquian-speaking tribes living in the area of Virginia loosely united under one government. Until their strength was broken by the Jamestown colonists in the 1600s, they were a powerful force in the southeast.

Santa Elena. Spanish name for a bay near Port Royal off the coast of North Carolina, now called Saint Helena.

Sara. Also called Suala or Cheraw. Known to the Cherokees as Ani-Suwali. A Siouan tribe in the North Carolina area.

Theocracy. A government by priests.

Weesock. Also, and more often, called Waxhaw. A South Carolina Siouan-speaking tribe.

❖

CHAPTER THREE

⟨⟩

Beginnings of Central Government

The observations of Gabriel Arthur in 1673 are the earliest descriptions of any substance of Cherokees that we have. So we might say that Cherokee history—that is, information written down about Cherokees—really begins with Arthur. In 1673, the Cherokee country was found to be a vast area, as mentioned earlier, covering all or parts of what are now the southern states of Virginia, West Virginia, North Carolina, South Carolina, Georgia, Alabama, Tennessee, and Kentucky.

This area was divided into three regions known as the Overhills (or Upper Towns), the Middle Towns, and the Lower Towns (or Valley Towns). Three major dialects of the Cherokee language were spoken, one in each of these regions. According to James Mooney, the Eastern dialect (Lower Towns) "was originally spoken in all the towns upon the waters of the Keowee and Tugaloo, head-streams of Savannah River, in South Carolina and the adjacent portion of Georgia." The chief distinction of this dialect was a rolling *r* in place of the *l* in the other dialects. For example, the word *Tsalagi*, in the eastern dialect becomes *Tsaragi*. The English speakers of South Carolina, perhaps, heard this word and in their mouths it became *Cherokee*.

Mooney says that the Middle dialect "might properly" be called the Kituwah dialect, and it was spoken "in the towns on the Tuckasegee and the headwaters of the Little Tennessee, in the very heart of the Cherokee country." The Western dialect (Overhills) was spoken "in most of the towns of east Tennessee and upper Georgia and upon Hiwassee and Cheowa Rivers in North Carolina."

Needham and Arthur visited the Overhills town of Chota, or Echota, in 1673, and Arthur later described a town built along the river, with high cliffs on the opposite side of the river, and a twelve-foot-high wall of logs around the other three sides of the town. There were scaffolds with parapets to defend the walls. He described the houses as being built along streets. At Chota, he said, there were 150 canoes, the smallest of which would carry twenty men.

During this time the Cherokees were at war with the Shawnees, the Catawbas, the Tuscaroras, and other neighboring tribes. They apparently made raids as far south as Florida, and they already had guns.

For the next several years following the visit of Needham and Arthur to Chota and the visit of the Cherokees from Chota to Fort Henry to take Arthur home again, Cherokees and English colonists visited each other frequently. Although it does not survive, a treaty was supposedly signed by the Cherokees from some of the Lower Towns with the colony of South Carolina during this period.

In 1711, the colonists of South Carolina were having troubles with the Tuscaroras. In exchange for the Cherokees' promise to help them fight the Tuscaroras, they gave the Cherokees guns. The Cherokees then joined with the colonists and drove the Tuscaroras north. For the next few years, the Cherokees were able to obtain guns and ammunition from South Carolina, and they used these weapons against their traditional enemies. In 1715, they joined with the Chickasaws to drive the Shawnees out of the Cumberland River Valley.

But later that same year, the Cherokees learned that the colonists of South Carolina had been playing an evil trick on them and on their enemies at the same time. The colonists had been supplying guns to various Indian tribes and provoking them to make war on each other. In exchange for the guns, the colonists simply asked both sides to deliver up to them all their prisoners of war. The colonists then shipped the prisoners to the West Indies to be sold into slavery.

When they made that startling discovery, some Cherokees allied themselves with the Yamassees and Catawbas in what has been called the Yamassee War and attacked Charlestown and surrounding farms, but the following year, the Cherokees made peace again with South Carolina. It was an uneasy peace, however, and it was during this time that the noted Cherokee Ada gal'kala (recorded in histories as Attakullakulla), or the Little Carpenter, first became known for his diplomatic skills.

In 1721, thirty-seven Cherokee chiefs went to Charlestown, South Carolina, to meet with Governor Nicolson, the royal governor of the colony. A number of very important things happened at this meeting.

In an attempt to settle a fixed boundary between the Cherokee country and the colony, Cherokees for the first time gave up land to English colonists. Because the colonists were frequently confused over having to deal with chiefs of different Cherokee towns, the Cherokee chiefs present agreed to select one man to represent them all in dealing with matters of trade with South Carolina. In turn, the colonial government agreed to appoint a commissioner of trade to oversee the various traders who dealt with the Cherokees. The Cherokees selected a man whose name was recorded as "Wrosetasatow," and the governor appointed Colonel George Chicken.

It has already been mentioned that Cherokee towns were autonomous, and that each had two chiefs, a Peace Chief and a War Chief. The Europeans seem to have been constantly frustrated by having to deal with each Cherokee town separately, and this appointment of "Wro-setasatow," who may also have been known by the war title "Mankiller," appears to have been the first step toward the central government that would eventually become the Cherokee Nation. Like each successive step in that process, it was necessitated by dealings with the Europeans (and later with the white Americans).

While most of the detailed records of this time period that have survived (or that were even kept in the first place) come from South Carolina, we know as well that the Cherokees were already pressed on two sides by the Englishmen of the southern colonies of Virginia, South Carolina, and Georgia. In addition, the French were also active in the area, having made their own trade alliances with both the Choctaws and the Creeks. The Spanish had withdrawn to the south, in Florida, southern Georgia, and on into the southwest, but they too were still players in the treacherous game of international intrigue being played out by European countries on foreign soil.

Each European country involved was competing with the others for dominance in what they were calling "the New World," and the English colonies were competing with each other as well. Finally, the colonies were already showing elements of that independent spirit that would eventually lead them into open rebellion against the British crown. For all the above reasons, Colonel George Chicken took immediate advantage of his new position as commissioner of trade, and the freedom of travel in the Cherokee country that it afforded him, to go from Cherokee town to Cherokee town to encourage the Cherokees to remain faithful to their new trade alliance with the British (in particular, the colony of South Carolina) and to avoid any dealings with the French. This was especially important to the British, if, as Mooney claims, the Cherokees were already "strongly disposed to favor the French" at the time.

For the next nine years, the historical record indicates relative calm, although the scheming and maneuvering of the various European political interests among the Cherokees must have been intense. The Cherokees were not satisfied with their trade situation, however, for they made numerous complaints regarding the bad behavior of the traders who came among them. Some of the complaints had to do with the general rowdy manners of the traders, and others had to do with the traders cheating the Cherokees in their trade deals.

In response to these complaints (and mainly because of the British fear that the Cherokees would turn to the French), the British sent Sir Alexander Cuming to visit the Cherokees to reaffirm their earlier agreement. Woodward calls Cuming "an unofficial envoy" from the king. Mooney simply says that Cuming "was dispatched on a secret mission" to the Cherokees. Whoever sent him, Cuming's arrival in Cherokee country resulted in a remarkable tale and a second step toward a Cherokee central government.

Cuming showed up at Keowee on March 23, 1730. There were present in Keowee at the time several British traders who were witnesses to what transpired. (Mooney says that Cuming arrived at Nikwasi. It probably doesn't matter much, for Cuming must have gone to several towns before he was done with his mission. At any rate, he began his excursion somewhere in the Lower Towns, near South Carolina.) The story as it has come down to us from Cuming himself and the traders who were present and through various historians is as follows:

Cuming entered the townhouse at Keowee wearing pistols and a sword, in spite of the Cherokee ban against weapons in the townhouse, and demanded that the Cherokees acknowledge themselves to be subjects of the king of England. The traders there claim to have been horrified at his boldness and astonished by its results. Woodward says the Cherokees "acknowledged the complete sovereignty of England over their people."

From there, according to the standard tale, Cuming went on to the Cherokee Middle Towns and then to the Overhills Towns and, using the same methods, exacted the same promise from them all. Along the way, he stopped by Tellico, where he selected "Moytoy" (probably Ama-edohi) to become "Emperor of the Cherokees." All of the Cherokee town chiefs, it is claimed, agreed to this preposterous demand, and "Moytoy" was "created Emperor" in a great ceremony.

The story is totally absurd. Certainly, Cuming visited the Cherokees, traveling from town to town and addressing the people assembled in their townhouses, and certainly he came away from the Cherokee country having reached some sort of agreement with them and having had "Moytoy" appointed as something. But whatever he accomplished, he certainly embellished the tale for the benefit of King George.

It is easy to believe that the egotistical King George II was taken in by Cuming's fabrication. What is astonishing is that almost all historians ever since writing about the Cherokees have also been gullible enough to accept it at face value. In the first place, it has always been extremely difficult, if not impossible, to get all Cherokees to agree on anything. In the second place, the Cherokees have always (at least since the time of the killing of the Ani-Kutani) been almost fanatical about democracy.

Cuming's interpreter, William Cooper, is supposed to have said that "if he had known beforehand what Sir Alexander would have order'd him to have said, he would not have ventured into the Town House to have been the interpreter, nor would the Indian Traders have ventured to have been Spectators, believing that none of them could have gone out of the Town House without being murdered, considering how jealous that People had always been of their liberties" (Woodward, p. 61).

Cuming's story was corroborated by several different English traders who were witnesses to the events of his remarkable trip through Cherokee country. They were British subjects, with licenses to trade with the Cherokees issued by a British colony under the authority of the king. Was it not to their advantage to back up Cuming's tale?

What the Cherokees probably agreed to was not much more than what they had already agreed to in Charlestown nine years earlier. That is to say, they probably agreed to trade with the British colonies and not with the French. And they probably selected one man ("Moytoy") as their trade representative. The difference in the new trade agreement from the old one was probably that all Cherokee towns, or at least towns from all three major divisions (Overhill, Middle, and Lower), agreed on this occasion, rather than just thirty-seven towns; the agreement included all the British colonies and not just South Carolina, and a new man was elected to the position of trade representative.

The event is certainly an important one in Cherokee history, one that moved the Cherokees a step closer to central government, and one that strengthened the Cherokee alliance with Great Britain, but it almost certainly did not happen the way it has been reported.

SOURCE LIST AND SUGGESTIONS FOR FURTHER READING

Foreman, Carolyn T. 1943. *Indians Abroad, 1493–1938*. Norman: University of
     Oklahoma Press.
Steele, William O. 1977. *The Cherokee Crown of Tannassy*. Charlotte, N. C.:
     Heritage Printers.

GLOSSARY

Ada gal'kala. A noted Cherokee leader, recorded in histories as "Attakullakulla,"
     and known to whites as "The Little Carpenter." Mooney explains the
     name thus: "It may be rendered 'Leaning Wood,' from *ata*, 'wood,' and
     gul kalu a verb implying that something long is leaning, without
     sufficient support, against some other object."

Catawbas. A Siouan-speaking tribe originally in what is now South Carolina.
     The Cherokees' nearest neighbor tribe to the east.

Cheowa. According to Mooney, this is a corruption of the Cherokee, *Tsiyahi*,
     meaning "Otter Place." A place name, it has been used several times
     throughout Cherokee history.

Chota. Variously spelled Echota, Chote, and more accurately, Itsodi, this was
     the name of the ancient capital and sacred peace town of the Cherokees.
     It has also been the name of several other towns, often with an adjective,
     such as Little Echota and New Echota (Mooney).

Cumberland River Valley. An area in southeast Kentucky and northern
     Tennessee along the 687 mile long Cumberland River.

Hiwassee. Corruption of *Ayuhwasi*, meaning a meadow or savannah, it was
     the name of at least two Cherokee towns. In the form Hiwassee, it is the
     name of a river in Tennessee and of an island in that river.

Keowee. The main town of the Lower Cherokee Towns in what is now South
     Carolina. Probably a corruption of *Kuwahiyi*, meaning Mulberry Place.

Kituwah dialect. The dialect of the Cherokee language spoken in the Middle
     Towns. According to Mooney, it is the dialect still spoken by most of the
     people living on the Qualla Reservation in North Carolina. Although it
     shares some characteristics with the Eastern dialect, like the Western, it
     has an *l* instead of an *r*.

Little Tennessee. River flowing out of the Tennessee River in eastern
     Tennessee into southwestern North Carolina.

Lower Towns. Towns occupied by speakers of the Eastern dialect of the
     Cherokee language, located along the Keowee and Tugaloo rivers in

what is now western South Carolina and eastern Georgia.

Middle Towns. Towns occupied by speakers of the Middle or Kituwah dialect of the Cherokee language and located along the Tuckasegee and Little Tennessee rivers, as Mooney says, "in the very heart of the Cherokee country."

Moytoy. The way in which Alexander Cuming recorded the name of the man he claimed to have made into the "Emperor" of the Cherokees. Traveler Bird (*Tell Them They Lie*, 1971, Westernlore Press, p. 19.) maintains, probably correctly, that it is a corruption of Ama Edohi, meaning something like "Water Traveler." And the name "Amahatoy," apparently an attempt at the same name, was recorded by Captain Christopher French in his "Journal of an Expedition to South Carolina," reprinted in the *Journal of Cherokee Studies* 2, no. 3, Summer 1977.

Overhills. The Overhills region of the Cherokee country was made up of those Cherokee towns on the west side of the Great Smoky Mountain Range in what is now eastern Tennessee.

Parapets. A defensive wall or elevation in a fort.

Savannah. A savannah is a plain characterized by coarse grasses and occasional trees, especially on the edge of a forest. It's also the name of a river that forms most of the boundary between Georgia and South Carolina; 314 miles long, it flows into the Atlantic Ocean. The name comes from the Savanna branch of the Shawnees who once lived in South Carolina.

Tellico. Also spelled Telliquo, Talikwa and Tahlequah. Different Cherokee towns at different periods of history have had this name. In spite of several popular stories that purport to explain how Tahlequah, Oklahoma, got its name, the real meaning of the word is apparently lost.

Tsalagi. The Cherokee form of the word "Cherokee." Most scholars agree that the word is not of Cherokee origin and is most likely from the Choctaw language and gained wide usage through the Mobilian trade language, which was based on Choctaw. The Choctaw word seems to mean "Cave People" or "Cave Dwellers."

Tsaragi. The same as above but in the Eastern or Lower Cherokee dialect.

Tuckasegee. Corruption of *Tsiksitsi* or *Tuksitsi*. The meaning of the word seems to have been lost, but it was the name of a Cherokee settlement in what is now North Carolina.

Tugaloo. Corruption of *Dugiluyi*, a Cherokee town in what is now Georgia on the Tugaloo River.

Tuscarora. A southern Iroquoian tribe that once lived in what is now North Carolina. When they were driven north in 1713, they became the sixth member tribe of the Iroquois League.

Wro-setasatow. The name, as recorded by the English, of the Cherokee man selected in 1721 to be the trade representative for the Cherokees to South

Carolina. Mooney suggests that it is an attempt at the same name record-ed elsewhere as Outacite, Otassite, Outassatah, Wootassite, and Outacity. He further suggests that the name ends in the suffix *dihi* or "killer." Then he quotes Timberlake who claimed the name to mean Mankiller. "Man" is *asgaya*, and in no way resembles the beginning of this name in any of its spellings. Elsewhere, Mooney records *atasi* or *atasu* as meaning war club. Perhaps the name is a combination of the words *atasi* and *dihi*.

Yamassee. A member tribe of the Creek Confederacy.

CHAPTER FOUR

Visits Back and Forth

When he at last left the Cherokee country and returned to England, Sir Alexander Cuming took seven Cherokee men with him. Their names were recorded as Oukah-Ulah, Oukanekah (called Owen Naken by the English, and later known as Ada Gal'kala), Kettagustah, Tathtiowie, Clogittah, Collanah, and Ounakannowie. "Moytoy" stayed behind because of a sick wife. Eleazar Wiggan, known to the Cherokees as "the Old Rabbit," went along as interpreter.

On May 4, 1730, they boarded the man-of-war, *Fox*, at Charlestown, and after almost exactly one month at sea, they arrived at Dover in England. They were taken from Dover to London, where Cuming got them rooms in the basement of the house of an undertaker named Arne, who sold tickets to allow curious passersby to peek through the windows to get a look at the unknowing Cherokees. They were wined and dined at fashionable spots in London, had their portraits painted, and were followed around town by curious crowds.

At Whitehall Palace, we are told by the British records, the seven Cherokees renewed the treaty they had signed with Cuming by acknowledging the sovereignty of England over all of the Cherokees, by binding the Cherokees to have no trade alliance with any nation other than England, by agreeing to allow no white people other than English to live among them, by promising to deliver into English hands any fugitive slaves or any white lawbreakers who might seek refuge among them, and by pledging themselves to English military service in the event England should engage in a war with France or any other foreign power.

Oukanekah, who, Woodward says, could speak a little English, is reported to have said to the king, "We look upon the Great King George as the Sun, and as our father, and upon ourselves as his children. For though we are red, and you are white yet our hands and hearts are joined together. What we have seen, our children from generation to generation will always remember it. In war we shall always be with you."

The Cherokees gave the king a "crown," five eagle tails, and four scalps. They received in return guns, ammunition, red paint, and promises of love and perpetual friendship. In September, they once again boarded ship and returned to South Carolina all in good health, and Oukanekah thereafter was a staunch supporter of the British and would have nothing to do with the French. That is the tale of the visit of the seven Cherokees to England in 1730 as it was recorded in England and as it has been passed down to us by various historians. It needs to be examined.

In the first place, we do not have any record of the way in which any of the seven Cherokees recalled that trip or their meeting with the king of England. The record is all based on the way in which the English set it down, and, as Jennings and others have pointed out, "Indians signed for what they had heard. The English held them to what was written." Is it not possible, even probable, that the Cherokee sense of what had transpired in England was very different from what the English recorded?

Let's begin by looking back at the speech Oukanekah is supposed to have delivered to the king. Woodward says that Oukanekah could speak "a little English." The context of her comment seems to indicate that the speech was delivered in English. If so, and if it was recorded accurately, he could certainly speak more than "a little English." But whether the speech was delivered in English or in Cherokee is really irrelevant, for we have no way of knowing that the speech was recorded as it was delivered.

A close examination of that speech reveals curiosities beyond the question of the speaker's command of the English language. According to the sources, Oukanekah said that the Cherokees "look upon the Great King George as the Sun, and as our father." A Cherokee would never have said such a thing without careful British coaching. The English considered the sun, at least metaphorically, as male, and called the king the Sun, as in the famous lines from Shakespeare's play, *King Richard the Third*: "Now is the winter of our discontent/Made glorious summer by this Sun of York." But to Cherokees, the sun was female and, therefore, no one's king or father. Then, according to the recorded speech, Oukanekah said, "we are red." The "redness" of American Indian skin is a European perception. Oukanekah would much more likely have said "brown."

Jennings's explanation of the Native American practice of exchanging gifts at treaty negotiations is also instructive here. According to Jennings, a large gift following negotiations was considered tribute, and the payment of tribute was "ceremonial recognition of a confederate relationship in which" the recipient of the tribute was "superior." With that in mind, does it make any sense to think that the Cherokees would have acknowledged the English to be their superiors, while at the same time accepting gifts of much greater value than those which they had given? It does not.

It seems reasonable, then, to say that Oukanekah certainly did not compose the speech as it has been handed down to us, and to say further, that he probably did not deliver it in such a form. He probably did make a speech in which he pledged friendship to the English, and in which he agreed to a trade alliance. He may even have agreed to some of the other terms of the treaty, such as turning over fugitives from English colonies to the colonial governments and agreeing not to deal with the French or other Europeans. As long as the trade with England remained beneficial to the Cherokees, there would be no harm in such an agreement. But it is very difficult, almost impossible, to believe that Oukanekah, or any Cherokee in 1730, would agree to make all Cherokees subjects of the British crown, or that he would use the kind of language attributed to him by the historians.

Most likely, the speech was delivered in Cherokee and translated, or interpreted as they said in those days, by Wiggan, and "the Old Rabbit," probably acting under instructions from Cuming, said those words, not Oukanekah.

Finally, according to Woodward, when the seven Cherokees arrived back home, they were "sharply questioned by the people concerning the promises they had made to 'the Man who lives across the Great Water.'" Among other things, the people wanted to know if Oukanekah had given away any land. The answers Oukanekah gave the people were apparently satisfactory, for not only was he not killed, he was elevated to the position of Peace Chief of his town, and he became know by his new name, Ada-Gal'kala. It is also interesting to note that while the English recorded Oukanekah as having referred to the king "as the Sun and as our father," the people back home called him simply "the Man who lives across the Great Water."

During this same period of time, the French were very active in the area and were meeting with success in establishing their own trade

relations with the Creeks and the Choctaws. They had established Fort
Toulouse on the Coosa River in Creek territory in what is now Alabama.
Around 1736, they began to more actively court the Cherokees, but
apparently Oukanekah—from now on known as Ada-Gal'kala—was successful in keeping the Cherokees loyal to the agreement with the British.

Another curious episode in Cherokee history began in 1736 when a
man known as Christian Gottlieb Priber came to stay at Tellico. He
became friends with Agan'stat' (known in most histories as Oconostota),
the War Chief of Tellico, and stayed there for several years. Again, the
historical record all comes down to us from the English. Here is the tale
that they told, which has been retold by historians ever since.

Priber came from Saxony and was a German Jesuit priest but was
almost certainly an agent of the French. Once established at Tellico, he
cut his hair and dressed like a Cherokee. He told the Cherokees that they
had been cheated out of a great deal of land by the English. He told them
that they should give up no more land, and that they should trade with
English and French alike.

He proposed a new system of government, under which all property, including wives, would be held in common, and children would be
public property. He urged the Cherokees to move their capital nearer to
the French and to admit anyone who agreed with their philosophy of
government into their society. He wrote a letter to the government of
South Carolina and signed it, "Prime Minister." Priber learned to speak
Cherokee and did his best to convince the Cherokees to hate the English
and to go over to the French. He crowned "Moytoy" of Tellico "Emperor,"
and called himself "his imperial majesty's principal secretary of state."

South Carolina sent Colonel Fox to Tellico to arrest Priber. Fox "laid
hold of him in the Townhouse," but the Cherokees defended Priber and
told Fox to get out of their country. They said that the country was theirs,
and that they could do what they wanted to do. They said that they
meant to continue to trade with the English as "free men and equals," but
that they also intended to trade with the French. Fox was then escorted
safely back out of Cherokee country.

After five years, according to Adair, Priber and a few Cherokees headed for the French garrison in Alabama. Their mission was to talk the
Creeks and Choctaws into becoming a part of their "red empire." Along
the way, English traders captured Priber. They took him to Frederica, in
the English colony of Georgia, where he was thrown into prison. Adair
says, "happily for us, he died in confinement."

During the time Priber spent in Tellico, he is said to have written a
Cherokee dictionary and a book describing his proposed governmental

system, which he titled *Paradise*. Neither of these books, nor any of Priber's letters, seem to have survived, and so we have left only the accusations of the English.

Once again, the English chroniclers and the historians who have blindly followed them have given us a tale full of contradictions. Priber was a German, but he was a French agent. He was a Jesuit priest, but he railed against religion. He was a dangerous French agent who urged the Cherokees to trade with both the French and the English. (Why both if he was a French agent? The English urged the Cherokees to trade only with them.) Among a matrilineal society, he spoke of wives as property, without being killed, thrown out of town, or even laughed at. Among a people with a strong clan system, he advocated that children be raised as "public property." He "crowned an emperor" among a society of equals. The man himself has been painted as a bundle of contradictions, and the ideas he is supposed to have proposed to the Cherokees and supposed to have influenced them with would never have been listened to by Cherokees. The entire tale is ludicrous.

And isn't it interested that Priber is supposed to have selected the very same man, "Moytoy" of Tellico, to crown as "Emperor" as had Cuming six years or so earlier?

Certainly there was a Priber, and certainly he lived at Tellico for some years and was well liked by Agan'stat' and the other residents of that town. And if he was really a friend to the Cherokees, he probably did advocate that they trade with the French as well as with anyone else who came along. He probably also cautioned them against making any more land cessions to the British or to anyone else.

And the English in their paranoia may have actually believed that Priber was an agent for the French, for they both hated and feared the French and saw themselves as being in fierce competition with the French for dominance in America. The rest of the story seems to have been carefully made up to justify their treatment of Priber. His arrest was made without just cause, and his death in prison was certainly convenient for the English.

GLOSSARY

Agan'stat'. War Chief of Tellico. See Oconostota below.

Clogittah. A garbled form of the name of one of the seven Cherokee men who went to England with Sir Alexander Cuming in 1730.

Collanah. (Also spelled Colaneh, Colona, Kolana, Golana, etc.) It's the
  Cherokee word for "Raven," and was a common war title. It's given as
  the name of one of the seven Cherokees who went to England in 1730.

Confederate. A member of a confederacy, a league or alliance of states, more
  or less permanent.

Jesuit. A member of a Roman Catholic religious order. The English considered
  them to be crafty and untrustworthy.

Kettagustah. Listed as one of the seven Cherokees who went to England in
  1730. It is garbled Cherokee.

Man-of-war. A warship.

Oconostota. More properly spelled, according to Mooney, Aganstata, meaning
  "Groundhog Sausage." War Chief at Tellico in 1736 and afterward.

Oukah-Ulah. The garbled name of one of the seven Cherokees who went to
  England in 1730. It could possibly be some form of *Uguku*, the hooting
  or barred owl.

Oukanekah. Another attempt by the English to spell the name of one of the
  seven Cherokees who went to England in 1730. He was the spokesman
  and leader of the group. His name has also been spelled "Oukandekah"
  and "Oukanaeka." The English sometimes called him Captain Owen
  Nakan. The name is probably some combination of *Uguku* (hooting
  owl) and *unega* (white). Oukanekah later became known as Ada-
  Gal'kala, the spelling of which was corrupted to "Attakullakulla." (See
  Glossary for Chapter 3.)

Ounakannowie. Another of the seven Cherokees who went to England in 1730,
  his name also mangled by English attempts to spell Cherokee words.
  The first part of the name would seem to be a version of *unega* or
  unaka, meaning white.

Saxony. At one time an independent state, Saxony later became a part of
  Germany.

Sovereignty. Supreme and independent power in a state.

Tathtiowie. Garbled name of another of the seven Cherokee travelers to
  England in 1730.

Tribute. Money paid by one sovereign state to another in acknowledgement of
  subjugation or as the price of peace.

◆

CHAPTER FIVE

"What Nation or People Am I Afraid Of?"

W hether or not Christian Gottlieb Priber was really an agent for the French, the events of 1736 and the years immediately following seem to have left the Cherokees divided on the issue of European alliances. The majority of Cherokees remained faithful to the agreements they had made with the English, but Agan'stat' and some of his followers had become anti-English and partial to the French.

Then, in 1738, a major disaster struck the Cherokees when their towns were swept by an epidemic of smallpox, brought into South Carolina by the slave ships. Smallpox was a disease introduced to America by Europeans, who had themselves developed an immunity to the disease. Since smallpox had not been in the Americas prior to the arrival of Europeans, Cherokees and other Native Americans had no such immunity and were therefore extremely vulnerable to its attack.

The traditional medicine people of the Cherokees had no experience with smallpox and therefore no way to fight it, and the epidemic was so overwhelming that it is said that within one year over half of the Cherokee population had died as a result of the horrible, disfiguring, and deadly disease. Mooney says, "As the pestilence spread unchecked from town to town, despair fell upon the nation. . . . Hundreds of the warriors committed suicide on beholding their frightful disfigurement." Adair says that "some shot themselves, others cut their throats, some stabbed themselves with knives, and others with sharp-pointed canes; many threw themselves with sullen madness into the fire, and there slowly expired, as if they had been utterly divested of the native power of feeling pain."

Agan'stat' himself was one of the victims. He survived, but he retained for the rest of his life the disfiguring smallpox scars. He accused the English of having deliberately planted smallpox germs in the trade goods they had shipped to the Cherokees. Whether or not the English deliberately or inadvertently spread the smallpox germs among the Cherokees, they were certainly guilty of having done the job. Agan'stat' hated the British thereafter and began spending more of his time with the French at Fort Toulouse. Ada-gal'kala, on the other hand, still loyal to the English, scolded Agan'stat' for this, and Agan'stat' is said to have replied, "What Nation or people am I afraid of? I do not fear the forces which the Great King George can send against me to these mountains."

In spite of the dissension of Agan'stat' and some others, Cherokee trading with the English colonists had increased by 1740 They were trading with Georgia as well as with South Carolina. And following up on their agreement to ally themselves militarily with England, they sent one thousand warriors to join Georgia colonists in attacking the Spanish at St. Augustine.

At this point in Cherokee history, it would be well to pause and reflect on the events, as sketchy as they are, and on the profound alterations to Cherokee society caused by those events. After over sixty years of contact and trade with the English, the Cherokees had already changed a great deal. They had possessed guns and ammunition for those guns since sometime before that initial contact. This means that their style of warfare and their manner of hunting had both changed. It also means that they had begun to abandon the use of their traditional weapons and that the making of those traditional weapons was being abandoned.

They had developed a hunting and trading economy. Whereas in the past Cherokees had hunted for food and clothing, they had begun to hunt for the purpose of accumulating furs and skins for trade. In the words of Jennings, writing about Native American trade with Europeans in general, they moved from "subsistence hunting" to "commercial hunting," and they "turned to hunting with an intensity previously unknown." And they had become dependent in many ways on this new economy. Jennings says further, "New commodities displaced old. Iron and steel implements made copper and stone obsolete."

Traditional skills were being abandoned. As more and more Cherokees began using weapons and ammunition of European manufacture, steel pots, cloth, and other items of trade, the products of the traditional crafts-people were in less demand. Bow makers, arrow makers, potters, basket makers, and others found their skills suddenly less necessary.

New behavioral patterns and new attitudes were being introduced as well. Hunters spent more of their time out hunting in order to accumulate more to trade, and women back home spent more and more time preparing the skins for the trade business. White traders settled in Cherokee towns and married Cherokee women. They brought with them not only implements of trade, but also foreign ideas and strong liquor. According to Adair, "the old magi and religious physicians" among the Cherokees blamed the smallpox epidemic of 1738 on drunkenness and adultery, habits apparently brought about by the influence of the whites among them.

Adair also tells us that the Cherokees all had horses by this time, and that some were even raising cattle and hogs. Cherokee bacon, he says, tasted better than any that could be acquired in the colonies. The raising of large, domesticated, grazing animals indicates more than a change in lifestyle for the owner of the animals. It brings about a major change in the environment. Sarah Hill (1997) has pointed out in great detail, for example, the devastating effects on the Cherokee basket-making industry of grazing cattle in the canebrakes.

Also as a result of the trade, a movement toward a centralized Cherokee government was underway. The thirty-seven chiefs who visited Charlestown in 1721 had chosen "Wro-setasetow" for a position that can only be called "trade commissioner," although, of course, it was not called that at the time. With that precedent, "Moytoy" was picked for what was surely a similar position in 1730 and seemingly chosen again in 1736. But, as we have already seen, the trade agreements carried along with them agreements of military alliance. The position of "trade commissioner" was therefore a very important one, and the trade agreements that were concluded became profoundly significant in terms of government. It is also at about this same time that we find the traders (Adair and others) referring to Tellico as the Cherokee capital city.

A mixed-blood population was developing among the Cherokees, also because of the presence of the traders. Cornelius Dougherty had been living with the Cherokees since 1690. Ludovic Grant moved to the Cherokee country about 1726, married a Cherokee woman, and stayed. And there were others. The ideas, beliefs, and behavior of these white residents were bound to have had some influence, if only, in the beginning, on the traders' own wives and children.

Although Mooney says that "up to this time no civilizing or mission work had been undertaken by either of the Carolina governments," it is

safe to say that some Cherokees had almost certainly heard some things
about Christianity, if not from the traders resident among them, certainly
from a Jesuit priest who had spent somewhere between five and nine years
in Tellico. We might also ask what Mooney means by "civilizing" work.

As Jennings has so brilliantly pointed out, the words "civilization"
and "savagery," used as absolutes, have no meaning whatsoever. Each is
simply defined as the opposite of the other. They are terms of propaganda. Therefore, any talk of "civilizing" Indians, really means "making
the Indians live like white people." So in spite of Mooney's statement,
quite a bit had already been accomplished along those lines by 1740.

New enemies and new dangers were all around. By 1740 the
Cherokees had already been involved in fights with the Spanish and with
the English. They had also engaged in wars with other Indian tribes that
had actually been instigated by the English. They had given up land to
the English, and they had been visited by a deadly disease imported by
the English. In their own homeland, they were in a much more dangerous position than they had ever experienced before.

Finally, factionalism had developed within Cherokee towns because
of Agan'stat's preference for the French at a time when Cherokees had
made trade alliances with the English. Such factionalism will continue to
grow throughout the remainder of Cherokee history.

SOURCE LIST AND SUGGESTIONS FOR FURTHER READING

Hill, Sarah H. 1993. "A Basket of History: Ecological Transformation in the
        World of Eighteenth Century Cherokee Women," Unpublished paper
        delivered at the Cherokee Nation Historical Convention in Tahlequah,
        September 3, 1993.
Hill, Sarah H. 1997. *Weaving New Worlds*. Chapel Hill: University of North
        Carolina Press.

GLOSSARY

Absolutes. Something independent of any outside conditions. For example,
        when someone says, "Indians had no civilization," he is using "civiliza-
        tion" as an absolute.
Civilization. Used as an absolute, "civilization" means the opposite of "sav-

agery." Jennings maintains that these two words have no meaning at all when used as absolutes, but, rather, both are propaganda words, words used as weapons.

Factionalism. Divisiveness within a group. The result of a large group dividing itself into smaller groups, or "factions."

Magi. (plural of "Magus") The three Wise Men who visited the infant Jesus in the Bible. By extension, any "Wise Men."

Savagery. Used as an absolute, "savagery" has no meaning beyond the opposite of "civilization." It's a propaganda word used as a weapon. There is no historical record of any group of human beings who ever lived in a state of savagery.

Smallpox. A highly contagious disease caused by a virus and characterized by pimple- or blister-like eruptions that often leave permanent scars or "pock marks" on the skin. Before the arrival of Europeans in America, smallpox was unknown here. The Europeans had been through earlier epidemics of smallpox and had developed at least partial immunity to the disease, but the American Indians, never having been exposed to it before, had no such immunity. Smallpox, as well as other European diseases, including measles, therefore proved to be deadly to Indians when first introduced.

CHAPTER SIX

"Let Him be Wary."

In 1754, France and England were at war in Europe, and the war was extended to American soil. Both the English and the French attempted to draw their respective Indian allies into the war on their side, and they did so at times successfully. The war, which would last in America until 1760, was named by the English, and so we still know it as the "French and Indian War." The designation reflects English bias, for, as mentioned, it was a war between France and England with Indian allies fighting on both sides.

British Lieutenant Colonel George Washington said that the war could not be won by the English without the assistance of Indian allies, and the Virginia colonists asked for Cherokee participation. The Cherokees had not dealt with Virginia since their unpleasant experience in 1654 when the Virginia colonists had attacked a new Cherokee town located nearby, just because they didn't want Indians living that close to them. (See Chapter 2.) The Cherokees refused to cooperate. At the suggestion of George Washington, therefore, because the colonies desperately needed Cherokee help, Governor Dinwiddie of Virginia sent Nathaniel Gist to beg for Cherokee assistance in fighting the Shawnees, allies of the French. Cherokees and Shawnees had long been enemies, and so some Cherokees at last agreed.

One hundred warriors from Chota and nearby towns, under the leadership of Ostenaco, agreed to attack the Shawnees, in exchange for the English promise to build forts in Cherokee country to protect the women and children from the French and their allies while the warriors were away. The agreement was made, with the assistance of Ada-gal'kala, and it included the cession of forty million acres more of Cherokee land to the English. Ada-gal'kala said, "We fear not the French. Give us arms, and we will go to war with the enemies of the Great King."

Governor Glen of South Carolina began construction of two forts, Fort Prince George, near Keowee on the Savannah River in the Lower Towns, and Fort Loudoun, near Chota, where the Little Tennessee and Tellico rivers come together, in the Overhills Towns. The Virginians built another fort across the Little Tennessee River from Chota. According to Woodward, the Virginia fort was not named, and it was not manned. Mooney calls it Fort Dobbs.

At any rate, when the forts were finally finished, Ostenaco and his one hundred warriors, along with two hundred Virginia troops under the command of Major Andrew Lewis, headed for the Shawnee country. The Virginia force was also strengthened by Creek, Tuscarora, and other allied Indian warriors. It was February of 1756. It was not the traditional time of year for Cherokees to go to war.

According to Mooney, "After six weeks of fruitless tramping through the woods, with the ground covered with snow and the streams so swollen by rains that they lost their provisions and ammunition in crossing, they were obliged to return to the settlements in a starving condition, having killed their horses on the way." The Indians were already disgusted by the way in which the Virginians had been treating them, and the Tuscaroras had already gone home. So the Cherokees turned around and headed back on foot toward Chota. Along their way, says Mooney, "finding some horses running loose on the range, they appropriated them, on the theory that as they had lost their own animals, to say nothing of having risked their lives, in the services of the colonists, it was only a fair exchange."

Angry Virginia settlers, either not knowing about the Cherokees' situation or not caring, banded together and attacked them, killing twenty-four, scalping them and further mutilating the bodies. They then took the scalps to Governor Dinwiddie, presented them as the scalps of enemy Indians and were paid for them, for Dinwiddie had offered a bounty for the scalps of enemy Indians.

Somehow the "mistake" was discovered, and Dinwiddie sent apologies and presents to Chota. The Virginians who had done the killings, however, excused their action by calling the Cherokees horse thieves. Ada-gal'kala was not pleased. He told the commander of Fort Loudoun, Captain Raymond Demere, that the Cherokees no longer wanted to be allied with the English. He was right. Some Cherokees, acting on their own, retaliated against the Virginia settlers, attacking lone cabins and killing Virginians in order to set things right for the Cherokees who had been killed and scalped. Some settlers in North Carolina were also killed by the Cherokees. It seemed that an all-out war was at hand. Ada-gal'kala continued to try to smooth things over, sending apologies to the governors of both Virginia and North Carolina, and in November of 1758 a party of chiefs went to Charlestown to meet with the governor and other officials. Peace was officially declared.

Then unexpectedly, in May of 1759, Governor Lyttleton, who had replaced Governor Glen of South Carolina, demanded that Ada-gal'kala send him for execution every Cherokee who had killed a white man in the recent fighting. At about that same time, the commander of Fort Loudoun made a similar demand, specifying twenty-four "chiefs" he "suspected of unfriendly action." All trading supplies to the Upper Towns were cut off.

After a delegation representing all of the Cherokee towns went to Charlestown to state their desire to live in peace with the English colonists, but to also explain that they could not give up their own chiefs to the English, war was declared on the Cherokees by Governor Lyttleton of South Carolina. He called out the troops and sent messages to neighboring tribes to help in attacking the Cherokees.

The Cherokees sent a second peace delegation, this one consisting of thirty-two men, including Agan'stat'. This time they met the governor at Fort Prince George, where he had them arrested and thrown into prison, all thirty-two confined in a room, according to Mooney, large enough for only six soldiers. At the same time, the governor ordered fourteen hundred soldiers to invade the Cherokee country.

But Ada-gal'kala continued to pursue the matter diplomatically. He succeeded in having Agan'stat' and two others released, after six others had signed a paper agreeing that the remainder could be held hostage until those the English wanted had surrendered themselves. They also agreed to kill or capture any Frenchman found in Cherokee country. Perhaps they knew what they had signed. Perhaps they did not.

But smallpox broke out once again in the Cherokee towns, and Lyttleton decided that he had triumphed. He returned to the safety of Charlestown.

It was February of 1760, and Agan'stat' was furious at the English. He laid siege to Fort Prince George, cutting them off from any supplies or communication from the colony. Then one day, according to Mooney, he sent word "by an Indian woman that he wished to speak to the commander, Lieutenant Coytmore. As the lieutenant stepped out from the

stockade to see what was wanted, Oconostota [*sic*], standing on the opposite [side] of the river, swung a bridle above his head as a signal to his warriors concealed in the bushes, and the officer was at once shot down."

In angry response, the soldiers in the garrison broke into the room
where the hostages were still being held and butchered them to the last
man. The war was on. Cherokees attacked the frontier settlements of South
Carolina, and the Cherokees living near Fort Loudoun laid seige to it.
Another new governor of South Carolina, Governor Bull, sent a desperate
plea for help to General Amherst, commander in chief of the British army
in America. According to Woodward, Amherst sent " a battalion of
Highlanders and four companies of Royal Scots commanded by Colonel
Montgomery." In South Carolina, she goes on, "he was joined by the whole
force of the province." Mooney puts the total number at sixteen hundred.

In April of 1760, Montgomery led his army into the Cherokee Lower
Towns. He drove the Cherokees away from Fort Prince George, and proceeded to destroy all of the Lower Towns, "burning them to the ground,
cutting down the cornfields and orchards, killing and taking more than
a hundred of their men, and driving the whole population into the
mountains before him. His own loss was very slight."(Mooney)

Feeling smug from his early victories, Montgomery sent messages
to the Middle and Upper Towns, telling them that if they did not surrender he would do the same kind of damage to them. He received no
reply to his bold messages, and therefore proceeded on his way to carry
out his threats.

On hearing of Montgomery's progress, George Washington wrote in
May of that year, "It seems he has a prosperous beginning...and he is
now advancing his troops in high health and spirits to the relief of Fort
Loudoun. But let him be wary. He has a crafty, subtle enemy to deal with
that may give him most trouble when he least expects it."

On June 27, 1760, Montgomery led his army toward the Cherokee
Middle Town of Echoee, undoubtedly thinking that he would have the
same easy time he had enjoyed in the Lower Towns, but the Cherokees
were ready for him this time. They had gathered all their strength there
at Echoee to await his arrival, and Montgomery found himself trapped in
a deep valley, the sides of which were covered by vegetation.

The Cherokees were concealed in the vegetation, and from their hiding places, they fired on Montgomery's advance guard, killing Captain
Morrison and others. Woodward says that Montgomery's Highlanders
"eventually forced the Cherokees to retreat," and she goes on to call the
battle a victory for Montgomery. Mooney calls it "a desperate engage-
ment...by which Montgomery was compelled to retire." Mooney seems

to be closer to the truth, for in spite of the excuses made by Montgomery for his retreat, the fact remains that he did retreat, abandoning both his planned rescue of the men at Fort Loudoun and his bold threat to burn down all the remaining Cherokee towns. He had lost one hundred men (killed and wounded), feared the spreading smallpox, and complained that the Cherokees had better rifles than did his army. He retreated by way of Fort Prince George back to Charlestown and from there to New York.

At Fort Loudoun, Captain Paul Demere, who had replaced his brother Raymond, commanded a force of about two hundred men. They had been cut off from any outside supplies or help for six months and were said to be starving. They had eaten their horses and dogs. Some of the men in the fort were said to have Cherokee wives or sweethearts who had been providing them with food, and according to Mooney, "When threatened by the chiefs the women boldly replied that the soldiers were their husbands and it was their duty to help them, and if any harm came to themselves for their devotion their English relatives would avenge them."

At last, on August 8, 1760, Captain Demere surrendered the fort to Agan'stat', on condition that the English would be allowed to leave unmolested with their guns and enough ammunition to make the trip back to the colony. Demere agreed to leave the remaining ammunition stores to the Cherokees. Demere and his men left the fort and traveled far enough to make camp for the first night of their journey.

In the meantime, the Cherokees went into the fort to see what they could find. They found ten bags of powder and some lead balls that had been buried inside the fort, obviously in an attempt to hide them from the Cherokees. They also found a cannon, small arms, and other ammunition that the English had thrown into the river. Angry because the English had broken their agreement, the Cherokees followed them and caught up with them at their camp. Early the next morning, they attacked, killing Captain Demere and twenty-nine others with their first volley. The rest were taken prisoner.

Ada-gal'kala barterd with Agan'stat' for the release of Captain John Stuart and that of William Shorey. Stuart, a Scot, was second officer of the fort and had apparently gotten along well with the Cherokees before the trouble had started. He was married to a Cherokee woman, a mixed-blood named Susannah Emory, and he had been nicknamed "Bushyhead" by the Cherokees. Shorey, also a Scot, was an interpreter and was married to a full-blood Cherokee woman. Later, Ada-gal'kala took Stuart into the woods and led him to the safety of friends in Virginia.

Back in the colonies, the officials decided that it was too late in the year, and they were too worn out to follow up with any further military expeditions against the Cherokees. They decided to wait until the following year, taking their time to prepare an all-out assault.

SOURCE LIST AND SUGGESTIONS FOR FURTHER READING

Atkin, Edmond. 1954. *The Appalachian Indian Frontier: The Edmond Atkin Report and Plan of 1755*, ed. Wilbur R. Jacobs. Columbia: University of South Carolina Press. Reprinted, Lincoln: University of Nebraska Press, 1967.

Timberlake, Lieutenant Henry. 1927. *Lieutenant Henry Timberlake: Memoirs, 1756-1765*, ed. Samuel Cole Williams. Johnson City, Tenn.: The Watauga Press.

Schroeder, John Frederick, and B.J. Lossing. 1903. *Life and Times of Washington*. 4 vols. Albany, N.Y.

GLOSSARY

French and Indian War. The war fought between France and England in North America between 1754 and 1760.

Ostenaco. English spelling of the name of a Cherokee War Chief.

Scalping. The practice of cutting and tearing the scalp from the head of an enemy for a trophy of war or for other purposes. Jennings says that scalping was "apparently Indian in origin," though not practiced by all tribes. When colonial governments adopted it "as a convenient way" of collecting bounties placed on Indians, the practice spread rapidly. The origin of this practice is, however, fiercely debated.

CHAPTER SEVEN

"President of the Nation"

For a thorough study of the difference in the concept of war as practiced by Native Americans and by Europeans, one need only turn once again to Jennings. And in order to really grasp the events of early Cherokee history, we must have at least a basic understanding of that difference. According to Jennings, first of all, Indian wars "were sporadic, individualistic affairs." He says that Native warfare would have been called "brigandage" (i.e., banditry) in Europe. Sometimes, he says, they fought for territory, but when they did they wanted to displace the occupants rather than rule over them. Sometimes they fought for dominance over another group, in which case the defeated tribe would pay tribute to the victor and would become a subordinate ally of the victor.

The most frequent motive for Indian war, however, Jennings says, was what is usually called by English-speaking writers "revenge." Hudson adds, more specifically of southeastern Indians, including Cherokees, "More than anything else it resembled clan retaliation." In other words, war was, more often than not, a manifestation of the deepseated belief that all things must be kept in balance. For example, if a Cherokee member of the Wolf Clan killed a Cherokee member of the Deer Clan, then the Deer Clan must retaliate and kill a member of the Wolf Clan in order to maintain the balance. By extension, if a Creek killed a Cherokee, the Cherokees must kill a Creek. If the English killed a Cherokee, the Cherokees must kill an Englishman. Once the balance had been restored, the matter was closed. Finally, as Hudson says, "Aboriginal Southeastern warfare was seasonal... the Indians waged war in late spring, summer, and in early fall." The English and other Europeans never understood the Indian concept of war.

European warfare was another matter entirely. Europeans fought to obtain territory or to subjugate or even to exterminate entire populations. They brought to America a concept of total war, wherein villages were burned and crops destroyed, so that anyone who might escape instant death during the battle would face death by exposure and starvation. Furthermore, they had a fondness for destroying their enemies' homes and stores of food in the middle of winter in order to make the results all the more devastating.

Following the surrender of Fort Loudoun and the killing of some of the soldiers there, the Cherokees were satisfied. They saw no purpose in carrying the war any further, and the English at Fort Prince George were not attacked. The French tried to talk the Cherokees into continuing the war against the English, but instead, the Cherokees asked for peace. Both Agan'stat' and Ostenaco spoke for peace at Nikwasi with a British flag flying over the town.

But the English had different ideas. General Amherst wrote of the surrender of Fort Loudoun, "I must own I am ashamed, for I believe it is the first instance of His Majesty's troops having yielded to the Indians." At this same time, the English were puffed up because of recent victories over the French. Amherst sent Colonel James Grant and two thousand men to Charlestown to prepare to invade the Cherokee country. In June of 1761, his army strengthened by an additional six hundred, including Chickasaws and Catawbas, Grant led his expedition forth on the same trail that had been followed the year before by Montgomery. Ada-gal'kala requested a meeting for a peace talk, but Grant refused.

Moving quickly through the already devastated Lower Towns, Grant met the Cherokee forces at a place within two miles of the site of the battle that had repulsed Montgomery. A fight followed that lasted for several hours, and Grant's losses were heavy, but he won the fight. From there he proceeded to methodically destroy all of the Middle Towns and their crops, driving the surviving Cherokees farther into the mountains and farther west.

Mooney says, "The Cherokees were now reduced to the greatest extremity. With some of their best towns in ashes, their fields and orchards wasted for two successive years, their ammunition nearly exhausted, many of their bravest warriors dead, the people fugitives in the mountains, hiding in caves and living like beasts upon roots or killing their horses for food, with the terrible scourge of smallpox adding to the miseries of starvation, and withal torn by factional differences which had existed from the very beginning of the war—it was impossible for even brave men to resist longer."

In September of 1761, Ada-gal'kala, Ostenaco, and seventeen other chiefs went to Fort Prince George to surrender and sign a new treaty of peace. Grant's terms were insulting. He wanted four Cherokees given to him for public execution. Ada-gal'kala refused to sign. He went instead to Charlestown to talk to Governor Bull.

Bull and Ada-gal'kala agreed, and a treaty was signed between the Cherokees and South Carolina. At Ada-gal'kala's request, his old friend Bushyhead (John Stuart) was made Indian agent for South Carolina and sent back with Ada-gal'kala to the Cherokee country. But Virginia would not cease hostilities against the Cherokees without its own treaty, and so in November, Standing Turkey and four hundred Cherokees met with Colonel Stephens of Virginia and signed a treaty with him. They also asked for a representative from Virginia to be sent among them, and a young lieutenant, Henry Timberlake volunteered for the duty.

The following year, after Timberlake had spent several months with the Cherokees, he decided to return to Virginia. Ostenaco, Stalking Turkey, and Pouting Pigeon accompanied him to Williamsburg, where they expressed their desire to visit the king in England. (George II had died in 1760 and been replaced by King George III.)

On May 15, 1762, Timberlake, interpreter William Shorey, and the three Cherokees left for England. Shorey died en route. The rest arrived at Plymouth on June 5, and they were taken to London by carriage. It took Timberlake three weeks to get an audience with the king, and during that long wait the three Cherokees, bored, took to drink. Because of the death of Shorey, Woodward says, "interpreting duties were taken over by Sir Alexander Cuming and two British officers who had mastered the Cherokee language when sent to the Nation years before." One wonders who these two "masters" might have been.

Sir Joshua Reynolds painted a group portrait of the three chiefs and an individual portrait that he titled "Syacust Ukah," presumably, Woodward says, Ostenaco; and Francis Parsons painted "Cunne Shote," or Stalking Turkey. The three Cherokees at last saw the king on July 8, were taken on sightseeing tours, and were exhibited around London. Overall, the trip was unsatisfactory for everyone involved, and the Cherokees left England on August 25 to return home.

On February 10, 1763, the Treaty of Paris marked the end of the French and Indian War, and, according to the terms of the treaty, all Indian tribes east of the Mississippi River came under the jurisdiction of England. Of course, no Indian tribes were party to the negotiations. It was November of that same year before anyone got around to explaining to the Cherokees and other Indian tribes the implications of that treaty. A general council was held in Augusta, Georgia, attended by "chiefs," presumably from all the southern Indian tribes, and the governors of Virginia, North Carolina, South Carolina, and Georgia. John Stuart was also there, newly appointed British Superintendent of Indian Affairs for all tribes south of the Ohio River. On November 10, 1763, a new treaty was signed.

But the establishment of peace between France and England did not greatly improve matters for the Cherokees. Settlers from both Virginia and South Carolina began moving onto Cherokee land, in spite of the king's Proclamation of 1763, which made it illegal for them to do so. There were border disputes between the Cherokees and the various colonies, and in 1765 Virginia settlers killed five Cherokees. War also continued between the Cherokees and the Iroquois League.

In 1768, with Governor Francis Fauquier of Virginia and Sir William Johnson, Superintendent of Indian Affairs in the north, acting as facilitators, Agan'stat' and Ada-gal'kala, both now in their late sixties, went to New York, and a peace was at last concluded between the Cherokees and their distant relatives and longtime foes, the northern Iroquois.

That same year, in the words of Kelly, "a torrent of settlers began flooding the valleys of the Holston." In response to Cherokee complaints, negotiations were held in 1770 that resulted in the Cherokees giving up the land on which the whites had settled. In 1772, more settlers moved onto Cherokee land and, attempting some compliance with the Proclamation of 1763, actually signed an eight-year lease with Ada-gal'kala. They built their settlements along the Watauga River in present-day Tennessee. Some went on to sell their leased land to ignorant buyers.

Mixed-blood families were proliferating. Woodward, while lamenting that the Cherokees did not "progress" much during this time, points out that Alexander Cameron, John McDonald, Edward Graves, John Adair, George Lowrey, and Bryan Ward had all married Cherokee women. And other white men, such as Nathaniel Gist and Richard Pearis, fathered children by Cherokee women but did not bother staying around to make their homes with them.

All of this had an impact on the culture. While Cherokees had always had matrilineal clans, tracing descent through the female line, the English men, true to their English traditions, usually insisted on being the heads

> By the 1770s we can see that the major changes that
> had begun to take place among the Cherokees a
> few years earlier were now intensifying. Treaties
> accompanied by the giving up of more Cherokee
> lands were coming more frequently, one following
> another with increasing speed. Royce lists them as
> follows: Treaty of 1721 with South Carolina; Treaty of
> 1755 with South Carolina; Treaty of 1768 with the
> British Superintendent of Indian Affairs; Treaty
> of 1770 at Lochabar, South Carolina; Treaty of
> 1772 with Virginia; Treaty of 1773 with the British
> Superintendent of Indian Affairs; Treaty of 1775 with
> Richard Henderson, et. al.; Treaty of 1777 with South
> Carolina and Georgia; Treaty of 1777 with Virginia
> and North Carolina. And there would be another
> in 1783 with Georgia. Each of these treaties involved
> the giving up of more land by the Cherokees.

of their households and passing along their surnames. This, then, was the beginning of the undermining of the Cherokee family structure.

The movement toward a central Cherokee government was growing as well, so much so that Ada-gal'kala, on whose authority we do not know, styled himself in 1775 as "president of the nation for more than half a century." And most of the English seem to have accepted and supported him in that role.

SOURCE LIST AND SUGGESTIONS FOR FURTHER READING

Cotterill, R. S. 1954. *The Southern Indians: The Story of the Civilized Tribes before Removal.* Norman: The University of Oklahoma Press.

Evans, E. Raymond, and Duane H. King. 1977. "Historic Documentation of the Grant Expedition against the Cherokees." *Journal of Cherokee Studies* 2:272–73.

French, Captain Christopher. 1977. "Journal of an Expedition to South Carolina." *Journal of Cherokee Studies* 2:275–301.

Kelly, James C. 1979. "Notable Persons in Cherokee History: Attakullakulla."

Journal of Cherokee Studies 3:221–38.

Kelly, James C. 1979. "Oconostota." *Journal of Cherokee Studies* 3:221–38.

Marion, Lieutenant Francis. 1977. "Sowing Tares of Hate." *Journal of Cherokee Studies* 2:332–33.

Monypenny, Major Alexander. 1977. "Order Book of the Grant Expedition." *Journal of Cherokee Studies* 2:302–19.

Monypenny, Major Alexander. 1977. "Diary of March 20–May 31, 1761." *Journal of Cherokee Studies* 2:320–31.

Royce, Charles C. 1887. "The Cherokee Nation of Indians: A Narrative of Their Official Relations with the Colonial and Federal Governments." Smithsonian Institution. Bureau of Ethnology. *Fifth Annual Report, 1883–84*, pp. 121–378. Washington, D.C.: U.S. Government Printing Office. Reprinted, Chicago: Aldine Publishing Co., 1975.

GLOSSARY

Aboriginal. Pertaining to the native, original, or earliest-known inhabitants of a country or region.

Cunne Shote. An English rendering of the Cherokee name of Stalking Turkey. The first part is obviously an attempt at *guhna*, turkey. The rest is anyone's guess.

Holston. An area along the Holston River in present-day Tennessee.

Subjugate. To bring under complete control.

Syacust Ukah. This name was given as the title of one of the portraits painted of the Cherokees in England and is assumed to be another name for "Ostenaco." With a little imagination, we might believe it possible that they are both bad attempts at spelling the same Cherokee name, and we might think that the "ukah" or "aco" part of the name could be a form of *uguku*, or owl.

Treaty of Paris. Treaty between France and England concluded in Paris in 1763, which marked the end of the Seven Years War, known in America as the French and Indian War.

CHAPTER EIGHT

"I Have My Young Warriors around Me"

They met at a place called Sycamore Shoals in the leased Watauga settlements in 1775, Richard Henderson and Nathaniel Hart, partners in a land company called the Transylvania Company, and Cherokees, including Ada-gal'kala, Agan'stat', Savanooka, Dragging Canoe (who was the son of Ada-gal'kala), Willinawa, Tuckasee, Terrapin, and the Tanase Warrior. The land desired by the Transylvania Company included most of what is now Kentucky, and middle Tennessee, and the price was two thousand British pounds and ten thousand pounds worth of trade goods, much of which was guns and ammunition. Neither side, though, had a legal right to make the deal.

The European countries exploring the world in those days had adopted a "Doctrine of Discovery" under which they agreed that the inhabitants of the land owned it and only the country of the "discoverer" could negotiate with them for purchase of their land. English law, agreeing with that doctrine, held that no one but the English government could buy land from Indians, and the Cherokees had promised by treaty that they would sell to no one but the English government. In addition, there seems to have been some question as to the rightful ownership of part of the land because of a Shawnee claim. But Henderson and Hart didn't care about all that, for Daniel Boone already had settlers on part of the land, and those settlers, like many colonists, were also boldly and openly talking about armed rebellion against the king.

Agan'stat' and Ada-gal'kala did not seem to care either. The Cherokees had recently suffered a defeat at the hands of the Choctaws because, Woodward says, "they were short of guns and powder." The old men wanted the guns and powder that were part of the trade goods offered as partial payment for the land.

But Dragging Canoe did care. He cared about Cherokee land. Even though Ada-gal'kala was his father, Dragging Canoe openly opposed both him and Agan'stat' at the council. He spoke out vigorously against the selling of the land, and when he saw that the old men would sign the treaty in spite of all his arguments, he turned to Henderson and said, "You have bought a fair land, but you will find its settlement dark and bloody" (Evans).

It was at this gathering at Sycamore Shoals that Dragging Canoe first became prominent in Cherokee history. Evans tell us that he "was born around 1740 in one of the Overhill Towns, on the Little Tennessee River." His father was Ada-gal'kala. Alexander Cameron, a Scottish assistant to John Stuart, the British Superintendent of Indian Affairs for the southern tribes, was his adopted brother. At a young age, Evans says, Dragging Canoe became the "Head Warrior" (War Chief?) of the town of Malaquo, or Big Island Town, on the Little Tennessee River.

Many of the followers of Dragging Canoe were mixed-bloods and some were pure white, and two white men present at Sycamore Shoals, Richard Pearis and John Vann, actually sided with Dragging Canoe and cautioned the old men against selling the land to the Transylvania Company.

Be all that as it may, Ada-gal'kala, Agan'stat', and others concluded the deal and headed home with their ill-gotten gains. Hard on the heels of the Sycamore Shoals affair came the news that the colonies were very near open rebellion against the British crown, and many of the frontiersmen living illegally on Indian land supported the rebellion precisely because they saw it as the only way to hang onto the land they had squatted upon.

John Stuart wrote to the Cherokees from Georgia telling them about the rebels among the colonists. He told them further that because he was loyal to the king, he had been run out of Charlestown, and that the rebel General Charles Lee had cut off the supply of trade goods to the Cherokees from South Carolina. Stuart promised to send thirty horse loads of ammunition for their protection to Chota by his brother, Henry, and his deputy, Cameron, as he himself was sick in bed.

On their way to Chota, Henry Stuart and Cameron were robbed of nine loads of ammunition by Illinois Indians, but Dragging Canoe and eighty men met them after that and escorted them and the remaining supplies safely the rest of the way. Dragging Canoe was ready to attack the illegal Wataugan settlements. "The white men have almost surrounded us," he said, "leaving us only a little spot of ground to stand upon, and it seems to be their intention to destroy us as a nation."

When Stuart replied that the Cherokees had sold the land to Henderson, Dragging Canoe snapped back, "I had nothing to do with making that bargin [sic]; it was made by some of the old men, who are too old to hunt or fight. As for me, I have a great many of my young warriors around me, and they mean to have their lands" (Evans).

Acting on his brother's instructions, Henry Stuart tried to keep the Cherokees from attacking. He was joined in this effort by Cameron, Ada-gal'kala, Agan'stat', and Cherokee Nancy Ward (either a sister or a cousin to Dragging Canoe, depending on which source we choose to accept, and known to historians as the "ghigau.") Together they were able to convince Dragging Canoe to at least wait a little while, to allow Deputy Superintendent Cameron and Ada-gal'kala time to try to persuade the Watauga settlers to move out peacefully.

In the meantime, Henderson, of the Transylvania Company, found himself in hot water back home, and according to Evans, he had "fled to the wilderness to avoid prosecution." It would take a successful revolution to save him too.

The "peace party" of Cameron, Stuart, and Agan'stat' followed up on their plans and sent letters to the Wataugan settlers offering several suggestions, including a move to west Florida. The Wataugans did not bother to respond. Instead, they circulated among other revolutionaries letters claiming that a large force made up of British soldiers, reinforced by Creeks, Choctaws, and Chickasaws, was marching from Florida to join the Cherokees in a massive attack on the frontier settlers. They signed the letters with the names of Cameron and Stuart. The forgeries had their desired effect. "In a matter of weeks," says Evans, "forces were being raised to destroy the Cherokees."

Later a delegation of northern Indians, including Shawnees, Delawares, and Mohawks, came to the Cherokee country. Headed by Shawnee chief Cornstalk, Evans says, "They urged the Cherokees to join them in war against the Americans."

"Nancy Ward," says Woodward, "treated the northern Indians coolly. Attakullakulla [sic] and Oconostota [sic] ... looked sad and dejected throughout the council, and, when presented with the northern Indians' war belts, both chiefs silently refused them." But Dragging Canoe accepted the belts.

And so Dragging Canoe emerged as the unquestioned leader of the Cherokees at what was certainly up until that point the most critical time in their history. The land base was dwindling; the Cherokees were surrounded by unruly white settlers; the old culture was slowly crumbling because of trade, governmental pressures from outside, intermarriage of Cherokees with whites and the resulting slow erosion of traditional Cherokee family structures, changes in the environment due to changed methods of agriculture, including the addition of grazing animals, the introduction of a cash economy, new notions of warfare, and deadly European diseases. The only hope for the Cherokees seemed to be to help England control its rebellious colonies. And Dragging Canoe was determined to do just that.

At about that time, the news came of the gathering of a large army of Virginia rebels who were preparing to attack the Cherokees in reaction to the forged letters from the Wataugan squatters. Henry Stuart left Chota to hurry back to Georgia and report to his brother. Dragging Canoe decided not to wait for the Americans to invade his country. He made his plans. One division, to be led by the Raven of Chota, would strike the settlers in Carter's Valley. A second division, led by Abram of Chilhowie, would attack the Watauga and Nolichucky River settlements, and Dragging Canoe himself would lead a third division against the Holston settlements.

At a council in Chota, Dragging Canoe told the people that they were not engaging in a war against all the whites, but only against the enemies of the king of England, in other words, against the American revolutionaries. The white men who lived among the Cherokees, most of whom had Cherokee wives, he said, he considered to be the same as the Cherokees. Then to those whites he said, "If any of you choose to join the war, I will be glad, but I will not insist upon any of you going. Those who do not go, however, will be expected to furnish the warriors with ammunition and supplies."

Woodward says that Nancy Ward, in her capacity as "ghigau," on the night of July 8, 1776, "prepared the black drink" for the warriors, then "returned to her seat next to the warriors and headmen." From that vantage point, she listened to Dragging Canoe's battle plans. After the ceremonies were done, she went straight to the homes of the traders Thomas, Williams, and Fawlings, told them the plans, and urged them "to sound the alarm from Wolf Hills (Abingdon, Virginia) westward." She then helped the three traders slip out of town to get started on their mission.

◈

SOURCE LIST AND SUGGESTIONS FOR FURTHER READING

Cox, Brent (Yanusdi). 1999. *Heart of the Eagle: Dragging Canoe and the Emergence of the Chickamauga Confederacy*. Milan, Tenn.: Chenanee Publishers.

Evans, E. Raymond. 1977. "Notable Persons in Cherokee History: Dragging Canoe." *Journal of Cherokee Studies* 2:176–89.

Gritts, Levi. 1971. *Dictionary of the Cherokee Language*, ed. J. T. Alexander. Privately printed.

Stoutenburgh, John, Jr. 1960. *Dictionary of the American Indian*. New York: Philosophical Library.

GLOSSARY

Black drink. Traditional ceremonial drink, brewed from the leaves of a variety of holly and containing significant amounts of caffeine, the black drink was often used to induce vomiting for purposes of purity. The actual Cherokee name for this liquid translates as "White Drink," with "white" symbolizing purity. In English it's always called the Black Drink because of its color.

Carter's Valley. An area of illegal white settlements along the Holston River in Tennessee.

Chilhowie. (or Chilhowee) Mooney identifies this as *Tsulunwei, Tsulunwe* or *Tsulawi*, "possibly connected with *tsulu*, kingfisher." Chilhowee Creek is a tributary of the Little Tennessee River in northern Tennessee. It was obviously also the name of a Cherokee town.

Dragging Canoe. This great leader's name in Cherokee is Tsiyu gansini, Mooney says, from *tsiyu*, "canoe," and *gansini*, "he is dragging it." Some early sources spelled the name "Cheu cunsene" and some "Kunnesee," and a few translated the name as "Otter Lifter." Otter is *tsiya*, so that particular confusion is easily explained. In Gritts we find *ganuhsidasdi*, "carrier," and *ganasinuhsdi*, "drag," obviously forms of the same verb, thus explaining the drag, carry, lift variation.

Ghigau. Usually translated as "Beloved Woman," "Pretty Woman," or "War Woman," the word may be a combination of either *giga*, "blood," or *gige*, "red," and *agehya*, "woman." Of the three popular translations, then, it would seem that "War Woman" is the most accurate. It would not be all three, for a War Woman was a leader of the Women's Red or War Council, and Pretty Woman was a leader of the women's White or Peace Council. Beloved Woman is a designation for respected female elders.

Malaquo. Sometimes also spelled "Mialaquo" and translated as "Great Island" or "Great Island Town," the word is more accurately spelled Amayeli egwa, according to Mooney, who describes it as a town "on Little Tennessee River, at Big Island, a short distance below the mouth of Tellico, in Monroe County, Tennessee."

Nancutas. This is apparently a terrible corruption of the name of some northern tribe of Indians. There is no listing of this word in either Stoutenburgh or Terrell.

Ottawas. An Algonquian-speaking tribe from the area of the Great Lakes, their name in their own language, *Adawe*, means "traders."

Pound. English monetary unit.

Savanooka. A Cherokee name garbled by the English. It could possibly be an attempt to spell the word *Sawanugi*, a Cherokee name meaning "Shawnee."

Sycamore Shoals. Location in the white-squatter settlements of Watauga where the Cherokees met with representatives of the Transylvania Company.

Tanase. Also spelled *Tanasi*. It was apparently both a place-name and a masculine name, and the meaning seems to have been lost. The word developed in English into "Tennessee."

Transylvania Company. Company formed by Judge Richard Henderson and Nathaniel Hart of North Carolina for the express purpose of illegally acquiring and then reselling Cherokee land.

Tuckasee. Corrupt version of a Cherokee masculine name, possibly the same as or a form of the place-name "Tuckasegee," which Mooney identifies as *Tsiksitsi*. He also says that the word has lost its meaning.

Watauga. Actually, *Watagi*. This was the name of more than one Cherokee town. Mooney identifies two in Tennessee. In its corrupt form, "Watauga," the name is also applied to the illegal white settlements that sprang up near a Cherokee town of that name. The meaning of the word seems to be lost.

Willinawa. A corrupt Anglicization of a Cherokee masculine name.

CHAPTER NINE

"Our Cry Is All for Peace."

Unaware of his sister's betrayal, Dragging Canoe staged the attack on the illegal Watauga settlements as planned. Evans describes the campaign as follows:

> On the morning of June 20, the two opposing forces began advancing toward each other. After an ineffective exchange of fire between the advance units, the main bodies closed up. The Cherokee battle line consisted of a wedge formation in the center led by Dragging Canoe with crescent shaped lines extending on both flanks. When the Cherokees emerged from the woods a number of the militiamen ... broke ranks and ran for the safety of the fort.
>
> When Dragging Canoe saw the whites running he was sure of victory. . . . However, not all the whites had fled. Most of them took shelter behind trees and directed a murderous rifle fire at the oncoming Cherokees. Dragging Canoe himself was hit, his right leg shattered by the bullet. His brother, Little Owl, was hit eleven times. . . . The battle was over in a matter of minutes. There was nothing for the Cherokees to do but withdraw with their wounded, leaving thirteen of their men dead on the field to be scalped and mutilated by

the white militiamen. Abram ... also failed to take the fort at
Watauga. The Raven ... destroyed several isolated cabins, but
did little military damage.

On his way back home, Dragging Canoe sent small parties out in different directions to do what damage they could and to balance things
out for the thirteen dead Cherokees. These small parties killed eighteen
whites and burned their cabins. Abram's group returned home with a few
prisoners including a Mrs. Bean and a "young boy" named Samuel Moore.
Moore was burned at the stake. Nancy Ward, exercising her prerogative as
"Ghigau," rescued Mrs. Bean, who rewarded the "Ghigau's" kindness by
teaching her slaves how to make butter and cheese. A little later, Ward
helped Bean make her way safely back to the white-squatter settlements.

Following the failed attacks on the Watauga settlements, Dragging
Canoe knew that the white Americans would retaliate, and he had to
prepare for their coming attack. When it came it was massive, and it
came with the purpose of totally destroying the Cherokees.

In July of 1776, two hundred Georgians led by Colonel Samuel Jack
attacked Cherokee towns on the Chattahoochie and Tugaloo rivers.
Colonel Andrew Williamson led eleven hundred South Carolinians into
the Lower Towns in August. And two thousand North Carolinians under
the command of General Griffith Rutherford invaded the Middle Towns,
and soon after joined forces with those of Williamson. One thousand
Virginians led by Colonel Christian prepared to attack the Overhill Towns.

Their express purpose, Evans says, was "the complete destruction of
the entire Cherokee nation." They burned towns, destroyed crops and
killed men, women, and children indiscriminately. Evans goes on to say,
"Prisoners who were not immediately murdered were put on the slave
block and sold like Blacks."

Forces under Dragging Canoe and Alexander Cameron did their best
to hold off this attack, but when they ran out of ammunition, they were
forced to retreat. Cameron went to Florida to seek reinforcements of
British Loyalists, and Dragging Canoe and other survivors of the onslaught
went to the Overhills Towns. Now the huge rebel army was all together
and prepared to invade the Overhills. Agan'stat' at last raised his head up
again and spoke for peace. This time he was joined by the Raven of Chota,
and by Caleb Starr and other white residents of the Cherokee Nation.

Dragging Canoe remained opposed to any reconciliation with the
Americans, which could only be accomplished, as he well knew, by complete surrender. Instead, he wanted to send the women and children
away to safety, burn the towns before the invaders even reached them,

A few words seem to be in order here on the practice of torturing captives. This practice, which most certainly did take place, has been a favorite topic of both historians and writers of popular fiction. It seems to be ready made to use as "proof" of Indian "savagery." But Francis Jennings has taken a closer look at historical records, and here is a little of what he has to say on the subject.

Many of the aspects of so-called savage war were taught to Indians by European example. As to torture, for example, a systematic examination of the documents of the early contact era, published by Nathaniel Knowles in 1940, found no references to torture by Indians of the southeast coast region until almost 200 years after white contact.

and wait in ambush with every available Cherokee warrior to meet the rebel army head on. He was outvoted, and envoys suing for peace were sent to the Virginia army. Agan'stat' and his followers, now called the Peace Party, agreed to sign a new treaty with the colonies. They also agreed to turn over to the Americans both Dragging Canoe and Alexander Cameron, and a reward of one thousand pounds each was offered for their capture.

On May 20, 1777, Agan'stat' and other members of the Peace Party signed a treaty with South Carolina and Georgia. On June 20, they signed another with Virginia. Altogether, with these two treaties, the signers, acting on behalf of all the Cherokees, gave away 5,000,264 acres of land in exchange for peace. Interestingly, while Agan'stat' and the other signers were from the Overhills Towns, the land they gave away was in the Lower and Middle Towns.

And the evidence of the events surrounding the illegal Sycamore Shoals deal with the Transylvania Company, remember, strongly indicates that the leaders of the Peace Party were no longer the recognized leaders of the Cherokee people. That made no difference, of course, to the whites who were getting the land. It was a pattern that would be repeated again. Finally, to give these new treaties an air of legality, the rebel colonies recognized Agan'stat' as the legitimate Cherokee chief and labeled Dragging Canoe and his followers "secessionists" and "outlaws." The coupling of those two words is particularly ironic, coming from British colonists in the process of open, armed rebellion against their own government.

In reaction to all of these events, Dragging Canoe and his followers, some of them British Loyalists, also called Tories, moved to a new location. Because their land had been given up by the new treaties, many of the now homeless people from the Lower Towns joined them. They built new towns near the home of the British commissary, John McDonald, along Chickamauga Creek in southern Tennessee near the Georgia line. Evans says, "Most of the traders and other permanent white residents in the Nation moved with Dragging Canoe to the new towns. . . . Many white refugees, fleeing the excesses of the revolutionists in the Carolinas and Georgia, sought safety in the same area. This mixed group came to be called the Chickamaugas, or the Chickamauga Cherokees."

Ignoring the new treaties as illegal, the Chickamaugas continued to fight the American colonial revolutionaries. They boldly attacked settlements near the very places where the treaties had been signed and in the land areas that the so-called treaties had given over to the Americans. Among the whites killed during this time were David Crockett and his wife, grandparents of the later famous Davy Crockett.

Continuing to deal with Agan'stat', North Carolina and Virginia each appointed new commissioners to the Cherokees. Joseph Martin, the commissioner from Virginia, married a daughter of Nancy Ward. The continental army commissioned trader Nathaniel Gist a colonel, and Gist took seventeen Cherokees with him to serve as scouts under General George Washington. There were now Cherokees on both sides of the war. The American Revolution had become for the Cherokees a civil war. It would not be their last.

The Watauga settlers, not content with the land they had already wrested away from the Cherokees, continued to trespass farther into Cherokee country. And though the Overhills Towns had made peace with the Americans and had just recently given them over five million acres of land, whites continued to invade their remaining land. And the rebellious colonies sent no trade goods in to the Overhills Cherokees. The British, on the other hand, continued to supply the Chickamaugas, and therefore many Overhills people left their homes to join up with Dragging Canoe. At this point, it seems, the Cherokees were all in favor of the British, but those living near the colonies were afraid to say so, and their leader, Agan'stat', and others, continued to cooperate with the rebels.

In 1778, Dragging Canoe and all the warriors of the Chickamauga towns went with John McDonald to join British forces in Georgia and South Carolina to fight the rebels. Taking advantage of their absence, six hundred volunteers from North Carolina and Virginia, under orders from Governor Patrick Henry of Virginia (famous for his inflammatory speech on liberty), and led by Colonel Evan Shelby, attacked the Chickamauga towns. The brave troops totally destroyed eleven towns without much effort, for Dragging Canoe and all the fighting men were away from home. Even so, only four Cherokees were killed, as almost all of the women and children were able to escape into the woods.

The Chickamaugas moved their towns again, a little farther to the west, in southern Tennessee and northern Alabama. This time, with permission of the Creeks, they built their towns on Creek land at the base of Chatanuga Mountain. The new Chickamauga towns were known as the Five Lower Towns, and they were named Nickajack, Running Water, Long Island, Crow Town, and Lookout Town. (Evans says that "because of shifts of occupancy, there were actually more than five," and he lists, in addition to the above, Tuskegee Island Town and Will's Town.)

The leaders of the Chickamaugas at this time, besides Dragging Canoe, were Doublehead, Pumpkin Boy, Bench (or Bob Benge, son of white trader John Benge), Will Webber (half-breed, known as Red-headed Will Webber), Bloody Fellow, Glass, the Bowl (red haired and half Scots), Middlestriker, John Watts, Little Owl, and the Badger.

Dragging Canoe met with Shawnee leaders from the north, also allies of the British, and successfully brought to an end the ages-old war between the Cherokees and Shawnees. They became friends and allies, and some Chickamaugas moved north to the Ohio Valley in the Shawnee country, and some Shawnees moved south to live with the Chickamaugas.

In 1780, Dragging Canoe and the Chickamaugas aided the British forces under Colonel Thomas Browne in recapturing Augusta from the rebels. They scattered the rebel army and destroyed American settlements. After that, Evans says, "the Chickamauga Cherokees were entrusted [by the British] with the mission of keeping the frontier militiamen occupied west of the mountains. Dragging Canoe and McDonald responded with vigor, staging a series of guerilla raids all along the North Carolina frontier and well above the borders of Virginia." The American response was to attack the defenseless Overhills Towns, occupied by the very people who had been cooperating with them all this time. The army that accomplished these cowardly attacks was led by Colonel Arthur Campbell and John Sevier.

In 1781, Dragging Canoe led an attack against the American settlements in the area of present-day Nashville, Tennessee, and very nearly
wiped them out, but the British suffered losses that year, because both
Spain and France came to the aid of the Americans. The war was getting
to be unpopular back in England, and in October of 1781, Lord Cornwallis,
in command of the British forces in America, surrendered at Yorktown.
Loyalists in the colonies began fleeing the country. In November of 1782,
a provisional peace treaty was signed between Great Britain and the new
United States in Paris.

But Dragging Canoe did not surrender. When the British army was
called home to England, he was left to fight alone. He continued to talk
with representatives of other Indian tribes with the goal of forming a
confederation of all tribes to hold back further encroachment of
Americans onto Indian land. He met with Shawnees, Creeks, Choctaws,
Chickasaws, and others. And in spite of the withdrawal of British troops,
some of the Englishmen who had been living with the Chickamaugas,
including John McDonald, chose to stay with Dragging Canoe.

The closing of the American Revolution is a good time to pause and
reflect on what the historians have done with respect to these characters
and events, and an analysis of their treatment of Dragging Canoe and
Nancy Ward is probably the quickest way toward a clearer picture of the
way in which facts have been purposefully distorted in order to justify
actions or to support pet theories or themes.

Dragging Canoe has been portrayed as a bloodthirsty leader of a
band of outlaw Cherokees who simply hated white people. He has been
called "the Savage Napoleon" and "the Dragon." (Notable exceptions to
this attitude toward Dragging Canoe can be found in Evans and Collier.)

Nancy Ward, on the other hand, has been the darling of historians
writing about Cherokees as well as the darling of the Cherokee genealo-
gists. She earned her title "Ghigau," they tell us, when in battle with the
Creeks, her first husband, Kingfisher, was killed, and she picked up his
rifle and fought bravely throughout the rest of the battle. She also
became, they say, the first Cherokee owner of a Black slave, a dubious
claim to distinction. After the death of Kingfisher, she married a white
man, the trader Bryan Ward, and thereafter was known as Nancy Ward.

In 1776, when Dragging Canoe (either her brother or her first cousin)
was preparing to attack the Watauga settlements, Woodward says, she
was present, mixing the black drink, and overheard his battle plans. As
soon as her part in the ceremony was done, she raced away to send a
warning to the settlers. As a result of her action, Dragging Canoe's attack
was successfully repulsed, Dragging Canoe was shot through the thighs,

Little Owl was shot eleven times, and thirteen Cherokee men were killed, their bodies left lying on the battlefield to be scalped and mutilated by the settlers.

And how has she been remembered? Starr says that she was "described even after she was an old woman as a person of remarkable beauty, poise 'with a queenly and commanding presence.'" Woodward calls her "a friend to both whites and Indians." Here we have the stories of two full-blood Cherokees who grew up together and were closely related to one another. (A cousin on the mother's side, in the clan system, would be called brother or sister.) When affairs between the Cherokees and the revolutionary colonists became critical, one chose to fight for Cherokee rights, the other chose to warn the Americans.

Is it any wonder that the white American recorders of history have made a monster of the patriot and a heroine of the "friend of the whites"? United States history, as well as popular fiction, is full of examples of "the good Indian" who is a friend to the whites: Uncas, Pocahontas, Shabbona, Sacajawea, Nancy Ward—Tonto. Dragging Canoe was pursued until his death. Nancy Ward settled down to run a profitable inn and, as Starr tells us, "became quite wealthy, her property consisting of stock, slaves and money."

Some Cherokees and some historians, reacting to the old slant put on this period of history, have reinterpreted the roles of these two giant figures in Cherokee history. They have said that Dragging Canoe was a patriot and Nancy Ward a traitor. But perhaps the truth is much more complex than either extreme has seen it.

There is no question as to Dragging Canoe's motives. He was adamant regarding the protection of Cherokee land, Cherokee lifeways and Cherokee sovereignty. There is no doubt, then, that he may properly be designated a Cherokee patriot. But what of Nancy Ward and her motives? During this period of Cherokee history, much was in turmoil. There had already been a tremendous amount of bloodshed. Many Cherokee women, not Nancy Ward alone, wanted an end to the fighting. In 1781, Nancy Ward had said to the Cherokee warriors present for the signing of the Treaty of Long Island, "We are your mothers. You are our sons. Our cry is all for peace" (Hill, 1997). And remember the Cherokee women who smuggled food in to their husbands and sweethearts at the siege of Fort Loudoun. So there seems to have been a male voice, or perspective, on the issues, and a female voice, different and distinctive.

Cherokee women had always had power and influence, but it seems they were not being listened to here. Perhaps Dragging Canoe should have responded more thoughtfully to his sister's advice. Perhaps he should not have planned an attack on the Watauga settlements without her blessing or consent. Perhaps the clash between Dragging Canoe and Nancy Ward is a lone illustration of a much larger clash between the sexes among the Cherokees of the time.

The proliferation of mixed-blood families and the influence of the European heads of household among the Cherokees was causing some changes in attitudes and in behavior. Traditional female power was being eroded. Nancy Ward and the other women were likely asserting their old rights. Dragging Canoe and others, especially his followers, seem to have been ignoring those rights. (Dragging Canoe's own son was called Young Dragging Canoe, a reflection of the European practice of naming a child after its father, a practice in direct conflict with the ages-old Cherokee tradition of tracing descent through female lines.)

So perhaps Nancy Ward's actions do not so much reflect a choice of the white settlers over her own people, but rather reflect a choice of female rights and prerogatives over the changing attitudes and habits that she saw growing around her.

SOURCE LIST AND SUGGESTIONS FOR FURTHER READING

Starr, Emmet. 1921. *History of the Cherokee Indians and their Legends and Folklore*. Oklahoma City: Warden Company.

GLOSSARY

Bench. Another name for Bob Benge, a Chickamauga leader.

Bowl. Translation of Diwali, the name of a Chickamauga leader. He was also known as Bowles, John Bowls, and Colonel Bowls.

Chatanuga. Alternate spelling of Chattanooga. Mooney says it is from *Tsatanugi*, a place name with no meaning in Cherokee as it seems to be of foreign origin. The present city of Chattanooga, Tennessee, is in about the same location and takes its name from this.

Chickamauga. From *Tsikamagi*, which Mooney says has lost its meaning and seems to be of foreign origin. The name was applied to a creek coming into the Tennessee River a few miles above Chattanooga. When Dragging Canoe and his followers moved their towns to this area, they became known as Chickamaugas or Chickamauga Cherokees.

Commissary. During the period of the American Revolution, a British agent in charge of trade relations with Indian tribes.

Loyalist. British colonist who refused to join the revolutionary movement, but rather, remained loyal to the king of England.

Militia. A body of civilian soldiers.

Nickajack. Ancient Cherokee place name, from *Nikutsegi*. Mooney says the meaning is lost, and the word is probably of foreign origin. It has also been corrupted, simply because of the sound, to "Nigger Jack," and it has been used as a masculine name.

Tory. Another name for a Loyalist.

Tugaloo. From *Dugiluyi*, a place-name occurring more than once in the old Cherokee country. Mooney says the meaning is lost, and the etymology is uncertain.

Tuskegee. *Taskigiyi*. Tuskegee Place. The Tuskegee were a small tribe that sought refuge with the Cherokees. "Tuskegee Place" was used as a place-name in towns where they settled.

CHAPTER TEN

"A Pipe and a Little Tobacco"

At the conclusion of the American Revolution, England gave up its claim to Florida to Spain, but the northern boundary line was not clearly drawn. The new Spanish governor of Florida, Don Esteban Miro, invited Choctaws, Chickasaws, Creeks, and Chickamauga Cherokees to a council, wherein he urged them all to continue fighting against the Americans and promised them Spanish support.

With the aid of the promised supplies from Spain, Dragging Canoe continued his war against the frontier settlements of Virginia and the Carolinas. At the same time, the Overhills Towns continued to try to get along with the new United States, in spite of the fact that the states had rewarded Revolutionary War heroes with tracts of Indian land, and five hundred families had built new homes within a day's march of Chota, now recognized as the Cherokee capital.

The Overhills Towns now had new leadership, for in 1782 Agan'stat' had resigned, intending to pass his leadership along to his son, Tuckasee. The Overhills people would have none of Tuckasee, however, and their new choice for chief was instead Old Tassel, with Hanging Maw as War Chief. Agan'stat' died in 1783 and was buried at Chota. (Ada-gal'kala had died in 1780.)

In 1784, the already notorious John Sevier and his friends and followers went onto Cherokee land in what is now western North Carolina and formed the state of Franklin, with Sevier as "President." Woodward describes Sevier as "handsome, hard-riding, fast shooting," and tells us that he was called "Nolichucky Jack" by the whites and "Little John" by the Cherokees. Sevier negotiated a treaty with an inexperienced delegation of young chiefs led by "Ancoo" in May of 1785.

In November of 1785, the Cherokees signed their first treaty with the new United States at a place called Hopewell in South Carolina. Woodward, citing the U.S. commissioners themselves, tells us that "36 chiefs and 918" Cherokees, including Old Tassel, were present at the treaty conference. Evans and Cotterill say that there were fewer than one hundred. Everyone agrees, however, that no one from the Chickamaugas was there.

Old Tassel explained the treaty with Franklin as a mistake, and he protested the old treaty with the Transylvania Company. Although the transaction with the Transylvania Company had clearly been illegal, the agents of the United States insisted that it was binding on the Cherokees. Amazingly, the Treaty of Hopewell did not ask the Cherokees to give up any additional land. Nancy Ward was there and offered the commissioners from the United States "a pipe and a little tobacco . . . to smoke in friendship."

The Treaty of Hopewell also gave the Cherokees the right to deal with trespassers on their land as they saw fit. John Sevier reacted simply. He sent an expedition of Franklin militiamen into the Overhills and forced Old Tassel and others to sign a new treaty with Franklin, called the Treaty of Coyatee. In this treaty, Old Tassel gave up all of the Cherokees' remaining land north of the Little Tennessee River. The Franklinites almost immediately moved in and started to build a new settlement on that land in a region known as Muscle Shoals, but Dragging Canoe led a force that destroyed the settlement before it had been completed.

In the summer of 1788, a militia of 250 men from Franklin, led by Sevier himself, invaded the Overhills Towns. They claimed to have exacted yet another treaty from the Cherokees, they burned towns, and they killed a number of Cherokee people, including Old Tassel, Abram, and Abram's son, while meeting under a flag of truce. The Overhills Towns moved their capital to Ustanali in Georgia, east of the Chickamauga towns, and the Cherokees were reunited under the leadership of Dragging Canoe.

Governor Johnston of North Carolina, clearly more concerned about the reunification of the Cherokees than about the senseless and brutal murders of Old Tassel and the others, ordered the arrest of Sevier and had him charged with treason. Most of the Franklinites then took an oath of allegiance to North Carolina, and, to gain his own freedom from prison, so did Sevier, in February of 1789. With the troublesome state of Franklin out of the picture, all was forgiven, and in the fall of that same year Sevier was elected to the North Carolina Senate. That same year, George Washington was inaugurated as the first president of the United States.

But the land that the state of Franklin had claimed did not go back to the Cherokees. Instead it went to the United States and was made into part of the new "Southwest Territory," with William Blount as territorial governor.

Dragging Canoe, no longer a young man, spent most of his energy at this time seeking alliances with other Indian tribes, still trying to build his confederacy. More and more, the Chickamauga raids were being led by younger men, particularly John Watts and Bob Benge.

In August of 1790, the U.S. Congress finally acted upon a recommendation President Washington had made a year earlier. Responding to a letter he had received from Secretary of War Henry Knox, Washington had requested Congress to appoint a commission to examine the case of the Cherokees and renew with them the provisions of the Treaty of Hopewell. This was called for because, according to Knox, "the disgraceful violation of the Treaty of Hopewell with the Cherokees requires the serious consideration of Congress. If so direct and manifest contempt of the authority of the United States be suffered with impunity, it will be in vain to attempt to extend the arm of government to the frontiers. The Indian tribes can have no faith in such imbecile promises, and the lawless whites will ridicule a government which shall, on paper only, make Indian treaties and regulate Indian boundaries."

And so the Cherokees once more met with representatives of the United States government. They met at White's Fort on the Holston River in Tennessee, on July 2, 1791. Woodward says that "twelve hundred Cherokees and forty chiefs" were there to negotiate the Treaty of Holston. This time Dragging Canoe and other Chickamauga Cherokees participated.

The treaty promised "perpetual peace and friendship between all the citizens of the United States of America, and all the individuals composing the whole Cherokee nation of Indians." The Cherokees acknowledged themselves "to be under the protection of the said United States" and agreed not to make treaties with any "foreign power, individual state, or with individuals of any state." Both sides agreed to an exchange of prisoners.

Boundary lines between the United States and the Cherokee Nation were defined, but they included the Muscle Shoals area in the United States so that the whites already illegally settled there would not be required to move. And the United States promised to "cause certain valuable goods, to be immediately delivered to the undersigned Chiefs and Warriors, for the use of their nation," and to pay the Cherokee Nation one thousand dollars annually.

The United States was given the right to regulate Cherokee trade, and U.S. citizens were given free use of a road through the Cherokee Nation and of the Tennessee River. The United States guaranteed Cherokee ownership of all remaining Cherokee land, and agreed that any person settling illegally on Cherokee land forfeited the protection of the United States "and the Cherokees may punish him or not as they please."

U.S. citizens were forbidden to hunt on Cherokee land or to enter Cherokee land without a passport from the governor of one of the states or organized territories or someone authorized by the president. The Cherokee Nation agreed to turn over to the authorities any Cherokee found guilty of robbery, murder, "or other capitol crime" against U.S. citizens or residents. However, if any white should commit a crime in Cherokee country against a Cherokee, the Cherokees were obligated to rely on the United States or one of the states to punish that person.

The greatest irony in the treaty shows up in Article XIV. "That the Cherokee nation," it says, "may be led to a greater degree of civilization, and to become herdsmen and cultivators, instead of remaining in a state of hunters, the United States will from time to time furnish gratuitously the said nation with useful implements of husbandry." In other words, they will attempt to make farmers of people who have only been hunters. And this language comes from people who had been fighting the Cherokees by destroying their crops and stealing their surplus food supplies.

The treaty was apparently at least satisfactory to all, for it was signed by forty-one Cherokees, a number of them Chickamaugas, including the Badger, John Watts, Bloody Fellow, Doublehead, Middlestriker, and "Cheakoneske, or Otter Lifter." That last is almost certainly Dragging Canoe. (See the discussion of Dragging Canoe's name in the glossary following Chapter 8.)

Before the year was over, a party of Cherokees went to Philadelphia, then the capital of the United States, to protest that they had been pressured into signing the treaty and giving up more land. The annual payment was increased. They further protested that white settlers had not moved off of Cherokee lands, and, furthermore, more were moving in. They asked that these illegal settlers be removed, according to the terms of the treaty. The settlers were not removed, and Cherokee raids on those settlers were resumed. The Cherokees had the right, of course, "to punish [them] or not as they please." In 1792, the Chickamaugas formally declared war.

Dragging Canoe, over sixty years old by this time, died later that same year, but Chickamaugas under the leadership of John Watts and Bob Benge, also known as the Bench, continued to fight. Then in June of 1793, in response to a request from President Washington, Governor

Blount and a federal peace commission met with Cherokee leaders, including new Overhills chief Hanging Maw, at the Cherokee town of Coyatee. Progress toward a peaceful resolution was being made when all of a sudden a company of mounted militia under the command of Captain John Beard came racing through the town and firing at anyone they saw, Indian or white. Several people were killed in the senseless attack. One of the dead was the wife of Hanging Maw.

The Cherokees protested, demanding satisfaction, and John Watts, says Evans, "waited to see what the authorities would do." Bob Benge had not been present at the scene, but when he heard about what had happened, he prepared to retaliate. Beard was arrested, tried, acquitted, and released. Outraged, John Watts joined Benge, but before they could move, a company of two hundred mounted men invaded the Middle Towns, killed fifteen Cherokees and captured another fifteen.

"Late in September," Mooney says, "seven hundred Creeks and three hundred Cherokees—under John Watts and Doublehead, crossed the Tennessee and advanced in the direction of Knoxville." They attacked a small blockhouse called Cavett's Station, which was defended by three men and thirteen women and children. The defenders of the blockhouse surrendered, only to be killed by Doublehead and his followers. One boy was saved by John Watts.

"Bob Benge," Evans says, "returned home from Cavett's Station, filled with disgust by Doublehead's excesses and by John Watts's inability to control the warriors." In April of 1794, with his brother Martin and a few more men, he set out for southern Virginia on a series of daring raids. On the return trip, taking captives along with him, Benge and his party were ambushed, and he was killed and scalped.

Because of the frequent raids, seven hundred men under the command of John Sevier were sent after the Cherokees, but they did not go into the Chickamauga towns. Instead, they rode into Ustanali and burned it to the ground. Then at Etowah, where the Cherokees were waiting for Sevier, there was a bloody fight, but the Cherokees were eventually forced to retreat. Sevier and his men then burned Etowah and several more nearby towns before heading for home.

Raids continued back and forth between American militiamen and Cherokees, and in early June of 1794, a group of Chickamaugas from Running Water under the leadership of the Bowl and Whitemankiller encountered some whites in a boat under the command of William Scott at Muscle Shoals on the Tennessee River. Historians differ on the matter of where the Chickamaugas had been, but they were apparently on their way home to Running Water, and they had money. The white men had a boat,

Mooney says, "laden with pots, hardware and other property." On the boats were six white men, three women, four children, and twenty Black slaves.

The white men, finding out that the Cherokees had money, invited them aboard the boats to look over the trade goods they were carrying. They gave the Cherokees whiskey, got them drunk, and sold them goods until the Cherokees had spent all their money. When the Cherokees woke up the next morning, sober, and looked at what they had bought and discovered that they had spent all their money, the Bowl went back to the boat and told Scott that the Cherokees wanted to give back the goods and get their money back. He offered to pay for the whiskey they had consumed. Scott refused.

Bowl went back to the other Cherokees on shore and told them what Scott had said. Some wanted to kill the white men right then, but Bowl talked them out of it. With two other men, he went back to Scott. He made the request again, and told Scott that he was trying to prevent a fight. The white men then attacked the three Cherokees with boat poles, killing two of them. The Bowl escaped. He quickly returned to the boats with the rest of the Cherokees. They killed all the white men, but did not harm the women, children, or the slaves. Following this incident, instead of returning to Running Water, this group of Chickamaugas continued west. They stopped in Missouri and built new homes there.

The reason for their move is unclear. Clarke says, "Afraid of what his tribe would think about the massacre [sic], since the Cherokee Indians were supposed to be abiding by a treaty of amity with the whites, Bowles and his band headed down the Tennessee River in boats." But the treaty had already been broken, war had been declared, and fighting was widespread. Whatever their reasons, the Bowl and his followers moved to Missouri.

That same month another treaty was signed, and after that, when a white man was killed by a Creek, the Overhills Cherokees, under the advice of Hanging Maw, captured the Creek and turned him in. The man was hanged for murder, and one hundred Creeks moved against the settlements in retaliation. Hanging Maw gave the alarm, and fifty-three Cherokees joined with federal troops in fighting and defeating the Creeks. The Cherokee unification that had so alarmed the United States had not lasted long. Cherokee leadership was once more fragmented, with Hanging Maw and the Overhills once more representing the Peace Party. Even among the Chickamaugas, without the charisma of Dragging Canoe to hold them together, things began to fall apart.

Benge was dead. The Bowl and his group had gone west. John Watts and Doublehead were not getting along with one another. They were especially vulnerable to the attack that finally came in September of 1794. The following is from Mooney:

> The Tennesseans... had long ago come to the conclusion
> that peace could be brought about only through the destruc-
> tion of the Chickamauga towns. Anticipating some action of
> this kind, which the general government did not think nec-
> essary or advisable, orders against any such attempt had
> been issued by the Secretary of War to Governor Blount. The
> frontier went about their preparations, however, and it is
> evident... that the local military authorities were in con-
> nivance with the undertaking.

General Robertson organized volunteers from Nashville, and Colonel Whitley brought a company from Virginia. Major Ore had been sent by Governor Blount for other reasons, but, as Mooney says, he "entered as heartily into the project as if no other orders had ever been issued." He assumed command of the whole expedition and added his detachment of troops to the volunteers already assembled. The army totaled 550 mounted men.

They attacked and destroyed both Nickajack and Running Water the same day, killing fifty Cherokees and capturing a good many more. After returning to Nashville, General Robertson sent a message to John Watts threatening a second invasion. Watts requested a conference at Tellico Blockhouse with Governor Blount.

They met there on November 7, 1794: Governor Blount, Hanging Maw (now styled Head Chief of the Cherokee Nation and supported in that role by the United States), and John Watts, chief of the Chickamauga towns. Peace was concluded at this conference without the aid of a for-mal treaty, and the long war between the Cherokees and the Americans was finally over.

SOURCE LIST AND SUGGESTIONS FOR FURTHER READING

Clarke, Mary Whatley. 1971. *Chief Bowles and the Texas Cherokees.* Norman: University of Oklahoma Press.

Evans, E. Raymond. 1976. "Notable Persons in Cherokee History: Bob Benge." *Journal of Cherokee Studies* 1:98–106.

CHAPTER ELEVEN

"Perpetual Friendship"

In 1798, the Cherokees yielded to pressure from the United States government to sign yet another treaty and to give up yet more land for the insatiable settlers. In exchange, the Cherokees received five thousand dollars worth of goods, an additional one thousand dollars on their annual payment from the previous treaties, and, of course, a renewed promise of perpetual friendship. Bloody Fellow, the Glass, and "Akooh" were three of the thirty-nine "chiefs" who signed the treaty.

By 1800 the Cherokees were at last really at peace with the United States. Their landholdings, mostly in Tennessee, with some in Georgia and Alabama, and a little in North Carolina, were down to approximately forty-three thousand square miles, and the Cherokee population was around twenty thousand. Mooney describes the Cherokees of this time in the following way:

They had been in possession of firearms for about one hundred years, and "had learned well their use.... hatchets knives, clothes, and trinkets had become so common...that [they] had declared that they could no longer live without the traders. Horses...had been introduced early in the [previous] century...[and some had] from two to a dozen each." They owned cattle, hogs, and poultry. "Peach trees and potatoes, as well as the native corn and beans, were abundant in their fields, and some had bees and honey and did a considerable trade in beeswax. They seem to have quickly recovered from the repeated ravages of war, and there was a general air of prosperity throughout the nation." Mooney continues:

> At a conference held [in 1801] we find the chiefs of the mountain towns complaining that the people of the more western and southwestern settlements had received more than their share of spinning wheels and cards, and were consequently more advanced in making their own clothing as well as in farming, to which the others retorted that these things had been offered to all alike at the same time, but while the lowland people had been quick to accept, the mountaineers had hung back."

These changes among the Cherokees, considered in those days and by numerous later historians as "advances in civilization," were more prevalent among the people of the lowlands, where there were more whites and more mixed-bloods in the towns. Mooney says, "Those of the mixed-blood who could afford it usually sent their children away to be educated, while some built schoolhouses upon their own grounds and brought in private teachers from the outside. [Around 1800] we find influential mixed-bloods in almost every town, and the civilized idea dominated even the national council. The Middle Towns, shut in from the outside world by high mountains, remained a stronghold of Cherokee conservatism."

These "lowlanders" who were becoming more "progressive," receiving more benefits from the treaties, and some of whom were to grow rich, were mostly former Chickamaugas, while the conservatives in the mountains were the remnants of the Peace Party. Ironically, at the conclusion of an Indian war, very often the U.S. Government dealt a worse hand to its friends than to its former enemies. This is just one of many such examples.

In 1801, the first mission was established in Cherokee country. With the permission of both the Cherokee National Council and the United States government, and at the invitation of David Vann, "a prominent mixed-blood chief," Moravians Abraham Steiner and Gottlieb Byhan started Spring Place near Vann's home in Georgia. In 1804, Reverend Gideon Blackburn started a Presbyterian school in Cherokee country.

But while the Cherokees were at peace with the United States, and the two governments had joined together in a pledge of "perpetual friendship," and many whites were praising the Cherokees for their rapid and remarkable "progress toward civilization," the Cherokees were not without dangerous enemies. Almost from the time of the signing of the last treaty, pressures were brought to bear on the Cherokees to sign again. And three more treaties, each taking more land, came one after another with almost dizzying speed in 1804 and 1805. Altogether they took almost eight thousand square miles of Cherokee land.

Cherokee haters were still popular in Georgia, Tennessee, and the Carolinas. Tennessee had sent Andrew Jackson to Congress. Jackson had fought in campaigns against the Cherokees and had personally profited from the sale of ill-gotten Cherokee lands. As senator from Tennessee, he actually introduced a bill to reimburse the state of Tennessee for the expenses incurred by John Sevier's unauthorized and illegal invasion of Cherokee towns, which Jackson maintained had been absolutely necessary. And Tennessee, admitted to the union as a state in 1796, had elected John Sevier its first governor. It seems the quickest road to fame and fortune in Tennessee during those times was to have killed Cherokees and to profess continuing hatred for Cherokees.

In 1802, President Thomas Jefferson signed an agreement, known as the Georgia Compact, with the state of Georgia, promising to acquire for the state of Georgia the title to all Indian lands "lying within the limits of that state" as soon as it could be done peaceably and at a reasonable cost. So the citizens of the states around the Cherokees continued to press on Cherokee land, the state governments wanted to be completely rid of the Cherokees, and the United States government was planning to remove the Cherokees to some as yet undisclosed location.

And President Jefferson had specific plans for accomplishing this goal. He created a government "factory system," whereby government factories, or trading posts, would take the place of the old traders. The "factors," or government traders in the stores, were instructed to give the Indians, "especially their leading men," unlimited credit. The idea was to allow the Indians to run up debts that they could not possibly pay. At that point, the United States government would offer to pay the debt in exchange for more land. Jefferson's other tactic was even simpler. It was to bribe "chiefs" and "leading men" to sign their names to treaties of land cession. Then when the United States "acquired" from France all of the land from the Mississippi River to the Rocky Mountains and from the Gulf of Mexico to Canada, in what became known as the Louisiana Purchase in 1803, Jefferson had a place to send the Cherokees and other unwanted eastern Indians. (Actually, the United States did not buy all that land from France, as France had never owned it. What the United States did buy from France was the exclusive right to negotiate with the Indians who owned the land.)

The Cherokees signed another treaty in 1806, giving up more land in Tennessee and in Alabama. This treaty was signed by Doublehead, James Vann, Tahlonteskee, John Jolly, and others, and bribes were involved in the negotiations. Woodward says that the treaty "incensed conservative Upper Towns Cherokees...they accused the Chickamaugans' treaty makers with willful violation of the ancient Cherokee law prohibiting the cession of lands without the National Council's consent, reminding them that the punishment for violating the sacred, unwritten law was death."

It was June of 1807 before the council decision was acted upon. Then the Ridge (later to be known as Major Ridge), Alex Saunders, and James Vann were chosen to carry out the execution of Doublehead for treason. Before they could get to him, Doublehead got into a quarrel with another Cherokee named Bonepolisher, who had accused him to his face of treason. Doublehead shot and killed Bonepolisher.

Then Doublehead went to a tavern at Hiwassee, near the government's Indian agency. When Ridge and Saunders arrived (Vann had supposedly fallen ill along the way.), they found Doublehead already drunk. Ridge walked over to the table at which Doublehead was sitting, pulled out a pistol, and shot him through the jaw. As Doublehead fell forward on the table, the two executioners made their escape. Later that night, they heard that Ridge's shot had not killed Doublehead. They trailed the wounded man to the loft of a nearby cabin, broke in, and climbed up into the loft. Wounded as he was, Doublehead got out of bed and struggled with Ridge. Saunders came up behind and drove his hatchet into Doublehead's skull to finish the job.

That same year, delegations from both the Upper Towns and the Lower Towns went to Washington City, as the new U.S. capital was being called, with two different purposes. The Upper Towns continued to complain that they were not receiving their fair share of annuities. They proposed that the Cherokee Nation be divided into two separate nations. The Lower Towns, on the other hand, wanted to exchange their lands for lands on the Arkansas River. Naturally the United States was more interested in the second proposal than in the first, but when the delegations returned home, and the people of the Lower Towns met, the majority of the people did not want to move west, and when the National Council met, amazingly, the differences between the two groups were resolved.

They wrote to their agent, Return J. Meigs, "It has now been a long time that we have been much confused and divided in our opinions but now we have settled our affair to the satisfaction of both parties and become as one—You will now hear from us not [as] from the Lower Towns nor [as from] the upper Towns but [as] from the whole Cherokee Nation."

They had begun to formalize the central government that had been slowly evolving ever since the selection of Wrosetasetow as trade commissioner way back in 1721. Accepting the advice of Thomas

Jefferson, they adopted written laws to replace the old clan laws, and instituted trials before the council, taxation of livestock, and a national police force called the Light Horse Guard. Ridge was made the commander of the Guard. Blackfox was Principal Chief. A new constitution was written, and it was formally adopted in 1827. The Cherokees "adopted a written code. . . . The first written law ever enacted by any tribal government . . . legalized the existing system of patrol, which had been in operation since 1797 and provided better law enforcement." Charles Hicks, Secretary, drafted the codes (Malone).

A little over a thousand of the Lower Cherokees under the leadership of Tahlonteskee still wanted to move west, and they made their wishes known to the federal government. Most historians assume that Tahlonteskee, as he had signed the same treaty as had Doublehead, simply feared for his life. Perhaps he did. However, it would be a few years before he and his followers would actually make the move west.

The American Revolution had ended back in 1782, but the British were still in Canada, and they had not forgotten their humiliating defeat at the hands of the "colonials." From Canada, British agents had been encouraging northern Indians to continue fighting the United States. The farsighted Shawnee Tecumseh, with a vision of Indian confederacy much like that of the late Dragging Canoe, visited the Cherokees.

"In August of 1811," says Van Every, "foreseeing the imminent outbreak of war between the United States and Great Britain, he embarked upon a tour of the southern nations to preach the absolute necessity of Indian union in the approaching crisis. With the prospective support of British military power, he maintained, there had appeared a last chance to require the Americans to recognize Indian right to what remained of their homeland."

SOURCE LIST AND SUGGESTIONS FOR FURTHER READING

Baker, Jack D., transcriber. 1977. *Cherokee Emigration Rolls: 1817–1835*.
    Oklahoma City: Baker Publisher Company.
Institute for the Development of Indian Law. N.d. *Treaties and Agreements of
    the Five Civilized Tribes*. Washington, D.C.: Institute for the
    Development of Indian Law.
Malone, Henry Thompson. 1956. *Cherokees of the Old South*. Athens:
    University of Georgia Press.
Van Every, Dale. 1966. *Disinherited: The Lost Birthright of the American Indian*.

New York: William Morrow.

Wilkins, Thurman. 1970. *Cherokee Tragedy: The Story of the Ridge Family and of the Decimation of a People*. New York: The Macmillan Company.

GLOSSARY

Akooh. A garbled Cherokee masculine name, perhaps the same as "Ancoo." (See Glossary for the previous chapter.)

Chief. In negotiations between the U.S. government and an Indian nation, often anyone who could be coerced into signing would be called a chief.

Conservatism. In general, the disposition to preserve what is established and to resist change. In terms of Indians, the disposition to hold on to tribal traditions and culture and to resist assimilation and acculturation.

Conservatives. Those individuals who believe in and uphold conservatism.

Factor. An agent or person who transacts business for someone else. Here, a government agent assigned to a "factory." See below.

Factory. An establishment for carrying on business in a foreign country. Here, a government trading post in Indian country.

Factory system. A scheme devised by President Thomas Jefferson wherein Indians would be given unlimited credit and strongly urged to make use of it in government factories. When the Indian debt had grown to unmanageable extremes, the government would pay it off in exchange for land.

Moravian. A Christian denomination descended from the Bohemian Brethren, formed in Bohemia in 1467 and reorganized in 1722 as the Moravian Church.

Tahlonteskee. Variously spelled Tollunteeskee, Taluntiski, Tallotiskee, Tallotuskee, the name is, according to Mooney, *Ataluntiski*, meaning "one who throws some living object from a place, as an enemy from a precipice."

CHAPTER TWELVE

Tecumseh and Red Eagle

Tecumseh visited the Creeks, because he had relatives among them. He was received at Tuckabatchee like a major celebrity. After a few days of celebration and meetings, Tecumseh delivered his speech. The Ridge was there visiting, and he listened to the message. Tecumseh told the Creeks that if the Indians failed to join together in a common cause, all their lands would eventually be taken from them. He recited a list of eastern tribes that had already vanished. He advocated a confederacy of all Indian tribes, the purpose of which would be to stop the western movement of the United States.

But Tecumseh's message was more than military. He was concerned with the survival of Indians as Indians. He urged all Indians to give up the ways of the white man and the things they had acquired from white men. Tecumseh's brother, Tenskwatawa, "the Open Door," known as "the Prophet," had seen a vision, and back up in the Shawnee country, to the north, the Prophet had given the people a new dance, "the Dance of the Lakes."

Tecumseh did not advocate war, at least not right away. He advocated a great Indian alliance that would hold the line against any further white encroachment onto Indian land, and he advocated a return to the traditional ways of Indians. He said that the time for war would come, and when it did the Indians would be aided by the British, who had commissioned him a general in the British army.

Tecumseh has been much misunderstood and misrepresented by historians. He did not hate white people. He did not advocate killing all the white people in America or even driving them all out of the country. He simply wanted Indians to remain Indian and white people to stop taking Indian land. And in order to accomplish these two purposes, he believed that they must put aside their tribal differences and band together in a powerful Indian confederacy.

Perhaps if Dragging Canoe had still been alive, with his influence things would have worked out differently. But far-reaching changes had already taken place in the southeast among both the Creeks and the Cherokees, and Tecumseh could not have foreseen the strength of the new so-called progressive element in both of those nations. Like the Cherokees, the Creeks had developed a split into two factions. The Creek Upper Towns, like the Cherokee Upper Towns, were mostly conservative, but also like the Cherokees, the progressive Lower Creek Towns constituted a majority of the nation.

Tecumseh's message was not well received by the Ridge nor by the Creek Big Warrior of Tuckabatchee. But both Creek and Cherokee Upper Towns received the message with excitement and anticipation. Immediately following Tecumseh's speech, however, the Big Warrior made a response which both insulted and angered Tecumseh, and the great Shawnee warned that when he arrived back home in the north, he would stamp on the earth and make it shake. He left the southeast, but he left behind among the Creeks a man named Seekaboo, who continued to work among the conservative Creeks. The Ridge went home to Ustanali.

Then on December 16, 1811, a tremendous earthquake struck. "Never before in man's memory," says Wilkins, "had such a quake occurred. It damaged buildings; springs belched muddy or clouded water. Fantastic reports arrived from the West, for the disturbance seemed to focus near the settlement of New Madrid on the Mississippi; how the water in the river had risen and fallen like a tide; how lake bottoms were elevated above the surrounding land; how the earth cracked in gigantic furrows and sulfurous fumes fouled the air; how flashes of lightning streaked from the earth, with noises like cannon fire at close range; and how the ground felt hot to one's foot."

In Missouri, the Bowl and his followers felt the wrath of the quake more than did those back in the old Cherokee and Creek countries. Fearing to stay longer in Missouri and believing it a bad place to live, they packed up their belongings and moved to new locations along the Arkansas and White rivers in what is now the state of Arkansas. Mooney says that there were probably "but few" Cherokees in Missouri and later in Arkansas in those days. Thornton says (p. 44) that Meriwether Lewis reported a Cherokee population along the St. Francis River of approximately one thousand in 1804.

Back in the southeast, conservatives among both Cherokees and Creeks remembered the threat of Tecumseh. Ridge sought his explanations from the missionaries, and at a large gathering at Ustanali, now the capital of the Cherokee Nation, continued to denounce the message of Tecumseh and the visions of his brother, the Prophet. Then an old Cherokee prophet, whose name has gone down in history only as Charlie, with two black wolves, one on each side, said to be spirits, appeared at the meeting. He preached the same message as had Tecumseh. He told the Cherokees gathered there to get rid of all the things they had acquired from white men. He told them to throw away their iron cooking pots, steel knives, guns, trade cloth, and beads. He told them to kill all their cattle, hogs, and cats. He said that Selu, Corn, the mother of the Cherokees, had abandoned them because they were living too much like the whites, and as he spoke, the clouds parted in the sky. Then he added that the spirits would strike dead anyone who dared to deny his message.

Ridge dared. He spoke against Charlie by saying that such talk would only lead to war with the Americans, and that war with the Americans would lead to the destruction of the Cherokees. He offered to test Charlie's threat with his own life. Angry conservative Cherokees attacked Ridge and tried to kill him. Some progressive Cherokees rushed to Ridge's aid, and eventually someone managed to restore order. No one was killed.

Charlie then threatened a terrible hailstorm that would destroy all of the Cherokees except those who chose to follow him and who believed in his message. He told them to join him at the highest peak in the Smoky Mountains on the day of the storm, and they would be safe. Many conservatives followed Charlie on the appointed day, and when the promised storm failed to materialize Charlie was totally discredited, and there was no more hope for Tecumseh's message among the Cherokees. The Ridge and the progressives had won the debate.

But the faith of the Creek conservatives was solid. If anything, Tecumseh and his assistant Seekaboo, with the help of the earthquake, had been too successful, for the conservative Creeks, now known as Red Sticks, did not want to wait any longer. When the progressive Creek government issued a proclamation of "unqualified and unanimous" friendship for the United States a civil war broke out among the Creeks. Conservative Red Sticks attacked progressive towns, and soon the civil war expanded into a war against the United States, when white Alabamans, fearful of an "uprising," attacked a Creek supply train.

In the meantime, war had officially been declared between the United States and England, and the War of 1812 began on June 28 of that year. General Tecumseh, at the head of fifteen hundred warriors, was fighting in the north. That same summer, a delegation of Creeks went north to visit the Shawnees, and on their way home they attacked white settlements and killed some settlers. In April 1813, the Creek Nation, to forestall war with the United States, hunted down eleven of the Creeks who had done the killings and executed them. The Red Sticks were furious, and even some who had been undecided joined them because of the executions.

Menawa and Red Eagle (William Weatherford), both mixed-bloods, emerged as the leaders of the Red Sticks, and on August 30, 1813, they led an attack on Fort Mims, a few miles north of Mobile, Alabama. DeRosier says, "The fort contained five hundred fifty-three Americans, two hundred sixty-five of whom were soldiers and the remainder frightened civilians who understood the need for refuge from the... Red Sticks. The fort was commanded by Major Samuel Beasley, who was so inept that he didn't even shut and lock the gates despite positive knowledge that Red Sticks were lurking about. At noon, on a prearranged signal, the Red Sticks attacked, overwhelmed the fort [and] killed all but thirty-six people who escaped."

In October of that same year, at the Battle of the Thames in Ontario, Canada, Tecumseh was killed. Wilkins says, "The news of Fort Mims reached the Cherokees while a friendly Creek named William McIntosh, the headman of Coweta... visited in their midst enlisting aid against the Red Stick insurgents." Ridge and others escorted McIntosh safely back home to Coweta where "they found the Creek council in emergency session.... They had already asked the United States for help." Now they sent the Ridge home with a message asking for Cherokee help.

At first the Cherokee council refused, but when Ridge declared that he would go to the aid of the progressive Creeks with volunteers, and a large number of Cherokees immediately volunteered to go with him, they voted again. This time the vote was in favor of assisting the Creeks against the Red Sticks.

Under the command of Major General Thomas Pinckney, the Americans planned a three-pronged attack on the Creek Upper Towns. General John Floyd led Georgia troops, combined with Lower Town Creeks under McIntosh and some Cherokees, from the east. Brigadier General Claiborne brought volunteers from Louisiana and Mississippi and Choctaws under Pushmataha, and three forces under the command of General Andrew Jackson came from Tennessee. The advance Tennessee contingent was led by Brigadier General James White. It and another division under Major General John Cocke came from eastern Tennessee, and

Jackson himself led the troops from the western part of the state. Five hundred Cherokees were divided to serve under all three Tennessee generals.

DeRosier says, "Claiborne's army met with success in western Alabama, winning the significant Battle of the Holy Ground. Floyd offered a severe test to the Red Sticks, but his army was eventually driven from the field. Even Andrew Jackson, plagued by bad health and an army of militiamen more intent on mustering out and returning home than killing Indians, suffered two initial defeats."

But at last, Jackson, with fresh reinforcements from Tennessee, and with two cannons, marched on the Red Sticks where they were gathered at the Horseshoe Bend of the Tallapoosa River. The Tallapoosa River took a sharp turn to the south, then curved around and headed back north, creating a large peninsula of around a hundred acres, open to the north. There was a town there called Tohopki, or Tohopeka.

Around one thousand fighting men were there and about three hundred women and children. They had built a breastwork of logs across the neck of the peninsula, so the only way for the enemy to get at Tohopki was over the breastworks or across the river on either the east or west sides or the far southern tip of the peninsula. On March 27, 1814, Jackson came at them with fifteen hundred Tennessee militiamen and five hundred Cherokees.

Menawa and William Weatherford were there for the Creeks. On the other side, besides Jackson, were a number of men who would become prominent, even famous, later on: Sam Houston and Davy Crockett; among the Cherokees, Ridge, John Ross, Junaluska (although he was not yet known by that name), Sequoyah, and others.

Mooney describes the layout and the beginning of the battle, which he calls a massacre, in the following way:

> Having arrived in the neighborhood of the fort, Jackson disposed his men for the attack by detailing General Coffee with the mounted men and nearly the whole of the Indian force to cross the river at a ford about three miles below and surround the bend in such manner that none could escape in that direction. He, himself, with the rest of his force, advanced to the front of the breastwork and planted his cannon upon a slight rise within eighty yards of the fortification. He then directed a heavy cannonade upon the center of the breastwork, while the rifles and muskets kept up a galling fire upon the defenders whenever they showed themselves behind the logs. The breastwork was very strongly and compactly built,

from five to eight feet high, with a double row of portholes,
and so planned that no enemy could approach without being
exposed to a crossfire from those on the inside.

After about two hours of firing the cannon at the breastworks and
the rifles and muskets at infrequent targets, Jackson sent the entire
mounted force of seven hundred troops and five hundred Indians (one
hundred were Creeks and the rest Cherokees) to cross the river and completely surround the peninsula.

From where the Cherokees were, they could see Creek canoes across
the river. Charles Reese, the Whale, and another Cherokee swam the river
to get canoes, but the Whale was wounded, so they brought back only
two canoes. Then Cherokees including the Ridge climbed into the canoes
and paddled across to attack in force. Each time they crossed, some
would take the canoes back for more, until all the Cherokees were on the
peninsula and in the town.

Then they fought their way through the town, driving the people all
north toward the breastworks and setting fire to houses as they went. With
the Red Sticks all driven up against the breastworks, and the Cherokees
firing at them from behind, Jackson had his men rush the wall. The Red
Sticks fought valiantly, but when about half of them had been killed, the
rest rushed into the river, only to be shot at by the soldiers on the other
side. Some ran into the brush and timber for cover, and the soldiers set it
on fire. As the Red Sticks came running out, they were shot down.

The entire battle lasted for about five hours and only ended with
darkness, but it was resumed again the following morning. However,
only sixteen Red Sticks were found and killed on the second day. Jackson
claimed that not more than twenty could have escaped. Three hundred
prisoners were taken, and only three of them were men. The American
forces must have killed nearly a thousand Red Stick fighting men.

Only twenty-six to thirty-two white soldiers were killed. Ninety-nine to
a hundred and seven were wounded. Eighteen Cherokees were killed and
thirty-six wounded. Five Creeks allied with the Americans were killed and
eleven wounded. Mooney says, "there is considerable truth in the boast of
the Cherokees that they saved the day for Jackson at Horseshoe Bend."

Two weeks later, William Weatherford came into Jackson's camp and
surrendered, and the Red Stick War was officially over. The war between
England and the United States would not come to a close until the following year.

A tale has been told that during the Battle of Horseshoe Bend, General
Jackson was about to be killed by one of the Red Sticks, when a Cherokee

named Gul'kalaski attacked the Red Stick and killed him, saving the general's life. Gul'kalaski would later go down in history as Junaluska.

SOURCE LIST AND SUGGESTIONS FOR FURTHER READING

Debo, Angie. 1941. *A History of the Creek Indians.* Norman: University of Oklahoma Press.

DeRosier, Arthur H., Jr. 1975. "The Destruction of the Creek Confederacy." In *Forked Tongues and Broken Treaties*, ed. Donald E. Worcester. Caldwell, Idaho: The Caxton Printers.

GLOSSARY

Gul'kalaski. The name of the Cherokee said to have saved the life of Andrew Jackson during the Battle of Horseshoe Bend. Mooney says it "denotes something habitually falling from a leaning position." This man later changed his name to Tsuhnuhlahuhski, corrupted in English to Junaluska. See below.

Junaluska. English version of the Cherokee name Tsuhnuhlahuhski, meaning, "He tries, but fails."

Menawa. Half-breed Creek leader of the Red Sticks.

Red Sticks. Conservative faction of the Creeks, 1811–1814, so-called, according to Debo, because of their adoption of Tecumseh's "magic Red Stick that would point out the direction of his enemies and confound and overwhelm them."

Seekaboo. Also spelled Seekapoo, this man accompanied Tecumseh on his 1811 visit to the Creeks, and when Tecumseh went back north, Seekaboo stayed with the Creeks. He has been called Tecumseh's Creek interpreter.

Selu. Cherokee for corn. Also the name of a character in Cherokee mythology, especially in the tale recorded by Mooney as "Kanati and Selu: the Origin of Game and Corn."

Sequoyah. The name of this famous Cherokee is the subject of much debate. Some say it cannot be translated and is not even a Cherokee word. Mooney calls it "Sikwayi." Some have called it "Pig Place" for "sikwa," pig or hog, and the locative ending "yi." It could as easily be "sikwa" for opossum, if the name predates the introduction of swine to America, and "ya," or real or original.

Tallapoosa. A river in Alabama. The name is from the Muskogee (Creek) language.

Tenskwatawa. The Shawnee name of Tecumseh's brother, meaning "the Open Door." He was called "the Prophet," or sometimes, "the Shawnee Prophet."

Tohopeka. Creek name of the town located on the peninsula called Horseshoe Bend in English. Perhaps it's also the name of the whole peninsula.

Tohopki. Alternate spelling for "Tohopeka," above.

Tuckabatchee. One of the Creek Lower Towns, it served as the national capital during the early 1800s.

Weatherford, William. Mixed-blood Creek leader of the Red Sticks, Weatherford's Creek name, according to Debo, was Lumhe Chati, or Red Eagle. He was a nephew of the great Creek chief, Alexander McGillivray

CHAPTER THIRTEEN

Five Treaties in Three Years

For the Cherokees, the immediate outcome of their participation in the Creek War was a certain amount of high praise from military and governmental authorities, and the spoliation of their own lands by white soldiers who traveled through the Cherokee Nation on their way home. The soldiers had "plundered their lands," says Collier, "stolen livestock, destroyed crops and set fire to some of their villages."

Then at Fort Jackson, hastily constructed and pompously named by Jackson during the Red Stick War, Jackson exacted more punishment on the Creeks in the form of a treaty. His attitude toward the Cherokees, who had almost certainly been responsible for his victory, was also revealed here, for the Cherokees wanted a precise boundary drawn between their land and that of the Creeks. Jackson wanted the land for himself, so, instead of accommodating the Cherokees, in the words of Woodward, he "audaciously suggested that while the United States troops were yet on the field it might be well to force cessions of all Tennessee lands from both Chickasaws and Cherokees." (The land to which he referred was the same land involved in the Cherokee-Creek boundary dispute.)

Unable to gain permission to pursue such a course, Jackson concerned himself with other boundaries. DeRosier says, "The Treaty of Fort Jackson was a victor's peace if ever there were one," and "it was the product of Jackson's own thinking." He says further that "it punished the friendly Lower Creeks more than it did the Red Sticks of the Upper Towns." Jackson took twenty-two million acres of land from the Creeks, mostly from the Lower Towns. The lesson of the Creek War, or Red Stick War, and of the treaty inflicted on the Creeks thereafter is that the United States government would use any means possible to take whatever land it wanted away from Indians, even going to the extent of punishing its own allies at the end of a conflict.

In 1816, a delegation of Cherokees was sent by the National Council to Washington to request compensation for the damages done by the white soldiers going through the Cherokee Nation at the end of the Creek War, and to request that the boundary line between the Cherokee Nation and the Creek Nation be fixed. They were able to accomplish those two goals, but at a cost. The Cherokee delegation consisted of Colonel John Lowrey, Major Ridge, Captain John Walker, Captain Richard Taylor, Cheucunsenee, and Adjutant John Ross, all veterans of the recent campaign against the Red Sticks. (The Ridge, having attained the rank of major during the war, thereafter used it as a given name.)

On March 22, 1816, they signed two treaties. In the first, they gave up all claim to their remaining land in South Carolina for five thousand dollars. In the second, the United States agreed to fix the boundary between the Cherokee Nation and the Creek Nation in a manner satisfactory to the Cherokees, and the Cherokees gave the United States the right to "lay off, open, and have the free use of, such road or roads, through any part of the Cherokee nation, lying north of the boundary line now established, as may be deemed necessary for the free intercourse between the States of Tennessee and Georgia and the Mississippi River." And the United States agreed to pay individual Cherokees for damages done by the soldiers, up to a total of 25,500 dollars.

In September of that same year, only six months later, there was yet another treaty. This time one of the three U.S. commissioners was Andrew Jackson, who had declared it his diplomatic ambition to undo what the previous treaty had done in terms of the Cherokee-Creek boundary. By offering bribes to Pathkiller, Glass, Boat, Sour Mush, Chulioa, Dick Justice, Richard Brown, and Chickasautchee, Jackson was able to obtain their signatures on a treaty in which they gave up their claim to the land in question. (It was also claimed by the Chickasaws, and later Jackson was able to get them to give it up as well. At last he had what he wanted at the time of the signing of the Treaty of Fort Jackson.)

Jackson was back in July of 1817, and he called a conference at Calhoun, the new agency, on the Hiwassee River. Fifteen "chiefs" from the Western Cherokees were there on their way to Washington. (Those

---

FROM THE PREAMBLE OF THE TREATY OF JULY 8, 1817

Whereas... a deputation from the Upper and Lower Cherokee towns, duly authorized by their nation, went to the city of Washington, the first named to declare to the President of the United States their anxious desire to engage in the pursuits of agriculture and civilized life... and to request the establishment of a division line between the upper and lower towns... the proposed to begin the establishment of fixed laws and a regular government: The deputies from the lower towns to make known their desire to continue the hunter life, and also the scarcity of game where they then lived, and, under these circumstances, their wish to remove across the Mississippi river, on some vacant lands of the United States... the President of the United States... answered those petitions as follows: "The United States, my children, are the friends of both parties, and, as far as can be reasonably asked, they are willing to satisfy the wishes of both. Those who remain may be assured of our patronage, our aid and good neighborhood. Those who wish to remove, are permitted to send an exploring party to reconnoitre the country on the waters of the Arkansas and White rivers....

When this party shall have found a tract of country suiting the emigrants, and not claimed by other Indians, we will arrange with them and you the exchange of that for a just portion of the country they leave.... Every aid towards their removal, and what will be necessary for them there, will then be freely administered to them; and when established in their new settlements, we shall still consider them as our children, give them the benefit of exchanging their peltries for what they will want at our factories, and always hold them firmly by the hand.

Cherokees who had settled in Arkansas following the 1811 earthquake had begun dealing with the U.S. as the Western Cherokees.) Jackson was blunt. He claimed that thirty-seven hundred Cherokees were already living on land in the West that the United States had given them. He demanded that the Cherokee Nation give an equal amount of land in the East in exchange. Furthermore, he wanted the entire Cherokee Nation to pack up and move west and trade all of their remaining land for western lands.

The Council of the Cherokee Nation was indignant, and far from agreeing to Jackson's incredible demands, they drew up a protest "against the whole policy of emigration," which was signed by sixty-seven "chiefs"

A LETTER FROM NANCY WARD TO THE CHIEFS AND WARRIORS OF THE CHEROKEE NATION, MAY, 1817

The Cherokee ladys [*sic*] now being present at the meeting of the Chiefs and warriors in council have thought it their duties as mothers to address their beloved Chiefs and warriors now assembled.

Our beloved children and head men of the Cherokee nation we address you warriors in council we have raised all of you on the land which we now have, which God gave us to inhabit and raise provisions we know that our country has once been extensive but by repeated sales has become circumscribed to a small tract and never have thought it our duty to interfere in the disposition of it until now, if a father or mother was to sell all their lands which they had to depend on which their children had to raise their living on which would be indeed bad and to be removed to another country which we have understood some of our children wish to go over the Mississippi but this act of our children would be like destroying your mothers. Your mothers your sisters ask and beg of you not to part with any more of our lands, we say ours you are descendants and take pity on our request, but keep it for our growing children for it was the good will of our creator to place here and you know our father the great president will not allow his white children to take our country away only keep your hands off of paper talks for it is our own country for if it was not they would not ask you to put your hands to paper for it would be impossible to remove us all for as soon as one child is raised we have others in our arms for such is our situation and will consider our circumstance.

Therefore children don't part with any more of our lands but continue on it and enlarge your farms and cultivate and raise corn and cotton and we your mothers and sisters will make clothing for you which our father the president has recommended to us all we don't charge anybody for selling our lands, but we have heard such intentions of our children but your talks become true at last and it was our desire to forewarn you all not to part with our lands.

Nancy Ward to her children Warriors to take pity and to listen to the talks of your sisters, although I am very old yet cannot but pity the situation in which you will hear of their minds. I have great many grand children which I wish them to do well on our land.

Nancy Ward

and delivered to Jackson. Cotterill says, "Outraged by receiving a remonstrance where he had asked only for acquiescence, Jackson called on the signers of the document to repudiate it and when only two, Tuckasee and Glass, did so, announced that he would make a treaty with the Arkansas delegation alone."

Probably afraid that the unscrupulous Jackson would do exactly as he had threatened, the Council broke down thus far: They signed a treaty in which they gave up large tracts of land in Tennessee, Alabama, and Georgia for the land on the Arkansas and White rivers "bordering on the Osage nation." The treaty also promised to give "all the poor warriors who may remove to the western side of the Mississippi river [sic], one rifle gun and ammunition, one blanket, and one brass kettle, or, in lieu of the brass kettle, a beaver trap, which is to be considered as a full compensation for the improvements which they may leave."

It also provided for "reservations," meaning parcels of land for individuals who, in effect, wished to remain in the East on their own privately owned land and remove themselves from the Cherokee Nation. Individuals accepting such "reservations" could pass their land on to their children, but would not be able to sell it. If they chose at some time to leave the land, it would revert to the ownership of the United States.

The United States acted almost immediately upon the tiny opening provided by the clause regarding western emigration. According to Cotterill, "Although ... the Cherokees had made evident the tribal opposition to emigration, ... the United States was apparently determined to bring [it] about.... the War Department contracted for boats to transport the prospective emigrants ... while it delivered to the agency rifles, lead, powder, kettles, blankets, and traps." Sam Houston was appointed special agent to promote removal, and Governor McMinn of Tennessee was placed in charge of emigration. Cherokees were subjected to persuasion, threats and bribery.

There were 2,190 Cherokees, including John Jolly, or Ahuludegi, the brother of Tahlonteskee, now Chief of the Western Cherokees, and adopted father of Sam Houston, signing up in 1817, and a little over half of them actually made the move later that year. While Jolly probably made his decision based on his close relationship to both Tahlonteskee and Sam Houston, others might have given in to the pressures applied on them from the U.S. agents. And there were other, perhaps equal, and opposite pressures being applied by the government of the Cherokee Nation. Those favoring emigration, Mooney says, "became the object of scorn and hatred to the remainder of the nation. They were made the subjects of a persecution so relentless ... that it was never forgotten."

In Arkansas the Western Cherokees were engaged in a bitter and bloody war with the Osage Nation that had been going on almost since the first Cherokees had arrived in Arkansas in 1811. While the United States maintained that it had traded land in Arkansas to the Western Cherokees, the Osages claimed that the land in question was theirs. In 1816, just the previous year, the agent for the Western Cherokees, William L. Lovely, had negotiated away from the Osages a large tract of land in what is now eastern Oklahoma for the use of the Western Cherokees, and an uneasy peace had been agreed upon by the two groups at the same time. But by 1817, the war was on again, and the Western Cherokees were anxious to have more Cherokees join them in Arkansas to increase their numbers and power.

It was also in 1817 that a white man who would become a significant figure in Cherokee history arrived in Tennessee. Representing the American Board of Commissioners for Foreign Missions (known as the ABC), in the company of Reverend D. S. Buttrick, Reverend Samuel A. Worcester established Brainerd Mission.

Then in February, 1819, the United States was back again, demanding yet another treaty and still more land. The treaty was concluded, and more land was lost, but from that time forward, the government of the Cherokee Nation seemed determined to hang on to the land they had left. From original holdings that had spread over all or parts of the present states of North and South Carolina, Virginia and West Virginia, Kentucky, Tennessee, Georgia, and Alabama, Cherokee landholdings had been reduced to ten million acres, an area that stretched but 200 miles east to west and 120 miles north to south, most of it within the boundaries of the state of Georgia.

SOURCE LIST AND SUGGESTIONS FOR FURTHER READING

Foreman, Grant. 1930. *Indians and Pioneers*. Norman: University of Oklahoma Press.

Hoig, Stan. 1991. *Jesse Chisholm: Ambassador of the Plains*. Niwot: University Press of Colorado.

Washburn, Cephas. 1971. *Reminiscences of the Indians*. New York: Johnson Reprint Corporation. (Reprint of Washburn's 1869 treatment of his experiences with the Western Cherokee Nation.)

GLOSSARY

Ahuludegi. Sometimes spelled Oolooteka and other ways, this is the Cherokee name of John Jolly, who was the brother of Tahlonteskee and the adopted father of Sam Houston. Mooney translates the name, "He throws away the drum."

Cheucunsenee. One of the various corrupt spellings of Tsiyu gansini, or Dragging Canoe. The person thus named in Chapter 13 is obviously not the famous war leader, but someone else using the same name. It could possibly be a son or grandson.

Chulioa. A corruption of some Cherokee masculine name.

Chickasautchee. Another corruption of a Cherokee name, the first part of which is obviously "Chickasaw."

Reservation. During the early part of the 1800s, this word did not carry the same meaning as it does for us today. Then it meant an individual piece of land, individually owned, but still under a certain amount of government control (i.e., the owner was prohibited from selling it). If an Indian wanted to move away from his tribe, he could stay in the East on an individual "reservation." The government later did away with this policy.

CHAPTER FOURTEEN

Many Changes Taking Place

Cherokees have often been praised only to the extent that the Cherokees learned to live like white people. Some look at the period between 1819 and 1827 as the single most remarkable period in Cherokee history. It is marked on the part of the Cherokees by two things: (1) a powerful impulse to hold the line against any further incursions on the Cherokee land base, and (2) a major push toward remaking the Cherokee Nation in the image of the United States.

Of course, the changes in Cherokee society had been taking place at least since 1673 when the first Englishmen visited the Cherokee country. We know that some changes had taken place even earlier than that, since those first Englishmen declared that the Cherokees already had guns when they met them. But, beginning in 1819, it seems that the Cherokees made a concerted effort at culture change. They built schools and hired teachers. They invited missionaries to move in among them. Those who could afford it sent their children away to school. The wealthier among them built fine plantation-style homes like the rich white southerners, and they bought Black slaves to work their plantations. And they reorganized and formalized their government.

Of course, Cherokees had always had a civilization. It was one that had developed over countless generations and was especially suited to the needs, beliefs, and circumstances of the Cherokees. In many ways it was a much more complex civilization than that of the white men. Certainly it provided a safer and more secure environment for women and children than that which would replace it.

Even so, for any group of people to consciously remake themselves, to reshape their social and governmental institutions according to a set of foreign beliefs and forms, and to do it so thoroughly, so well, and so quickly is a remarkable occurrence in the history of the world. Leaders of this unprecedented movement were Major Ridge and John Ross. Ridge's son John and his nephew (John's cousin) Buck Oowatie were both sent to school at Cornwall, Connecticut, and both young Cherokee mixed-bloods married white girls from Cornwall, "thereby," Woodward says, "incurring the wrath of Cornwall's bluestocking citizenry to the extent of their closing the mission school and burning John Ridge and his bride in effigy."

John Ridge and Buck Oowatie, his name now changed to Elias Boudinot in honor of a benefactor, returned to the Cherokee Nation with their new wives. John Ross himself was but one-eighth Cherokee by blood, but his Cherokee blood came down to him through the female line. He had therefore been born into a clan, and that was what really mattered to Cherokees in those days. He had been educated in Kingsport, Tennessee, and, like Major Ridge, he was a veteran of the Creek War.

In addition to the mission schools already established in the Cherokee Nation, others came in: Presbyterians, Baptists, and Methodists. Catherine Brown, a Cherokee educated at Brainerd, opened her own mission school at Creek Path in Alabama. A Baptist mission was established in 1817 at Valley Town, and in 1821 it was taken over by the Welshman Evan Jones. A second Baptist mission was built at Tinsawattee. Jones especially was successful. One of his converts, full-blood Kaneeda, became the first Cherokee ordained Baptist minister. The Methodists began moving in around 1825, building mission schools at Will's Valley, Ustanali, Coosawattee, Mount Wesley, Ashbury, Chattooga, Sullacoie, Neeley's Grove, and Conasauga. A veteran of the Creek War, Turtle Fields, became the first Cherokee Methodist minister.

While all these changes were taking place in the East, out among the Western Cherokees in Arkansas another phenomenal event occurred. Tahlonteskee had died, and his brother John Jolly had been elected chief. The war with the Osage Nation had heated up again, and the flamboyant Cherokee Captain Dutch (Tahchee), spurred on by the fiery Degadoga, had led a massive raid in 1817 against the Osages at Clermont's Town. The U.S. government was trying to entice all Cherokees to move west, but not only was a war raging out there, the U.S. government was not leaving the Western Cherokees alone. In 1819 government surveyors told some of the Western Cherokees that they had settled on the wrong side of the Arkansas River. They were ordered to move. Bowl, who had been one of the earliest to move west back in 1794, angered at being told to move again, and anxious to escape the jurisdiction of the United States, took sixty families with him, and they moved—all the way to Texas.

In the midst of all this, Creek War veteran Sequoyah, revealed to the Western Cherokees the Cherokee syllabary, a method for reading and writing the Cherokee language. Sequoyah has been praised as a native genius and a Cherokee Cadmus. All alone, it is said, in the face of scorn, and with no more knowledge of reading and writing than that the white men could do it, Sequoyah worked diligently until he had perfected his system, a syllabary of eighty-five characters, each of which represented the sound of a syllable in the Cherokee language. This standard story is, at least, controversial, for some have suggested that the syllabary is in reality an ancient system of Cherokee writing that had fallen into disuse and secrecy and had been all but forgotten. Sequoyah, these say, knew the secret and simply made it public. (Remember the Cherokee who in 1717 told Alexander Long that "when we first came on this land...the priests and beloved men was writing.") Whatever the truth of the matter, and we can probably never know the truth, Sequoyah is certainly responsible for having made the syllabary available to Cherokees.

Following a demonstration in 1821 to show how it worked, Cherokees began learning the syllabary "almost overnight," and its use became widespread. Then Sequoyah made a trip back east carrying letters written in the syllabary from Western Cherokees to friends and relatives and thus made the syllabary known there. The Cherokee Nation was quick to take advantage of the new writing system, for not only did almost everyone learn to read and write in their native language, but the National Council voted to establish a newspaper and a national academy. In 1825, Elias Boudinot was appointed the first editor of *The Cherokee Phoenix*. He immediately launched a lecture tour in Philadelphia and New York to raise money to finance the paper.

Boudinot's lectures had a double purpose. While raising money, he was also informing the white citizens of the northern states about the "progress" of the Cherokee Nation and about the persecution of the Cherokee Nation by the state of Georgia. And he gained a great deal of support for the Cherokee cause. He also made money. A printing press was secured, and on February 21, 1828, the first issue of *The Cherokee Phoenix* appeared, printed in Cherokee and in English. "We will invariably state the will of the majority of our people," it said, "on the subject of the present controversy with Georgia, and the present removal policy of the United States Government."

In the area of government, the Cherokee Nation took on a new shape with the constitution that had been adopted in 1827. It was formed, like that of the United States, into a tripartite system. That is to say, it had three branches: executive, legislative, and judicial, with a separation of powers. Like the president, the Principal Chief was the chief executive of the nation. He was backed by a Deputy Principal Chief, comparable to the vice president. The legislative branch of the government (like Congress) was the Cherokee National Council, bicameral, like Congress. The National Committee corresponded to the U.S. Senate, and the National Council to the U.S. House of Representatives. The judicial branch, like the U.S. Supreme Court, was the Supreme Court of the Cherokee Nation.

The Cherokee Nation was divided into eight judicial districts, each with a judge, a marshal, and a local council. There was a company of "Light Horse" and a circuit judge for each two districts. A poll tax of fifty cents was levied on each head of a family and on each single man under sixty years of age, and it was collected by the marshals. A new capital was established at New Echota, "commonly referred to as Newtown," according to Cotterill, and a written constitution was adopted in 1827. New Echota had a two story log capitol building with brick chimneys and fireplaces, a plank floor, glass windows, and a staircase. It had a Superior Court Building with a judge's bench on a raised platform and benches for jurors, witnesses, officials, and the general public.

It was as if the Cherokees had said, "The white people don't want us for their neighbors because they think that we're savage. Therefore, if we can show them that we are really civilized, they won't mind having us nearby." If that was indeed the Cherokee intention, they badly misread the Georgia mentality of the time. Far from being impressed by Cherokee "advancement," in the words of Woodward, "Georgia flew into a mighty rage. Denouncing the Cherokees as savages, Georgia abandoned both dignity and ethics and through her government, press, and courts began, in 1820, a vicious attack upon the Cherokees that was to continue for eighteen years."

SOURCE LIST AND SUGGESTIONS FOR FURTHER READING

Foreman, Grant. 1938. *Sequoyah*. Norman: University of Oklahoma Press.

GLOSSARY

Bicameral. Having two branches, chambers or houses, as a legislative body.

Cadmus. In Greek mythology, a Phoenician prince who introduced writing to the Greeks and founded the city of Thebes.

Chattooga. Also spelled Chatuga. More accurately Tsatugi. Mooney thinks that this word, a place-name, is of foreign origin.

Clermont. English corruption of the Osage name Gra-Mo'n, Gle'Mo'n, or Gleh-Mo'n, meaning "Arrow Going Home," he was an important Osage chief who died in 1827 or 1828. The city of Claremore, Oklahoma, is named after him, in yet another corruption of his name.

Conasauga. Gansagi or Gansagiyi. According to Mooney, several Cherokee towns carried this name, which cannot be analyzed.

Coosawattee. Kusawetiyi. Mooney translates this as "Old Creek Town," from Kusa (Creek), weti (old) and the locative yi.

Degadoga. A Western Cherokee prominent in the Osage wars. In his later years, he advocated a union of all Indian tribes west of the Mississippi with the aim of keeping all the whites east of that river. His name has been variously spelled: Ta-kah-to-kuh, Takatoka, and even Tick-e-toke. Mooney translates the name as "they (meaning two men) are standing together so close in sympathy as to form but one body."

Echota or Itsadi. This word has also been spelled Chota, Chote, and even Choquata. Mooney says that the name occurs in several places in the old Cherokee country and cannot be translated. The primary town of Itsadi was the ancient capital and sacred peace town of the nation. The name was used once again when the capital was established at New Echota.

Kaneeda. An English spelling of a Cherokee masculine name.

Oowatie. Uweti. Old.

Poll tax. Also called a capitation tax. A uniform tax for each person.

Sullacoie. Corrupt English spelling for a Cherokee place-name.

Tahchee. One of several English spellings for the Cherokee name of the man known as Captain Dutch. Variations are Tatsi, Datsi, and Tuch-ee. A Western Cherokee prominent during the Osage war.

Tinsawattie. Corrupt spelling of a Cherokee place-name. The ending is probably uweti.

Tripartite. Divided into or consisting of three parts.

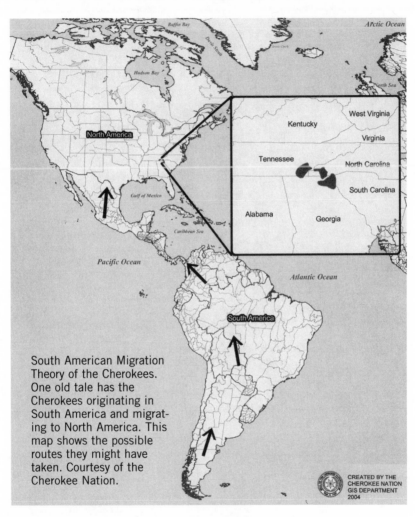

South American Migration Theory of the Cherokees. One old tale has the Cherokees originating in South America and migrating to North America. This map shows the possible routes they might have taken. Courtesy of the Cherokee Nation.

CREATED BY THE CHEROKEE NATION GIS DEPARTMENT 2004

1673 Cherokee Country. This map shows the old homelands of the Cherokees. Courtesy of the Cherokee Nation.

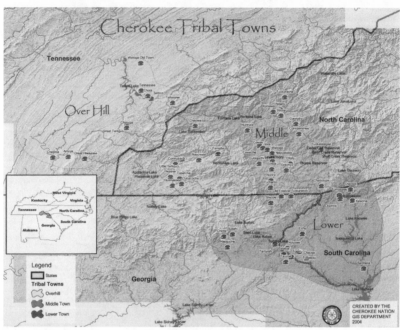

Cherokee Tribal Towns. Cherokee country and tribal towns before the
Removal in 1838–1839. Courtesy of the Cherokee Nation.

The Cherokee Nation in the West, in what is now Northeast Oklahoma. The
way the Cherokee Nation was laid out following the Trail of Tears. Courtesy of
the Cherokee Nation.

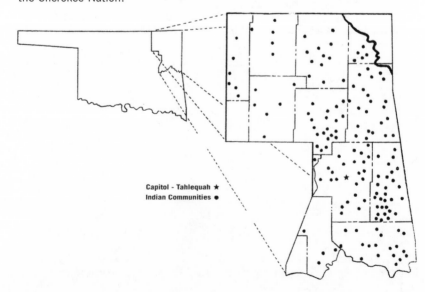

John Ross.
Principal Chief from
1828–1866, Ross saw
the Cherokee Nation
through the Trail of
Tears and the Civil War.
He was Chief for
thirty-eight years,
the longest term ever
for a Principal Chief.

W. P. Ross.
Nephew to Chief John
Ross, W. P. was twice
appointed Chief by the
Council but was never
elected to the position.
He served from
1866–1867 and again
from 1872–1875.

Lewis Downing.
Full-blood Cherokee
and Baptist preacher,
Downing was Chief
from 1867–1872.

Charles Thompson.
Half Cherokee,
Thompson was Chief
from 1875–1879.

Dennis Wolfe Bushyhead.
A '49er, Bushyhead
returned to the Cherokee
Nation to be elected
Chief and serve from
1879–1888.

Joel Bryan Mayes.
Mayes was chief
from 1888–1891.

Thomas Mitchell Buffington. Buffington was appointed Chief by the Council following the death of Chief Mayes while in office. In 1899, he was elected Chief and served until 1903.

Colonel Johnson Harris. Harris was Chief from 1891–1895. The activities of the Dawes Commission began during this time.

Samuel Houston Mayes.
Brother of Chief Joel
Bryan Mayes, Samuel
Houston Mayes was
Chief from 1895–1899.

William Charles Rogers.
Chief from 1903–1917,
Rogers was elected,
impeached, put out of
office and reinstated by
the U.S. Government.

Jesse Bartley Milam. Chief from 1941–1949, Milam had been elected by grass roots Cherokee organizations. The election was not recognized by the U.S. Government but was rubber stamped when the Roosevelt administration appointed Milam Chief.

W. W. Keeler. Chief from 1949–1975, Keeler was the last of a string of nine Chiefs appointed by the federal government. He was an elected Chief for his last four years in office.

Ross Swimmer.
Chief for ten years
(1975–1985), Swimmer
resigned to accept an
appointment as head
of the Bureau of
Indian Affairs.

Wilma Mankiller.
Swimmer's Deputy Chief,
Mankiller became Chief
upon his resignation.
She won reelection
twice, thus serving
for ten years, from
1985–1995.

Joe Byrd.
Byrd was Chief from
1995–1999. His admin-
istration was fraught
with controversy.

Chad Smith.
Smith was elected in
1999 and reelected in
2003. He is Principal
Chief of the Cherokee
Nation at this writing.
Photo by D. L.
Birchfield.

Ostenaco, one of the Cherokee "Chiefs" who traveled to England in 1762. He was a War Chief.

Cunne Shote, or Stalking Turkey, went to England in 1762. While there he was painted by Parsons.

George Lowrey, or
Agili, was Sequoyah's
cousin. He served as
Deputy Principal
Chief under Chief
John Ross for a time.

John Jolly, the adopted
father of Sam Houston,
Jolly was also the
Principal Chief of the
Western Cherokees in
Arkansas from
1819–1838.

Captain Dutch, or Tahchee, shown here in a portrait by George Catlin, was one of the main war leaders of the Western Cherokees in their war with the Osages.

Sequoyah

Sequoyah was the first major Cherokee celebrity. He presented the Cherokees with a syllabary and practically turned the entire Cherokee Nation literate "overnight."

Cherokee Alphabet.

D a	**R** e	**T** i	**δ** o	**O** u	**i** v
S ga **O** ka	**F** ge	**y** gi	**A** go	**J** gu	**E** gv
T ha	**P** he	**J** hi	**F** ho	**Γ** hu	**Φ** hv
W la	**δ** le	**P** li	**G** lo	**M** lu	**A** lv
T ma	**O** me	**H** mi	**5** mo	**y** mu	
O na **t** hna **G** nah	**Λ** ne	**h** ni	**Z** no	**∃** nu	**O** nv
T qua	**O** que	**P** qui	**V** quo	**O** quu	**E** quv
U sa **ω** s	**4** se	**b** si	**∓** so	**δ** su	**R** sv
L da **W** ta	**S** de **T** te	**J** di **J** ti	**V** do	**S** du	**G** dv
δ dla **L** tla	**L** tle	**C** tli	**∜** tlo	**∜** tlu	**P** tlv
G tsa	**V** tse	**Ir** tsi	**K** tso	**J** tsu	**C** tsv
G wa	**W** we	**Θ** wi	**O** wo	**δ** wu	**6** wv
ω ya	**β** ye	**δ** yi	**fi** yo	**G** yu	**B** yv

Sounds Represented by Vowels

a, as a in father, or short as a in rival ||| o, as o in note, approaching aw in law

e, as a in hate, or short as e in met ||| u, as oo in fool, or short as u in pull

i, as i in pique, or short as i in pit ||| v, as u in but, nasalized

Consonant Sounds

g nearly as in English, but approaching to k.   d nearly as in English but approaching to t. h k l m n q s t w y as in English. Syllables beginning with g except **S** (ga) have sometimes the power of k. **A** (go), **S** (du), **G** (dv) are sometimes sounded to, tu, tv and syllables written with tl except **L** (tla) sometimes vary to dl .

Cherokee Syllabary, the system for reading and writing the Cherokee language as presented by Sequoyah and redesigned by committee in preparation for casting type.

Major Ridge, prominent Cherokee who became a leader of the Treaty Party and was killed for having signed the Removal Treaty.

Major Ridge

John Ridge

John Ridge, son of Major Ridge, killed for having signed the Removal Treaty.

Stand Watie became a general in the Confederate Army and was the last Confederate general to surrender. He was styled the Principal Chief of the Confederate Cherokee Nation.

Corntassel, photographed here as an old man, Corntassel walked the Trail of Tears as a child.

Rose Cottage, the home of Principal Chief John Ross at Park Hill (now Oklahoma), was destroyed by Confederate forces during the Civil War.

Cherokee National Capitol in Tahlequah.

Zeke Proctor became the center of a jurisdictional conflict between the Cherokee Nation and the U.S. in 1872.

Beck-Hildebrand Mill. The site of Zeke Proctor's killing of Polly Beck.

Ned Christie (left) was falsely accused of killing a deputy U.S. marshal and successfully avoided the deputy marshals for four and a half years before they finally killed him.

Dawes Commission Office in Muskogee.

Will Rogers was the
second major Cherokee
celebrity. The only two
Indians represented in
the National Statuary
Hall of Fame are
Rogers and Sequoyah.

Wes Studi, successful
Cherokee film actor.

Scene on the Back Porch
of the old capitol build-
ing, August 13, 1997.

Note: All photos not individually credited are
courtesy of the Cherokee Honor Society

CHAPTER FIFTEEN

"The Cherokee Are Not Foreigners"

Tired of waiting for the United States government to enforce the 1802 Georgia Compact, the governor and legislature of Georgia presented a memorial to Congress in 1820 pressing for faster action. Congress was sympathetic. So was President James Monroe. In 1822, he appointed commissioners to treat with the Cherokee Nation for its Georgia land, which, of course, was almost all of the land remaining to the Cherokees in the East. The Cherokee Council agreed to meet with the commissioners, but only in New Echota. The meeting convened on October 6, 1823. Present at the meeting was the newly appointed agent for the Cherokee Nation, the former Governor McMinn of Tennessee. The Cherokees refused to even discuss giving up any more of their land, in spite of twelve thousand dollars worth of bribes offered to John Ross, Alexander McCoy, Charles Hicks, and others. On October 27, the Cherokees declared the conference to be at an end.

The council then sent a delegation to Washington to present its case directly to the president. The delegates, John Ross, Major Ridge, Elija Hicks, and George Lowrey, encountered a stubborn Madison, who recited to them the terms of the Georgia Compact and demanded that they give up their land and move to Arkansas. The Cherokees refused, and the conference accomplished nothing. They did leave Madison with the following statement:

"Sir, to these remarks we beg leave to observe and to remind you that the Cherokee are not foreigners but original inhabitants of America, and that they now inhabit and stand on the soil of their own territory and that the limits of this territory are defined by the treaties which they have made with the government of the United States, and that the states by which they are now surrounded have been created out of land which was once theirs, and that they cannot recognize the sovereignty of any state within the limits of their territory."

While in Washington, the Cherokee delegates were staying at the Tennison Hotel. In the dining room one day, they found themselves seated across the table from a Georgia congressman who had made a speech on the floor of Congress in which he had referred to the Cherokees as "savages subsisting upon roots, wild herbs, disgusting reptiles." When a waiter approached with a platter of sweet potatoes, George Lowrey took some and said, "We Indians are very fond of roots."

Georgia continued to agitate for Cherokee removal, and in 1827, Pathkiller, the Principal Chief of the Cherokee Nation, died. He was succeeded by Charles Hicks, but Hicks did not live long after that. In 1828, a national election was held, and John Ross was elected Principal Chief. George Lowrey was elected Deputy or Second Chief. One month later, Andrew Jackson was elected president of the United States.

One of the first things Principal Chief John Ross had to deal with was the so-called White-path Rebellion. Nunna-tsunega, White-path, from Ulunyi, or Turniptown, was a full-blood member of the National Council, and in 1828, in an echo of the message of Tecumseh and of the Red Stick movement among the Creeks, he began to advocate a complete rejection of all white culture, including Christianity and the new written laws, and a return to the old ways of the Cherokees. Mooney says, "He soon had a large band of followers, known to the whites as 'Red Sticks,'... From the townhouse of Ellijay he preached the rejection of the new constitution, the discarding of Christianity and the white man's ways, and a return to the old tribal law and custom... under the rule of such men as Hicks and Ross, the conservative opposition gradually melted away. Whitepath was deposed from his seat in council, but subsequently made submission and was reinstated."

The following year, on December 8, 1829, in his first annual address to Congress, President Andrew Jackson announced his intention to introduce a bill to Congress with the purpose of removing all Southeastern Indians to lands somewhere west of the Mississippi River. With its new and powerful ally in the White House, and because gold had been discovered on Cherokee land, Georgia intensified its efforts. On December 11, the Georgia legislature passed its infamous "anti-Cherokee laws." They annexed a large portion of Cherokee land and nullified Cherokee laws within that area. They forbade the Cherokee Council to meet within the defined area of the state of Georgia. They made it illegal for Cherokees to talk against emigration to the West. They made contracts between Cherokees and whites illegal unless witnessed by two whites. They made it illegal for a Cherokee to testify against a white man in court, and they forbade Cherokees to dig for gold on their own land. Violation of these laws could result in imprisonment for four years.

The intentions of the Georgia state legislature were plain and simple. If they could make life miserable enough for the Cherokees, perhaps the Cherokees would get fed up with it all and move west voluntarily. But they were not relying on that method alone. Covering all their bases, they were strong supporters of and lobbyists for Jackson's removal bill. Then, acting under their own anti-Cherokee laws, the state divided the Cherokee country up into "land lots" of 160 acres each and "gold lots" of 40 acres each and passed them out by lottery to Georgia's white citizens.

Another Georgia law made it illegal for any white man to live in Cherokee country without having first taken a special oath of allegiance to the state of Georgia. The penalty for violation of this law was four years in prison. The law was aimed at the white missionaries who were living with and teaching the Cherokees. The Cherokees went to President Jackson for help, but he said that there was nothing that he could do. He refused to interfere with the laws of the sovereign state of Georgia.

Then on May 28, 1830, the U.S. Congress passed Jackson's removal bill into law by a narrow margin. In general, northern lawmakers were opposed to the measure while southerners supported it. An exception was Congressman Davy Crockett from Tennessee, famous as an Indian fighter. Often someone will attempt to defend the actions of people of the past by saying that we cannot in fairness apply the standards of our time to the beliefs and actions of one hundred or more years ago. In other words, for example, they might say that in 1830 everyone thought that it was all right to drive Indians from their land, so we can't blame Andrew Jackson for feeling that way. Davy Crockett's example gives the lie to that line of reasoning. Crockett wrote that when he was elected in 1827, he was "without disguise, the friend and supporter of General Jackson, upon his principles as he had laid them down, and as '*I under-stood them*,' before his election as President." He goes on to say that during his first two sessions in Congress, under the Adams administration, he "worked along with what was called the Jackson party pretty well." But that all changed. In Crockett's words:

His famous, or rather I should say his in-*famous*, Indian bill
was brought forward, and I opposed it from the purest
motives in the world. Several of my colleagues... told
me... that I was ruining myself. They said this was a favorite
measure of the president, and I ought to go for it. I told them
I believed it was a wicked, unjust measure, and that I should
go against it, let the cost to myself be what it might; that I
was willing to go with General Jackson in everything that I
believed was honest and right; but, further than this, I
wouldn't go for him or any other man in the whole creation;
that I would sooner be honestly and politically damned,
than hypocritically immortalized.... I voted against this
Indian bill, and my conscience yet tells me that I gave a
good honest vote, and one that I believe will not make me
ashamed in the day of judgment. I served out my
term.... When it closed, and I returned home, I found the
storm had raised against me sure enough.

To further weaken the Cherokee Nation, Jackson suspended payment of the annuities specified in the treaties the Cherokee Nation had
signed with the United States. This was payment due in exchange for
lands already given up to the United States.

In 1831, William Wirt, attorney for the Cherokee Nation, filed suit against
Georgia in the United States Supreme Court, on the grounds that the state
of Georgia could not enforce its laws on the Cherokee Nation, an independent, sovereign nation. The case was dismissed on the grounds that
the Cherokee Nation was not a foreign country, and in its far-reaching decision, known as the *Cherokee Nation* v. *Georgia*, the Court defined Indian
tribes in the United States as "domestic, dependent nations."

In 1832, the Creeks, Choctaws, Seminoles, and Chickasaws all gave in
to the pressures and agreed to remove. Only the Cherokees held out. That
same year, Reverend Samuel Worcester, Elizur Butler, and nine other white
men were arrested in the Cherokee Nation for having refused to sign the
oath of allegiance to Georgia. Nine took the oath and were released, but
Worcester and Butler refused. They were tried, found guilty, and sentenced
to four years in the penitentiary at hard labor.

Chief Ross and the Cherokee Council again retained Wirt, who was
willing to wait for or even forego his fees, this time to appeal the case of the
missionaries to the Supreme Court. With no money to operate on, the
Cherokee Nation had Boudinot soliciting funds to support continued publication of the paper, a necessity in presenting the Cherokee case to the rest

of the country, and a delegation made up of John Ridge, John Martin, and William Shorey Coodey was in Washington pleading the case of the Cherokees to Secretary of War John Eaton. At just that same time, a delegation of Western Cherokees passed through the Cherokee Nation on its way to Washington. James Starr and John Walker, Jr., both mixed-bloods, joined them and accompanied them the rest of the way to Washington.

Worcester's case (*Worcester* v. *Georgia*) was heard by the U.S. Supreme Court. This time the Court ruled in favor of Worcester and ordered his release, saying that in matters dealing with Indian nations, the laws of the state must give way to federal law. On hearing the news, Elias Boudinot, in Boston, wrote to his brother Stand Watie: "It is glorious news. The laws of the state are declared by the highest judicial tribunal in the country to be *null & void*. It is a great triumph on the part of the Cherokees."

But Georgia refused to release Worcester and Butler, and when Andrew Jackson heard of the decision, he is supposed to have said of the court's chief justice, "John Marshal has made his decision, now let him enforce it." Probably discouraged by this news, tired of dealing with the Georgians, around six hundred Cherokees voluntarily moved west that year, but upon their arrival in the West, they wrote letters back home encouraging the rest to stay put. The government had failed to live up to its promises of rations and supplies for the trip, and people had gotten sick and died along the way.

On July 23, 1832, a council was held at Red Clay, Tennessee, to avoid the persecution of Georgia back at New Echota. United States commissioner Elisha Chester was there to offer the Cherokees a removal treaty. The council refused to consider it. But Chester's arguments that removal would save the Cherokees from the suffering they had been forced to endure under the harassment of Georgia must have made sense to some. Chester soon had a list of names of "protreaty advocates," and the list included the names of James Starr, John Walker, Jr., William Shorey Coodey, William Rogers, William Hicks, Andrew Ross (brother of the chief), Elias Boudinot, and John Ridge. The Cherokee Nation's unified resistance to removal had come to an end.

SOURCE LIST AND SUGGESTIONS FOR FURTHER READING

Crockett, David. 1955. *The Life of Davy Crockett*. New York: New American Library.

Filler, Louis, and Allen Guttman. 1977. *The Removal of the Cherokee Nation:*

Manifest Destiny or National Dishonor? Huntington, New York: Robert
E. Krieger Publishing Company.

Young, Mary Elizabeth. 1961. *Redskins, Ruffleshirts and Rednecks: Indian
Allotments in Alabama and Mississippi 1830–1860.* Norman: University
of Oklahoma Press.

GLOSSARY

Ellijay. Elatseyi. Mooney suggests that this word might be a combination of
Ela, or Eloh, earth, and itseyi, green. He translates it "Green Earth." It's
the name of several different Cherokee towns.

Nunna tsunega. Whitepath. Cherokee leader of a revivalist movement.

Ulunyi. Mooney translates this "Tuber Place." The Cherokee town was called,
in English, "Turnip Town."

CHAPTER SIXTEEN

The Treaty of New Echota

Out west in Arkansas, things were happening too. In 1820, in response to a request from Tahlonteskee, the American Board of Commissioners for Foreign Missions sent Reverend Cephas Washburn to Arkansas to establish a mission for the Western Cherokees. As their relatives in the East, the Western Cherokees were more interested in a school than in the religious work of the missionaries, but, of course, the two came together. Reverend Washburn established Dwight Mission on the banks of the Arkansas River in what is now Pope County, Arkansas. By the time the mission was in place, Tahlonteskee was dead, and John Jolly was chief, but like his brother, the former chief, Jolly supported the efforts of the missionary. Washburn was opposed, however, by Degadoga, who scornfully said that the reverend was trying to get the Indians to "wear breeches."

In 1818, in response to the Cherokee-Osage war, the government had established Fort Smith, called at the time Cantonment Smith, in what is now Arkansas, but was at the time part of Missouri Territory. In 1820, most of what are today the states of Arkansas and Oklahoma were organized into Arkansas Territory. In 1824, the U.S. Army moved farther into Osage country with the establishment of Fort Gibson at the Three Forks, the place where the Arkansas, Illinois, and Verdigris rivers all converge. That same year, Captain Dutch was informed by the military authorities that he was living on the wrong side of the Arkansas River, and in keeping with the order of 1819 he would have to move. Dutch reacted in the same way as had the Bowl. He moved, but not just across the Arkansas River. He moved to Texas just south of the Red River, outside the jurisdiction of the United States, and established two settlements there.

In 1825, Degadoga died on a trip to the East. He was working on his effort to unite all Indian tribes west of the Mississippi River. No one took his place, and his grand scheme died with him. But Dutch took the place of Degadoga in the arena of the war with the Osages. From his settlements on the Texas side of the Red River, Dutch led raids north into Osage country. The Western Cherokees disenfranchised Dutch so that they would not be held accountable for his actions, and the U.S. Army is said to have put a five-hundred-dollar bounty on his head. Any time the military authorities talked to the Osage leaders about ending the war, the Osages responded that they must have Dutch first. Then they wanted all Osage captives taken by the Cherokees to be returned to them.

The Western Cherokee response was that Dutch was an outlaw, and they were not responsible for his actions; and that all the Osage captives were free but did not want to return to the Osage Nation. They were all women and children, the Cherokees said. The women had married Cherokee men, and the children were all in school back east.

In the meantime, white people had been moving into Arkansas in large numbers. They had even crossed over into Lovely's Purchase (now eastern Oklahoma). The settlers in Lovely's Purchase had gone so far as to establish a post office, and they petitioned the territorial governor to give them the status of a county, to be called Lovely County. In 1828, the Western Cherokees sent a delegation made up of Blackfox, John Rogers, Thomas Graves, Thomas Maw, George Morris, Tobacco Will, and Sequoyah to Washington to protest the creation of Lovely County. They protested that Agent Lovely had negotiated Lovely's Purchase away from the Osages for the use of the Cherokees. At the same time a group of white settlers from Lovely County were in Washington to plead their side of the case. Neither side was prepared for the response they got from Washington.

The government gave the Western Cherokee delegation a choice. They said that either Lovely County would stand and the white settlers could stay, or the Western Cherokees could all relocate and build new homes in the area in question. The delegates signed a treaty to that effect. The Lovely County whites were furious at being forced to move back across the line into Arkansas, and the Western Cherokees were angry with their delegates for having signed the treaty giving up their land in Arkansas.

In the end though, in 1829, everyone involved made the move, and the Western Cherokees were all established in what is now eastern

Oklahoma. Reverend Washburn followed them, moving Dwight Mission to a new location in what is now Sequoyah County, Oklahoma. That same year, Clermont died, and Sam Houston moved west to live once again with his adopted father, John Jolly.

In 1830, Captain Dutch and John Smith, a Cherokee from near Fort Gibson, led a major raid against a town of Tawakoni Indians in Texas who had killed three Cherokee hunters. It was almost certainly the last of the old-time Cherokee war parties. Based on a report from Smith himself, as told to John Ridge, Foreman describes it in *Indians and Pioneers.*

At the home of Dutch on the Red River in Texas, "they danced the war dance for four nights, and the women prepared food for the men on the march; they parched corn and pounded it into meal, then gave each warrior a bagful. Dutch shaved his hair close to the skin, leaving only a small tuft on the top of his head in which to fasten his headdress made of the short feathers of the hawk. He painted his shaved head red and half the length of the feathers, leaving them tipped with white in the original color."

Sixty-three Cherokee warriors traveled ten days to reach the Tawakoni village, which they attacked early in the morning. The fight was over about ten o'clock. When the Cherokees returned victorious to their own settlements, they "cut a long pine sapling, peeled the bark off and painted it red, leaving on the end a bunch of green leaves. On this pole they strung the scalps of the hapless Tawakoni which they had dried and now combed out and painted red with vermilion, like the pole. They then painted themselves the same color." They carried the pole into the settlements where "Dutch sang the war song and gave as many whoops as they had scalps." They then shook hands with all the men and women present, told their tales of the exploit, and then joined in a great feast.

In 1831, with the help of Sam Houston's diplomatic skills, the U.S. Army at last successfully negotiated a treaty of peace between the Western Cherokees and the Osage Nation. Furthermore, the Osages actually agreed that if the Cherokees from the Red River settlements would move back up with their relatives within one year of the signing of the treaty, they would be included in the peace. Both the U.S. government and the Western Cherokees rescinded Dutch's outlaw status. The Western Cherokees sent people and wagons to Dutch's settlements to help move him back home, and Dutch cooperated, making the move. The long Cherokee-Osage war was finally at an end.

In 1832, Sam Houston left the Western Cherokees to go to Texas. The Bowl had settled on Caney Creek, about fifty miles north of Nacogdoches, where, according to Clarke, they "formed a loose confederacy with other refugee Indians, including Shawnees, Delawares, Kickapoos, Choctaws,

Biloxis, Alabamas, and Coushattas" under the name of the Texas Cherokees. Sometime after their arrival in Texas, the Cherokees had elected a new chief, Richard Fields. On behalf of the Texas Cherokees, Fields had applied to the government of Mexico for a grant to the land they were living on. Whether or not the grant was ever issued is a subject of controversy among historians. Apparently it was under consideration.

Even here, however, whites were pressing on the Cherokee lands, and a white man named John Dunn Hunter came to live with the Cherokees. Chief Fields had just spent a year in Mexico City trying unsuccessfully to get a title to the Cherokee lands. Hunter then went on the same mission. He too came back disappointed. Fields was ready to go to war, but Hunter talked him into waiting a little while.

Hunter then went to Nacogdoches where he met with the brothers Hayden and Benjamin Edwards. They planned a rebellion against the Mexican government to establish the Republic of Fredonia. The Texas Cherokees were to be their allies in this effort, and the white Fredonians signed a compact pledging that the Cherokees, following a Fredonian victory, would have their lands.

But the Bowl refused to take part in the Fredonian scheme, and before the Fredonians could take any decisive action, their plans were discovered. With the Mexican army coming after them, the Edwards brothers ran away to the safety of the United States. John Dunn Hunter and Richard Fields were both killed in the Cherokee settlements, some say by the Bowl. Big Mush was elected to the position of Peace Chief, and the Bowl was elected War Chief. For his part in putting down the Fredonian rebellion, the Bowl received a Mexican army officer's hat and the title of lieutenant colonel. After that he became known as Colonel Bowles. He kept working to secure a title to the Cherokee lands, and he was still engaged in that effort when Houston arrived in Texas and contacted him. The Texas Revolution began in 1835, and Sam Houston was made general of the Texas army.

Back in the old Cherokee country, the new protreaty faction of the Cherokee Nation had begun to solidify in 1832 with Elias Boudinot's letter of resignation from the editorship of *The Cherokee Phoenix*. In his letter, he told Chief Ross that he thought that the *Phoenix* had done its job of presenting the case for the rights of Cherokees, but that it was now time to tell the people the truth about the dangers of their continued resistance to removal. Ross accepted Boudinot's resignation and replaced him as editor of the newspaper with Elijah Hicks. Then at a council meeting in October of that same year, John Ridge, president of the National Committee, introduced a resolution that revealed his new sentiments. He proposed that a delegation be sent to Washington to negotiate a removal treaty. The resolution was not passed, but Ridge's new position was now clear.

Georgia continued to harass the Cherokees, and John Ross led a delegation to Washington to continue to protest the situation. Jackson offered the Cherokee Nation, through Ross, three million dollars to sell out and move, and Ross refused. After that, John Ridge turned vehemently against Ross with personal attacks. Then the leaders of the protreaty faction, now known more formally as the Treaty Party, began secret negotiations with both the state of Georgia and the United States regarding removal. Governor Lumpkin of Georgia ordered that their homes be protected. At the same time, Chief Ross's home was taken over by lottery winners, and he was forced to move to Tennessee for safety.

Andrew Ross, John Walker, Jr., and other members of the Treaty Party tried to negotiate a removal treaty in 1834, but the Cherokee Council rejected it. Feelings were high, and Walker was killed for introducing "disunity into the Nation" (Woodward, p. 177). Andrew Jackson said that Chief Ross and the Cherokee Council would be held responsible for all murders of protreaty Cherokees. Treaty Party delegations were fawned over in Washington, while official Cherokee Nation delegations were ignored and treated rudely.

At last, on December 29, 1835, following several failed attempts at pushing through a removal treaty, U.S. government negotiators met with "not more than three hundred [Cherokees], including women and children," at New Echota. John Ross was in Washington, and the majority of Cherokees refused to attend the meeting. Out of the three hundred or so gathered there, only about one hundred were voters. A committee of twenty was appointed to negotiate (Royce, p. 163). There, headed by Major Ridge, John Ridge, Elias Boudinot, Andrew Ross, James Starr, Stand Watie, James Rogers, and others, the Treaty Party signed the Treaty of New Echota, a treaty of total removal. None of these men had been authorized by the government or the people of the Cherokee Nation to sign a treaty. The entire procedure was illegal, but it was what the United States government wanted, and it was accepted by the U.S. Congress as legal and binding on the entire Cherokee Nation. The price for all of the Cherokee lands left in the East was five million dollars.

In its preamble, the treaty says that "the Cherokees are anxious to make some arrangements with the Government of the United States whereby the difficulties they have experienced by a residence within the settled parts of the Untied States under the jurisdiction and laws of the State Governments may be terminated and adjusted; and with a view to

The treaty was made up of twenty articles. In the first article, the Cherokee Nation gave up all rights to all of their lands and property east of the Mississippi River for five million dollars.

Article 2 outlined the western land that was to be set aside for the Cherokees. It included the area known as Lovely's Purchase on which the Western Cherokees were now located.

Article 3 gave the United States the right to continue to man Fort Gibson within the boundaries of the new Cherokee Nation.

In Article 4 the United States agreed to pay the Osages for any "reservations" they might have remaining in the land being signed over to the Cherokees.

Article 5 guaranteed that the new Cherokee Nation in the West would never be included in any state or territory without the consent of the Cherokees.

Article 6 promised perpetual peace and friendship between the United States and the Cherokees, and in this article the United States also promised to protect the Cherokee Nation from both domestic strife and from outside enemies.

Article 7 stated that the Cherokee Nation "shall be entitled to a delegate in the House of Representatives of the United States whenever Congress shall make provision for the same."

In Article 8 the United States detailed how it would pay for the removal of the Cherokees to their new homes.

Article 9 was a promise by the United States to appoint "suitable agents" to determine the value of improvements on Cherokee land, to adjust any Cherokee debts out of money due to the Cherokees, and to handle the money appropriated for removal expenses.

In Article 10 the president of the United States promised to invest money for the Cherokee Nation for a permanent fund.

Article 11 provided for the investment of money for a Cherokee school fund.

Article 12 made provisions for those Cherokees who might want to remain behind as individual citizens of the states of North Carolina, Tennessee, and Alabama. However, this article was stricken from the treaty when it was ratified by the U.S. Congress.

Article 13 made reference to the "reservations" of previous treaties, and allowed those Cherokees who had applied for and accepted them to remain on them as private citizens. This article too was stricken from the final treaty.

Article 14 promised pensions to Cherokee veterans of the Creek War.

Article 15 stated that the Western Cherokees would also share in the money derived from the sale of the Cherokees' eastern lands.

Article 16 gave the Cherokees two years in which to make the move.

Article 17 stated that any claims arising out of the treaty would be examined by commissioners appointed by the president, and stated that all previous treaties would remain in force except where specific items in them were canceled by specific items in the present treaty.

In Article 18 the United States agreed to pay for the support of the "poorer Cherokees" for two years after the removal.

Article 19 was a statement that the treaty would be in full force as soon as it was ratified by the U.S. Congress. No mention was made of ratification by the Cherokee Council.

reuniting their people in one body and securing a permanent home for themselves and their posterity in the country selected by their forefathers without the territorial limits of the State sovereignties, and where they can establish and enjoy a government of their choice and perpetuate such a state of society as may be most consonant with their views, habits and condition; and as may tend to their individual comfort and their advancement in civilization."

The treaty was signed by twenty members of the Treaty Party, and it was reported that Major Ridge, who had himself helped execute Doublehead for the same offense twenty-seven years earlier, as he put his mark on the document, said, "I feel as if I had just signed my own death warrant." His words would prove to be prophetic.

SOURCE LIST AND SUGGESTIONS FOR FURTHER READING

DeRosier, Arthur H., Jr. 1975. "The Cherokee Indians: Disaster through Negotiations." In *Forked Tongues and Broken Treaties*, ed. Donald E. Worcester. Caldwell, Idaho: Caxton Printers.

Gregory, Jack, and Rennard Strickland. 1967. *Sam Houston with the Cherokees: 1829–1833*. Austin: University of Texas Press.

GLOSSARY

Alabama. A Muskogean-speaking southeastern Indian tribe, once a member
tribe of the Creek Confederacy.

Biloxi. A Siouan-speaking Gulf Coast Indian tribe.

Cantonment. A military camp.

Coushatta. A southeastern Indian tribe, once a member of the Creek
Confederacy. Also spelled Koasati.

Disenfranchise. To deprive of the rights of citizenship.

Fredonia. Name given to a planned republic in Texas, prior to the Texas
Revolution. The revolution to establish Fredonia was put down without
a shot being fired.

Kickapoo. Algonquian-speaking American Indian tribe of the central prairies
and woodlands.

Phoenix. A bird from Greek mythology that was said to live for five hundred
years, burn itself to death, and rise again from its own ashes.

Ratification. Confirmation. A treaty negotiated on behalf of the United States
is not legal until the U.S. Senate has ratified it. Occasionally Indian
tribes claimed the same privilege, saying that treaties they had signed
were not binding until ratified by their tribal councils.

Tawakoni. A Caddoan-speaking Texas Indian tribe.

Territory. A region not admitted as a state to the union, but having its own
governor and legislature appointed by the president.

CHAPTER SEVENTEEN

"Living upon the Roots and Sap of Trees"

In Texas, the rebels organized a provisional government, and on November 13, 1835, the officers of that government met and unanimously adopted a "Solemn Declaration" which read in part as follows:

> Be it solemnly decreed, that we...solemnly declare that the Cherokee Indians, and their associate bands,...have derived their just claims to lands included within the bounds hereinafter mentioned from the Government of Mexico, from whom we have also derived our rights...
>
> We solemnly declare that we will guarantee to them the peaceful enjoyment of their rights to their lands, as we do our own;...
>
> We solemnly declare that it is our sincere desire that the Cherokee Indians and their associate bands, should remain our friends in peace and war, and if they do so, we pledge the public faith for the support of the foregoing declarations."

The declaration was signed by Sam Houston and other members of the convention, and in February of 1836, a formal treaty was negotiated with the Cherokees at Bowl's settlement. The land promised to the Cherokees was approximately the equivalent of the present Cherokee

County, Texas. Mooney says, "The treaty provoked such general dissatis-faction among the Texans that it was not presented to the convention for ratification. General Houston became President of Texas in November, 1836, but notwithstanding all his efforts in behalf of the Cherokees, the treaty was rejected by the Texas Senate in secret session on December 16, 1837. Texas having in the meantime achieved victorious independence was now in position to repudiate her engagements with the Indians."

Back in Washington, the U.S. Senate ratified the fraudulent Treaty of New Echota on May 23, 1836, "by a majority of only one vote over the nec-essary number" (Mooney) and set May 23, 1838, as a deadline for Cherokee removal. Andrew Jackson notified Chief Ross through the Secretary of War that he "had ceased to recognize any existing government among the east-ern Cherokee." At that point, many Cherokees recognized defeat and made the move on their own. "Between 1836-38 approximately 2,000 Cherokees joined the 'Old Settlers' or 'Cherokees West' in what is today eastern Oklahoma" (Woodward). And in the first month of 1837, she continues, "600 aristocratic members of the Treaty party availed themselves of the provisions of the New Echota treaty authorizing Cherokees to remove themselves. Accompanied by Negro slaves, saddle horses, and droves of fat oxen, these Cherokees traveled overland ... reaching their destination in time to put in spring crops" (Woodward).

In March of the same year, a second group of Treaty Party members made the move under the supervision of the U.S. government. This group of 466 included Major Ridge and his family, and they took the river route, traveling by boat. Starr and other Treaty Party members, about 365 of them, left in October, also under government supervision. They stopped along the way "to pay a respectful call on Jackson" (Woodward). Fifteen of them (eleven children) died along the way.

But Chief Ross continued to fight against the treaty, and the major-ity of Cherokees, approximately sixteen thousand, stood firmly behind him. Jackson sent U.S. troops under the command of General Wool to Cherokee country. Resolutions signed by nearly all of Ross's followers, declaring the treaty to be fraudulent, null and void, were presented to General Wool, who forwarded them to Jackson. Jackson's response was "surprise that an officer of the army would have received or transmitted a paper so disrespectful to the Executive, the Senate, and the American people" (Mooney).

Major Davis, who had been assigned the task of enrolling the Cherokees for removal and appraising the value of the improvements on their property, wrote the Secretary of War as follows: "Sir, that paper, ... called a treaty, is no treaty at all, because not sanctioned by the great body of the Cherokee and made without their participation or assent. . . . The most cunning and artful means were resorted to in order to conceal the paucity of numbers present at the treaty. No enumeration of them was made. . . . The business of making the treaty was transacted with a committee appointed by the Indians present, so as not to expose their numbers. . . . The delegation . . . had no more authority to make a treaty than any other dozen Cherokee accidentally picked up for the purpose. . . . The Cherokee are a peaceable, harmless people, but you may drive them to desperation, and this treaty cannot be carried into effect except by the strong arm of force."

General Wool himself, charged with disarming the Cherokees and distributing rations, wrote that not one of them, "however poor or destitute, would receive either rations or clothing from the United States lest they might compromise themselves in regard to the treaty. [They] preferred living upon the roots and sap of trees . . . and thousands . . . had no other food for weeks. Many have said they will die before they will leave the country." He wrote further, "The whole scene since I have been in this country has been nothing but a heart-rending one, and such a one as I would be glad to get rid of as soon as circumstances will permit. Because I am firm and decided, do not believe I would be unjust. If I could, and I could not do them a greater kindness, I would remove every Indian to-morrow beyond the reach of the white men, who, like vultures, are watching, ready to pounce upon their prey and strip them of everything they have or expect from the government of the United States. Yes, sir, nineteen-twentieths, if not ninety-nine out of every hundred, will go penniless to the West."

No one was safe from the land-hungry Georgians. Major Ridge himself, before he left for the West, had written to Jackson as follows:

> We now come to address you on the subject of our griefs and afflictions from the acts of the white people. They have got our lands and now they are preparing to fleece us of the money accruing from the treaty. We found our plantations taken either in whole or in part by the Georgians—suits instituted against us for back rents for our own farms. . . . Thus our funds will be filched from our people, and we shall be compelled to leave our country as beggars. . . . the lowest class of white people are flogging the Cherokees with cowhides, hickories, and clubs. We are not safe in our houses—our people are assailed by day and night by the rabble. Even justices of the peace and constables are concerned in

> this business. This barbarous treatment is not confined to
> men, but the women are stripped also and whipped without
> law or mercy.

Rumors of a Cherokee uprising spread, and Tennessee sent troops under the command of General Dunlap to prevent such a thing from happening or to put it down if it did actually occur. When Dunlap arrived in Cherokee country and saw for himself what was going on, he said that "he had given the Cherokees all the protection in his power, the whites needing none" (Mooney).

In 1837 Andrew Jackson was replaced as president of the United States by Martin Van Buren, and Wilson Lumpkin had been succeeded as governor of Georgia by George R. Gilmer. The policy of neither administration changed, however, and the question of Cherokee removal had become a heated national debate. On the one hand, it had become a partisan issue, with the Democrats in favor of removal and the Whigs opposed to it. On a slightly more philosophical level, it had become an argument between states-rights advocates and federal jurisdiction.

Ralph Waldo Emerson, later to become a famous and prominent American philosopher, wrote a letter to President Van Buren. "Such a dereliction of all faith and virtue," he wrote, "such a denial of justice, and such deafness to screams for mercy were never heard of in times of peace and in the dealing of a nation with its own allies and wards, since the earth was made. Sir, does this government think that the people of the United States are become savage and mad? From their mind are the sentiments of love and a good nature wiped clean out? The soul of man, the justice, the mercy that is the heart's heart in all men, from Maine to Georgia, does abhor this business."

Other prominent white citizens of the United States were strongly and openly opposed to the Cherokee removal: Henry Clay, Daniel Webster, and Edward Everett were a few. Chief John Ross continued to lobby and protest in Washington, but the process continued.

When it became clear that the remaining Cherokees, standing behind and depending on Chief Ross, were not going to remove themselves voluntarily, in spite of all the harassment from Georgians, General Wool, too sympathetic to the Cherokees, was replaced by General Winfield Scott. Scott had orders to start the Cherokees west as soon as possible, and he had under his command seven thousand men, a combination of regular army, state militia, and volunteers. Perhaps sixteen thousand Cherokees remained in their homelands, and they had already been disarmed by General Wool.

Scott established headquarters at New Echota in 1838, and from there he issued a proclamation stating his determination to accomplish the total removal of the Cherokees. "Will you...compel us to resort to arms," he asked, "or will you by flight seek to hide yourselves in mountains and forests and thus oblige us to hunt you down?" Scott then stationed his troops at various points around the Cherokee country. He had stockade "forts" built. Actually they were prisons, large holding pens for Cherokees who would be rounded up and herded like cattle into these "forts" and to be held there until the army was ready to start marching them to the West.

"From these," says Mooney, "squads of troops were sent to search out with rifle and bayonet every small cabin hidden away in the coves or by the sides of mountain streams, to seize and bring in as prisoners all the occupants, however or wherever they might be found. Families at dinner were startled by the sudden gleam of bayonets in the doorway and rose up to be driven with blows and oaths along the weary miles of trail that led to the stockade. Men were seized in their fields or going along the road, women were taken from their wheels and children from their play. In many cases, on turning for one last look as they crossed the ridge, they saw their homes in flames, fired by the lawless rabble that followed on the heels of the soldiers to loot and pillage. So keen were these outlaws on the scent that in some instances they were driving off the cattle and other stock of the Indians almost before the soldiers had fairly started their owners in the other direction. Systematic hunts were made by the same men for Indian graves, to rob them of the silver pendants and other valuables deposited with the dead."

While Chief Ross had urged the Cherokees to resist removal, he had also urged them to do so without resorting to violence, and the disarmed Cherokees for the most part followed his advice. Only once did Cherokees turn on the soldiers, and even then, only one soldier was killed. The story is controversial, but the hero of the tale has become legendary. The following version of the story has been repeated many times, by Mooney and others.

The roundup of the Cherokees was almost completed, when an old man named Tsali (Charlie) and his family were being driven from their home toward the nearest stockade. A soldier prodded Tsali's wife with a bayonet, trying to make her move faster. Furious, Tsali attacked the soldier. At the same time, his brother and his sons attacked the other soldiers. One soldier was killed, and the others ran away. Tsali and his family escaped into the mountains.

On hearing the report of this incident, General Scott sent a message to Tsali by the trader Will Thomas. Thomas was a white man who had been raised by Cherokees, spoke the language, and was generally well thought of among the Cherokees. He managed to locate Tsali hiding in the mountains with hundreds of other Cherokees who had managed to escape the roundup. The message from Scott was that if Tsali and his party would surrender themselves for punishment, Scott would abandon the search for more Cherokees. Mooney says, "Charley voluntarily came in with his sons, offering himself as a sacrifice for his people." Tsali, his brother, and his two oldest sons were shot to death by a firing squad, which Scott had put together from one of the stockades. Thus, in a final gesture of complete power over the Cherokees, he made Cherokee prisoners kill them.

A very different tale is told by French and Hornbuckle. "The Appalachian Cherokees," they say, "notably the villages of Alarka, Aquorra, Stekoih and Cheeoih, consisted of conservative Cherokees who neither participated in nor endorsed the Cherokee Nation. They clung to the traditional ways, placing great emphasis on the old village and clan system." These Appalachian, or North Carolina, Cherokees, they tell us, were allowed to avoid removal by special arrangements made with the state of North Carolina on their behalf by Will Thomas, acting as their legal counsel. Younaguska was the "Regional Chief of this area."

These North Carolina Cherokees, they say, remained behind "legally and not as fugitives." Some other Cherokees did manage to escape from the soldiers and join Younaguska's group. Altogether they were about one thousand. "Tsali," they say, "apparently was attempting to avoid the roundup... only to be detected while camping along the Little Tennessee River by a detachment of General Scott's soldiers. In the ensuing altercation, some soldiers were killed and others wounded, while Tsali and his band sought refuge in the rugged Appalachian mountains.... General Scott decided to make an example of Tsali. Younaguska, fearing that federal troops would have a difficult time distinguishing between his people... and the wanted refugees, consented to aid in the search for Tsali... General Scott was receptive to this plan, sending Euchella and an armed contingent of Cherokees... to find and punish Tsali. Euchella's group caught Tsali and, under federal pressure, executed him and all male members of the group with the exception of Tsali's youngest son.... As a reward for his services, Euchella and the rest of his men and their families were allowed to remain east with Younaguska's Cherokees."

**EXCERPT FROM A LETTER WRITTEN BY PRINCIPAL CHIEF
JOHN ROSS, IN WASHINGTON, TO HIS BROTHER, LEWIS,
FEBRUARY 26, 1838.**

On Saturday last the 24th inst. a duel with rifles was fought between Mr. [William J.] Graves of Ky. And Mr. [Jonathan] Cilly [Cilley] of Maine both of the House of Repves. In Congress. On the 3rd fire the latter fell and expired. Upon the meeting of Congress this morning and the annunciation of the death of Mr. Cilly, both Houses adjourned, the funeral will take place on tomorrow—and perhaps nothing more will be done, until the next day when it is supposed a motion will be made by Mr. [John Quincy] Adams to expel all members of the House who were in any way engaged in the tragical [*sic*] affair. Should this motion be made it will unquestionably produce much excitement among the members, and perhaps lead to further acts of hostility, if not to the use of powder and ball, to blows in some other way—if so, let them go on according to their own sense of honor through the scientific refinements of civilized life.

SOURCE LIST AND SUGGESTIONS FOR FURTHER READING

Bedford, Denton R. 1972. *Tsali.* San Francisco: Indian Historian Press.

Corn, James F. 1978. "Conscience or Duty: General John E. Wool's Dilemma With Cherokee Removal." *Journal of Cherokee Studies* 3, no.1:35–39.

Ehle, John. 1988. *Trail of Tears: The Rise and Fall of the Cherokee Nation.* New York: Doubleday.

Evans, E. Raymond. 1977. "Fort Marr Blockhouse: Last Evidence of America's First Concentration Camp." *Journal of Cherokee Studies* 2, no. 2:25663.

Finger, John R. 1984. *The Eastern Band of Cherokees: 1819–1900.* Knoxville: University of Tennessee Press.

———. 1991. *Cherokee Americans: The Eastern Band of Cherokees in the Twentieth Century.* Lincoln: The University of Nebraska Press.

French, Laurence, and Jim Hornbuckle, eds. 1981. *The Cherokee Perspective: Written by Eastern Cherokees.* Boone, N.C.: Appalachian Consortium Press.

Frizzell, George E. 1982. "Remarks of Mr. Thomas, of Jackson." *Journal of Cherokee Studies* 7, no. 2:64–68.

Vipperman, Carl J. 1978. "'Forcibly If We Must': The Georgia Case for the Cherokee Removal." *Journal of Cherokee Studies* 3, no. 2:103–10.

Whitmire, Mildred E., ed. 1990. *Noland's Cherokee Diary: A U.S. Soldier's Story from inside the Cherokee Nation*. Spartanburg, S.C.: The Reprint Company.

Williams, Walter L., ed. 1979. *Southeastern Indians since the Removal Era*. Athens: University of Georgia Press.

GLOSSARY

Alarka. Yalagi, according to Mooney. The meaning of the name is lost.

Aquorra. Possibly the same as in Mooney, Aquona, which he identifies as "probably a corruption of egwani, river."

Cheeoih. Also spelled Cheowa and Cheeowhee, Mooney identifies this place name as Tsiyahi, meaning "Otter Place."

Democrats. The Democratic Party of the early 1800s was not the same party as the one going by that name today, although the current Democratic Party, particularly in the South, retains at least a couple of major similarities with the old one. It was a party of the "common man," and it was a strong proponent of states rights.

Euchella. A Cherokee masculine name, in corrupt English spelling.

Old Settlers, also called "Early Settlers" and "Cherokees West." These were the names later given to the Cherokees who moved west voluntarily and organized the Western Cherokees.

Stekoih. Also spelled Stekoa, Stecoe, Steecoy, Stekoah, and Stickoey, Mooney identifies this as Stikoyi and says that it was the name of several Cherokee settlements, and the meaning of the name is lost.

Tsali. Cherokee masculine name, "Charlie" in English.

Ward. A person who is under the protection or control of another, usually of a legal guardian. In his decision on the case of *The Cherokee Nation* v. *Georgia*, Chief Justice Marshal said that the relationship between the Cherokee Nation and the United States was like that of a ward to his guardian, giving rise to the often repeated statement that Indians are "wards of the government."

Whigs. American political party of the 1800s organized in opposition to the Democratic Party.

Younaguska. Also spelled Yonaguska. Mooney spells it Yanugunski and translates it, "The Bear Drowns Him (Habitually)." The name is usually translated and simplified in English as "Drowning Bear."

CHAPTER EIGHTEEN

Hundreds of Babies Died

The Cherokees at the concentration camps found themselves imprisoned in a space two hundred by five hundred feet, enclosed by sixteen-foot-high walls. Inside the walls there was no shelter and no privacy. They slept on the bare ground. Evans says, "There were no provisions for sanitation, and the water supply was inadequate and questionable. The prisoners received a daily ration of flour and salt pork, but few had cooking utensils. Eating the salt pork raw, or poorly cooked, made the shortage of water all the more apparent."

The summer heat made the camps almost unbearable, and people began to die, especially the very old and the very young. Then traders came with illegal whiskey, ready to take anything in exchange for their wares. Evans says:

> The tempting chance to escape, however briefly, from the heartbreaking reality of the camp, even if only to drift into an alcoholic coma, was too much for many of the Cherokees to resist. They gulped the raw alcohol quickly, eager to block out the ugly reality, and made the nights hideous with their screaming and shouting. Brawling followed such bouts, resulting in broken bones and several deaths. Unable to do a thing to prevent it, [missionary] Daniel Buttrick looked on

with despair as the whites lured Cherokee girls into the wild orgies. They went after... the ones who had been to the mission schools and could speak English, causing Buttrick bitterly to regret that any Cherokee had ever been taught a word of that language. The white men induced young girls to drink from their bottles, and after a few rounds the girls forgot their upbringing, their mission training, and all the afflictions that had come upon their people. Robbed of their reason by the whiskey, they yielded to the whites and were passed from man to man before the sorrowful eyes of their parents.

A sickness that missionary physician Elizur Butler called a "putrid dysentery" then swept the camps and became epidemic in proportion. Seventeen died in one week at one camp. Hundreds of babies died, and altogether at least two thousand Cherokees died in these concentration camps. The following chilling entry is recorded in an old family Bible passed down to Evelyn Snell Conley on the pages headed "Family Record."

"A.M. Wofford born December 8th 1836. departed this life August 1838. while imprisoned on the Hiwassee River, old agency by the US Troops ordered by Maj Gen. Scott."

With nearly seventeen thousand people suffering the deplorable conditions in these camps for as much as two months, early in June of 1838, five thousand were at last brought out, broken into smaller groups, and loaded onto steamboats to be transported down the Tennessee and Ohio rivers to west of the Mississippi River. From there the journey continued by land. It was a hot summer, and many of the people were sick. Many died along the way.

Second Chief George Lowrey petitioned General Scott to delay further emigration until September to avoid the misery of the summer heat and drought. Scott relented, but before September came around Chief John Ross had convinced Secretary of War Joel R. Poinsett to allow the Cherokees to manage and control their own removal. Ross then divided the remaining Cherokees into groups of one thousand each and submitted a budget to Scott. From the prison camps he gathered what he could of the Cherokee government and held a council, at which he was given full authority to proceed.

Conductors, wagon masters, physicians, and contractors were assigned to each of the thirteen detachments. The contractors were supposed to supply the detachments with food and other necessities at various points along the way. The thirteen detachments, their conductors, or captains, their dates of departure and of arrival in what is now eastern Oklahoma, are outlined as follows by Starr.

The first detachment was led by Hair Conrad. It started on August 28, 1838, with 729 Cherokees and arrived at its destination on January 17, 1839, after 143 days on the road, with only 654. Deaths and "desertions" accounted for the difference. Nine births were recorded along the way.

William Shorey Coodey was present when this first detachment got underway. He wrote, "I glanced along the line and the form of Goingsnake, an aged and respected chief whose head eighty winters had whitened, mounted on his favorite pony passed before me and led the way in advance, followed by a number of young men on horseback.

"At this very moment a low sound of distant thunder fell on my ear. In almost an exact western direction a dark spiral cloud was rising above the horizon and sent forth a murmur I almost fancied a voice of divine indignation for the wrongs of my poor and unhappy countrymen, driven by *brutal* power from all they loved and cherished in the land of their fathers, to gratify the cravings of avarice."

Elijah Hicks led the second detachment, from September 1, 1838, until January 4, 1839. They were 126 days on the road, and though 858 strong at the beginning, only 744 finished the trip. Five births and thirty-four deaths were recorded. On October 24, Hicks wrote to Chief Ross, "I am almost without officers. . . . My first wagon master died at Woodbury. . . . Whitepath has been in the first stages of sickness . . . and cannot last but a few days. Necowee has given himself up to the bane of death and I have altogether lost his services." Hicks and his detachment found themselves stranded in southern Illinois between the frozen waters of the Ohio and Mississippi rivers because of an early and severe winter.

The third wave was headed by Reverend Jesse Bushyhead. They left on September 3, 1838, and arrived on February 27, 1839. They were 178 days making the trip. Of the 950 who started the trip, 898 finished. Six births, thirty-eight deaths and 148 "desertions" were recorded. Bushyhead wrote to Chief Ross on October 21, "We have a large number of sick and very many extremely aged and infirm persons in our detachment that must of necessity be conveyed in wagons."

The fourth wave was led by John Benge and left on September 28, 1838, arriving on January 11, 1839, after 106 days. 1,200 people started this trip. 1,132 finished. Thirty-three deaths and three births were recorded.

Situwakee led the fifth wave beginning on September 7, 1838, and traveling for 149 days to arrive on February 2, 1839. Of the 1,250 who started the trip, 1,033 made it to the end. Seventy-one deaths and five births were recorded.

The sixth wave was led by Captain Old Field. It left on September 24, 1838, and arrived on February 23, 1839, after 153 days of travel. Of 983 Cherokees, 921 finished the trip. Fifty-seven deaths and nineteen births were recorded.

Moses Daniel was conductor of the seventh wave. They left on September 20, 1838, and arrived on March 2, 1839. They traveled 164 days. Of 1,035 people, only 924 finished the trip. Forty-eight deaths were recorded and six births. Having left fully nineteen days after Elijah Hicks's second detachment, this group caught up with them and was stranded with them between the two rivers.

Choowalooka led the eighth wave, leaving on September 14, 1838, and arriving on March 1, 1839, after 162 days. 1,150 people started this trip. 970 finished. Details were not recorded.

James Brown, leading the ninth wave, left on September 10, 1838, and arrived on March 5, 1839, having traveled for 177 days. He left with 850 people and arrived with 717. Thirty-four deaths and three births were recorded. Brown's ninth wave was also stranded in southern Illinois along with the second and seventh detachments.

The tenth wave left on September 7, 1838, and arrived on March 14, 1839. Their captain was George Hicks. They were on the road for 189 days. Having left with 1,118, they arrived with 1,039. Hicks wrote Chief Ross, on November 4, that "since we have been on our march many of us have been stopped and our horses taken from our teams for the payment of unjust...debts."

Richard Taylor led the eleventh wave, starting on September 20, 1838, and arriving on March 24, 1839, after 186 days. Starting out with 1,029, he arrived with 942. Fifty-five deaths and fifteen births were recorded. Taylor and his detachment caught up with the others in southern Illinois only to be stranded with them between the two rivers.

The twelfth wave was led by Peter Hildebrand. They were on the road for 154 days, from October 23, 1838, until March 25, 1839. At the start, they were 1,766. 1,311 made it all the way. No further details were recorded. Hildebrand's twelfth was the last detachment to be stranded between the rivers in southern Illinois. His group brought the total to over four thousand destitute people in severe weather stranded outdoors and running low on supplies. Many of the deaths occurred here before the people could cross the waters to resume their journey.

John Drew led the thirteenth and final detachment. They left on December 5, 1838, and arrived on March 18, 1839. They were on the road for 104 days. Starting out with 231 people, they arrived with 219. No further details were recorded.

With all thirteen waves on their way west, "in early December Ross and his family joined a small group of about two hundred invalids for water passage to the West." (Moulton) On a riverboat near Little Rock, Arkansas, Ross's ailing wife died, possibly of tuberculosis. It has been said that nearly four thousand Cherokees died along the Trail of Tears. The figures above show that 1,584 fewer arrived at their destination than left the old Cherokee country. The recorded details show a total of 424 deaths and 182 "desertions." That leaves 988 unaccounted for. Some probably died. Some probably slipped away in the night. But some had died on the earlier "voluntary" migrations, and at least two thousand had died in the concentration camps awaiting removal. Even though the figures don't all add up, four thousand deaths is probably a reasonable figure. The record keeping left a great deal to be desired.

There were 645 wagons and 5,000 riding horses used for the removal of the Cherokee Nation, and the total cost of the removal of the thirteen waves under Cherokee supervision was $1,263,338.38. It was deducted from the amount paid to the Cherokees for the land in the East.

SOURCE LIST AND SUGGESTIONS FOR FURTHER READING

Moulton, Gary E., ed. 1985. *The Papers of Chief John Ross, Vol. I: 1807–1839.* Norman: University of Oklahoma Press.

GLOSSARY

Benge. Cherokee family name that originated with Bob Benge, the red-haired Chickamauga war leader who succeeded Dragging Canoe and was sometimes called "Bench."

Bushyhead. Cherokee family name, originating as a nickname for John Stuart, the Tory friend of the Chickamaugas.

Choowalooka. Cherokee name in corrupt English spelling.

Necowee. English spelling of a Cherokee name.

Quatie. English spelling of a Cherokee woman's name, the Cherokee equivalent of "Betty." It might more accurately be spelled "Gweti."

Situwakee. English spelling of a Cherokee man's name.

CHAPTER NINETEEN

Killings on Both Sides

A t this point in history, we have five distinct groups of Cherokees to consider. (1) There is the Cherokee Nation under the leadership of Chief John Ross recently forcibly removed from their homes in the East, by this time known as the National Party. (2) There is the Treaty Party, relocated to the West just shortly before the Cherokee Nation. (3) There are the people who comprise the Western Cherokees, sometimes called the Arkansas Cherokees, but from here on to be called the Old Settlers. (4) There are the Texas Cherokees with Bowles as chief, and (5) there is Younaguska and his band, still in the mountains of North Carolina.

The Treaty Party, upon their arrival in the West, made it clear that they were perfectly willing to live under the government of the Western Cherokees. But when Chief Ross arrived, a conflict immediately appeared. Ross maintained that the United States had moved not so many individual Cherokees but the Cherokee Nation. He further maintained that the Cherokee Nation was the one legitimate government for all Cherokees, and that the western lands had been given to the Cherokee Nation by treaty.

The Western Cherokees, on the other hand, did not want to dissolve its government and be absorbed by the larger Cherokee Nation. The Western Cherokees, many of them, had been functioning under their own government since 1794, and they were perfectly happy with it. Furthermore, they too had treaties in which the U.S. government had given them the land they lived on. However, even with the Treaty Party swelling their ranks, they were still outnumbered by the followers of John Ross by three to one.

Those people who had suffered over the "Trail of Tears" were naturally bitter and resentful, and needing someplace to release their anger and frustrations, some of them, on July 12, 1839, killed Major Ridge, his son John Ridge, and Elias Boudinot for their part in the signing of the Treaty of New Echota. Old Major Ridge was ambushed and shot to death as he rode his horse down a lane. John Ridge was dragged from his sick bed and stabbed to death in front of his terrified wife and young son. Elias Boudinot was lured down a shady lane under the pretense of asking his help for a sick neighbor. Then he was hacked and stabbed to death.

Three weeks later, the Council of the Cherokee Nation declared that the three men had been outlaws because they had signed the treaty. Therefore, it decreed, their killings had been legal executions. In the same session, the Cherokee Council declared that the Treaty of New Echota, having been negotiated and signed illegally, was "null and void." On July 12, 1839, the Cherokee Nation convention met again. This time they invited the government of the Western Cherokees to join them. Instead, the Western Cherokees called their own convention. However, some of the "Old Settlers" went to the meeting of the Cherokee Nation and there took part in an "Act of Union," declaring that the Cherokees were all once again united under the government of the Cherokee Nation. The government of the Western Cherokees declared that action to be illegal, "null and void."

Meanwhile, in Texas, back in December of 1838, Sam Houston had been defeated in the presidential election, largely because of his defense of the Cherokee position. He was replaced by Mirabeau B. Lamar, who called the Cherokees "Houston's pet Indians" and maintained that "the sword should mark the boundaries of the republic." President Lamar sent agents to Chief Bowles telling him to pack up and move out of Texas. The Cherokees should go to the new Cherokee Nation in the West, he said, to live with their relatives there. Bowles held out until Lamar sent Texas troops to his settlements to drive him out.

At that point, Bowles, following a council with other Texas Cherokees, agreed to leave. The Texas army then demanded that he surrender all his gunlocks and said that the army would accompany him to the border. Bowles refused to surrender the gunlocks and said that he and his people did not need an army escort to leave Texas. On July 15, the Cherokees were leaving their Texas homes heading north when the Texas army attacked. They fought until dark, resuming the battle the next morning. Bowles, eighty years old, rode into battle wearing the Mexican army hat and carrying a sword that had been presented to him by Sam Houston. His horse was shot out from under him. The old man got up to his knees, and a Texan walked up close to him, put a pistol to his head, and shot him.

The Texans killed fifty-five Cherokees during that battle and wounded another eighty. The surviving Cherokees scattered. Some, including John Bowles, the chief's son, went north to the Cherokee Nation where they were received by Captain Dutch at his new home on Dutch's Creek. Some others found their way into Mexico and settled in Guadalajara and Lake Chapala.

On September 6, 1839, another meeting was held by the Cherokee Nation. A new constitution was adopted, and Tahlequah was designated the capital city of the Cherokee Nation. The decree of outlawry that had been placed on the heads of the treaty signers was rescinded. Old Settlers also attended this meeting, and thus, the Act of Union previously passed, due partly to the efforts of Sequoyah among the members of the Western Cherokees, was somewhat solidified and became, in effect, the organic act of the Cherokee Nation. That did not mean, however, that all was calm in the Cherokee Nation. Certain members of the Old Settlers group, particularly certain Treaty Party members, remained unsatisfied. Stand Watie, a brother of Elias Boudinot, and others still blamed John Ross for the killings of the two Ridges and Boudinot. Stand Watie vowed revenge against Ross. According to Grant Foreman, John Ross "reported that Stand Watie . . . had determined on raising a company to take Ross's life as punishment. . . . Ross said that his friends to the number of several hundred had surrounded his home for his protection."

Then, in May of 1842, Stand Watie shot and killed James Foreman in Arkansas. He was tried in Arkansas for the killing but acquitted on the grounds of self-defense. Foreman had been a member of the Ross Party, as the majority was now called, and, according to Watie, he had also been one of the killers of the three treaty signers.

Plagued with internal problems, the Cherokee Nation could ill afford troubles with its neighboring Indian tribes. Chief Ross called for a "Grand Council," a large intertribal meeting, at Tahlequah, in June of 1843. Its purpose was to "perpetuate peace between tribes; and to encourage agriculture, education; and all useful arts that would in the future promote the comforts of women and children."

The historic meeting was attended by members of twenty-one different tribes and lasted for one month. The Grand Council became a kind of United Indian Nations, and it passed a number of laws under which "major intertribal conflicts became practically nonexistent . . . [and] Minor disagreements were settled by laws" (Woodward).

On August 7, 1843, elections were held in the Cherokee Nation, and "a lawless element that was opposed to the government," says Foreman, "proceeded to terrorize the voters and election officials in some of the precincts.... they destroyed the election papers, attacked and killed Isaac Bushyhead at the polls and severely wounded David Vann and Elijah Hicks." Outstanding among this "lawless element" were Tom Starr, son of James Starr, one of the treaty signers, and his brothers, Ellis and Bean. In 1843, the Starr brothers were accused of the brutal murders of a trader named Vore, his wife, and a visitor at their home. The three victims were all white people, and the Starrs were arrested for the crimes and held in jail in Arkansas, but they managed to escape. Later that same year, while driving stolen horses to Texas for sale, the Starrs were attacked by a group of Cherokee police, and Bean was shot. He died later from his wound.

It is difficult to determine whether this outlawry grew out of political unrest, or the outlaws simply made use of the political unrest as a cover for their activities. There were political differences remaining between the two major factions of the Cherokee Nation: the Ross Party on the one hand and the Treaty Party (now under the guise of the Old Settlers) on the other. And the "outlaws" were all representatives of the Treaty Party.

In the summer of 1842, Sequoyah left the Cherokee Nation. Somewhere between sixty-five and eighty years old at the time, and accompanied by the Worm and a few others, he did not tell them where he was going until they were well on the way. Then he said that he was going on a trip to trade with western Indian tribes and to look for the Cherokees in Mexico to invite them to rejoin their tribesmen in the Cherokee Nation. According to a report eventually brought back to Tahlequah by the Worm, Sequoyah did succeed in finding the Cherokees in Mexico, but he died and was buried there among them.

On October 30, 1843, the Council of the Cherokee Nation passed a law declaring all salines, or salt works, in the Cherokee Nation but one (the one that had been operated by Sequoyah) to be the property of the Cherokee Nation. Since the Old Settlers had been in the area longer than the majority, Old Settlers had located and begun to operate the salines even before the Trail of Tears. A movement was begun by disgruntled Old Settler saline operators and Treaty Party members to call for the creation of two separate Cherokee Nations. They held meetings in Arkansas and sent a delegation to Washington, complaining that they were being discriminated against by the government of Chief Ross and saying that the two groups could not live together in peace. For a time, there was some fear that they were organizing an effort to overthrow the government of the Cherokee Nation. One of the worst offenders was General

Arbuckle of Fort Gibson, who was working hard to undermine Chief Ross. An investigation by the U.S. government determined that everyone was being treated fairly, and that most of the complaints from the Old Settlers were actually coming from white men who had been living with them for some years.

In 1845, Tom Starr, Ellis Starr, Washington Starr, Suel Rider, and Ellis West rode into Park Hill to the home of R. J. Meigs. They attempted to kill Meigs, but he escaped, so they contented themselves with looting and burning his home. For some reason, they also killed two full-blood Indians in the neighborhood. Perhaps they had been witnesses. Meigs identified the killers. Outraged, "a posse of citizens," according to Foreman, "armed themselves and went to Flint District to the home of James Starr, the father of the notorious sons. The posse killed the elder Starr and wounded his fourteen year old son Washington, and another son William. They then proceeded half a mile to the home of Suel Rider whom they killed."

The Cherokee Council quickly passed a measure to raise a company of Light Horse. Rumors spread that the Ross Party meant to wipe out the entire Starr family, and legends began to grow. It was said that Tom Starr set about killing all the members of the posse that had killed his father, and before it was all over, he was said to have killed one hundred men. Many of the Starrs and their friends and supporters moved across the line into Arkansas for safety. Killings continued in the Cherokee Nation on both sides, and in time the refugee group in Arkansas became large and practically unmanageable. They were being kept at U.S. government expense, and it was claimed that many joined them just to get a "hand-out." They were also joined, apparently, by outlaws seeking a safe haven.

In Washington, a delegation of Treaty Party members very nearly suc-ceeded in getting the Cherokee Nation divided. President Polk recommend-ed the move, and a bill to that effect was introduced in Congress by the House Committee on Indian Affairs. Chief Ross was also in Washington, and he strongly opposed the bill. Ross managed to win the fight, and the entire controversy was finally concluded by means of a new treaty.

The Treaty of 1846 was negotiated in Washington and signed by repre-sentatives of the United States, the Cherokee Nation, "that portion of the Cherokee tribe of Indians known and recognized as the 'Treaty Party,'" and "that portion of the Cherokee Tribe of Indians known and recognized as 'Western Cherokees' or 'Old Settlers.'" John Ross, William Shorey Coodey, R. Taylor, Stephen Foreman, John Drew, and Richard Fields signed for the Cherokee Nation. For the Treaty Party, Stand Watie and others signed, and for the Old Settlers, Captain Dutch, John Brown, and others. The purpose of the treaty was set forth in its preamble as follows:

> serious difficulties have, for a considerable time past, existed
> between the different portions of the people constituting
> and recognized as the Cherokee Nation of Indians, which it
> is desirable should be speedily settled, so that peace and
> harmony may be restored among them; and . . . certain
> claims exist on the part of the Cherokee Nation, and por-
> tions of the Cherokee people, against the United States;
> Therefore, with a view to the final and amicable settlement
> of the difficulties and claims before mentioned, it is mutual-
> ly agreed by the several parties to this convention as follows.

The first article of the treaty declared "that the lands now occupied by the Cherokee Nation shall be secured to the whole Cherokee people for their common use and benefit," and that the United States would "forever secure and guarantee to them, and their heirs or successors, the country. . . . Provided always, That such lands shall revert to the United States if the Indians become extinct or abandon the same."

The second article stated that "all difficulties and differences hereto-fore existing between the several parties of the Cherokee Nation are hereby settled and adjusted, and shall, as far as possible, be forgotten and forever buried in oblivion. All party distinctions shall cease." It declared a general amnesty, pardoning all crimes committed by a Cherokee against another Cherokee or against the Cherokee Nation, and called for any future crimes to be punished only after conviction by a jury and sentence of a court. It abolished the Light Horse and any "military organization," leaving law enforcement to "civil authorities." In the Cherokee Nation, this meant district sheriffs and a "High Sheriff" of the Cherokee Nation.

In Article 7 the Cherokee Nation agreed to either return the confiscated salines to the original owners or to pay for them, the amount to be determined by a commissioner appointed by the U.S. government.

In Article 8 the United States agreed to pay the Cherokee Nation for the loss of its printing press, to pay individual Cherokees for the loss of any firearms confiscated by the U.S. Army, and "twenty thousand dollars, in lieu of all claims of the Cherokee Nation, as a nation, prior to the treaty of 1835."

The remaining articles dealt with various claims of the Cherokee Nation or of individual Cherokees against the United States, the amounts of money the United States agreed to pay to adjust those claims and the manner in which the money would be paid.

The unrest that had plagued the Cherokee Nation since before the removal seemed to be at an end, and the Cherokee Nation entered into a period of prosperity that has been called, by some historians, "the Golden Age of the Cherokee Nation."

SOURCE LIST AND SUGGESTIONS FOR FURTHER READING

Foreman, Grant. 1934. *The Five Civilized Tribes*. Norman: University of Oklahoma Press.

GLOSSARY

Dutch's Creek. Creek in the southwestern Cherokee Nation named because Captain Dutch at last settled there. The reason for its name has been all but forgotten, as the creek is now known as "Duchess Creek."

Guadalajara. City in southern Mexico, west of Mexico City. It was to this area, according to Mooney, that some of the remnants of the Texas Cherokees moved.

Lake Chapala. Lake in southern Mexico near Guadalajara, in the area where some of the Texas Cherokees settled.

Saline. As used here, a salt works, or a manufacturing facility constructed at a place where salt is found in nature, for purposes of producing salt for commercial use.

Tahlequah. Established in 1839 as the capital of the Cherokee Nation, the name, in spite of several popular explanations, cannot be translated. It is an old place-name that appeared a number of times in the old Cherokee country in the Southeast as Talikwa, Tellico, or Telliquo.

Watie. Surname of Stand Watie, from *uweti*, meaning "old."

CHAPTER TWENTY

The Golden Age

The period from 1846 until the beginning of the Civil War has been called "the Golden Age of the Cherokee Nation" for two reasons. First, it was a period of relative peace and prosperity. The violent domestic strife within the Cherokee Nation seemed to be at an end. People were building new homes and establishing new businesses, and the federal government was not coming around demanding new treaties and more land cessions. But the main reason this period has been called a "Golden Age" is because of the tremendous strides made by the Cherokees during this time toward becoming a so-called modern nation. At the time it was called becoming "civilized," and the Cherokee Nation, along with the Creek Nation, the Chickasaw Nation, the Choctaw Nation, and the Seminole Nation became known as the "Five Civilized Tribes." In other words, the period here under discussion became known as the Cherokee Golden Age purely and simply because during that time the Cherokees adopted more and more of white culture, and the Cherokee Nation became more like the United States. Some might very well feel that the real Golden Age of the Cherokees was before the arrival of Europeans on the North American continent.

Be that as it may, and whatever one's point of view, Cherokee accomplishments during this time are impressive. The new Cherokee Nation was divided into eight districts: Delaware, Goingsnake, Flint, Skin Bayou, Illinois, Canadian, Tahlequah, and Saline. Two members of the National Committee and three of the National Council were elected from each

district, and each district had its own sheriff, judge, and court. The Principal
Chief and Deputy Principal Chief were also elected. The constitution and
laws were printed and distributed throughout the nation. In Tahlequah a
two-story brick Supreme Court building was constructed, and the large
shed on the capitol square was replaced by a log capitol building.

Reverend Worcester had set up the printing press at Union Mission in
1835, and in 1837 he had moved it to Park Hill. There he published books
and pamphlets in the Cherokee, Creek, and Choctaw languages. In 1844,
the publication of a Cherokee newspaper had been resumed. Still bilingual, this time it was called *The Cherokee Advocate*. The mission schools
established earlier continued to operate, and more mission schools were
established throughout the Cherokee Nation. In addition, the Cherokee
Nation established its own free, compulsory, public school system, with
eleven schools in the eight districts, and built two new "seminaries," the
equivalent of high schools, one for males and one for females. It has been
said that the public school system was the first of its kind anywhere, and
that the seminaries were the first institutions of higher education west of
the Mississippi River. Education was the single largest line item on the
national budget. And while some teachers were white, brought in from
outside the Cherokee Nation, many of the teachers were native Cherokee.

Many Cherokees, especially in and around Tahlequah, became successful, even prosperous, merchants. Others were farmers, some operating with the use of slave labor. Some went into the business of trade with
the western Indian tribes. Notable among these was Jesse Chisholm,
after whom the famous Chisholm Trail was named. Cherokee women
became spinners and weavers, manufacturing their own cloth, so much
so that the demand for spinning wheels could not be kept up with.
Tahlequah had a Masonic lodge, and the Cherokee Nation had a strong
Temperance Society. The majority of Cherokees lived in log cabins, much
like those of frontier whites of the time, but some of the wealthier citizens
had fine, two-story, southern plantation-style homes. It seems that, having decided to imitate the lifestyle of the white man, the Cherokees went
even further than imitation. They improved on what they imitated.

For recreation, Cherokees were fond of reading, in English and in
Cherokee. Tahlequah had a literary society that met regularly, and occasionally traveling Shakespearean companies stopped in Tahlequah to give
their performances. The old ball game was still played, and many engaged
in raising and racing fine horses. This last was, of course, a combination of
business and pleasure. Tahlequah and Park Hill "became to the Indian
Territory what Boston became to New England at this same date—a center
of culture and industry, and a symbol of progress" (Woodward).

But the Cherokee Nation during this all too brief period was not a Utopia. There was still domestic strife. The worst violence, however, was confined to two locations and was mostly associated with the importation of illegal whiskey. Around Fort Gibson and near the Arkansas border just across from Fort Smith, white Arkansans and Missourians dealt in a lucrative whiskey trade, and in those areas, drunkenness, fights, and murders were common. The Cherokee Nation tried in vain to get the states of Arkansas and Missouri to cooperate in controlling this illegal business. The killings back and forth between the members of the Ross Party and the members of the Treaty Party seemed to have come to an end with the Treaty of 1846, but bitterness and resentment still smoldered in the hearts of some, waiting for an excuse to set them off again.

In 1849, word of the California gold rush reached the Cherokee Nation, and Cherokees, like others, caught the gold fever. "Forty-niners" on their way to California passed through Tahlequah, and Tahlequah merchants sold them supplies. But some Cherokees packed up to go with them or follow them to the California gold fields.

In 1859, Cherokee Agent Butler reported on the condition of the Cherokee Nation. According to Foreman, Butler said that "There were... 21,000 Cherokees, 4,000 voters, 1,000 whites and 4,000 Negroes; 102,500 acres in cultivation, 240,000 head of cattle, 20,000 horses and mules, 16,000 hogs and 5,000 sheep; an average of twenty-five bushels of corn produced to the acre, thirty of oats and twelve of wheat. There were thirty schools attended by 1,500 pupils; and of the teachers all but two were Cherokee."

That same year, Reverend Samuel Worcester died, having given much of his life and energies to the Cherokees. He was buried in the Mission Cemetery at Park Hill.

In spite of all this "advancement," or perhaps because of it, there were still white people clambering for Cherokee lands, and in the process they still used the same kind of rhetoric they had used years before. Three years earlier, in 1856, John Ross had quoted from a speech by Governor Walker of Kansas in warning the Cherokee people to remain vigilant. "Upon the south Kansas is bounded by," the governor had said, "the great south western Indian Territory. This is one of the most salubrious and fertile portions of this continent. It is a great cotton growing region, admirably adapted, by soil and climate, for the products of the south; embracing the valley of the Arkansas and Red Rivers; adjoining Texas on the south and west, and Arkansas on the east; and it ought speedily to become a state of the American Union. The Indian treaties will constitute no obstacle... for their lands, valueless to them... would be most cheerfully given."

For thirteen short years, things had been going very well for the
Cherokee Nation, but another major interruption was about to take
place, one that would help along the process longed for by whites like
Governor Walker. In the East, tensions were growing between the
northern and southern states of the United States. There was talk of a
coming civil war. Although the issue of slavery was the most talked
about and the most inflammatory, it was not the only point of difference, and some historians have maintained that it was not even the
most important.

The southern states had long been proponents of states rights over
federal authority, and Georgia had even threatened to secede from the
union back in the 1830s over the issue of Cherokee removal, and had,
in fact, openly defied the U.S. Supreme Court. Major problems between
the states and the federal government were averted at that time, largely because of the presence in the White House of Andrew Jackson, a
man sympathetic with the views of the southern states righters.

Aware of the growing controversy, Chief John Ross, seventy years
old in 1860, spoke to Cherokees and to chiefs of other tribes on the
importance of remaining neutral in the coming battle. "Our duty," he
said, "is to stand by our rights, allow no interference in our internal
affairs from any source, comply with all our engagements, and rely
upon [the] union for justice and protection."

SOURCE LIST AND SUGGESTIONS FOR FURTHER READING

Abel, Annie Heloise. 1993. *The American Indian and the End of the
Confederacy: 1863–1866.* Lincoln: University of Nebraska Press. Reprint
of *The American Indian under Reconstruction,* 1925.
Cherokee Nation, The. 1969. *The Constitution and Laws of the Cherokee Nation,
Passed at Tahlequah, Cherokee Nation, 1839–1851.* Tahlequah: The
Cherokee Nation. (This is a photolithographic reprint of the original.)
Crow, Vernon H. 1982. *Storm in the Mountains: Thomas' Confederate Legion of
Cherokee Indians and Mountaineers.* Cherokee, N.C.: Press of the
Museum of the Cherokee Indian.
Gaines, W. Craig. 1989. *The Confederate Cherokees: John Drew's Regiment of
Mounted Rifles.* Baton Rouge: Louisiana State University Press.
Mihesuah, Devon A. 1993. *Cultivating the Rosebuds: The Education of Women
at the Cherokee Female Seminary, 1851–1909.* Urbana: University of
Illinois Press.

Moulton, Gary E., ed. 1985. *The Papers of Chief John Ross, Vol. II: 1840–1866.* Norman: University of Oklahoma Press.

GLOSSARY

Masonic. Having to do with Freemasons, an international secret society founded on the principles of brotherliness, charity, and mutual aid.

Park Hill. Town five miles from Tahlequah and begun by Dr. Samuel Worcester as a mission station in 1836. After the Trail of Tears, Chief John Ross and other prominent and wealthy Cherokees settled there.

Secede. To withdraw formally from a group or organization, as a state from the union.

Seminary. A private school.

Temperance. Self-restraint or moderation. The "temperance movement" and "temperance societies" called for restraint in the use of alcoholic beverages.

Union Mission. According to Foreman, "Union Mission was established in 1820 by the United Foreign Mission Society of New York and in 1826 was transferred to the American Board of Commissioners for Foreign Missions; it was intended to minister to the Osage Indians and was located in their country, one mile west of the Neosho River and about twenty miles north of Fort Gibson."

CHAPTER TWENTY-ONE

Confederates and Pins

In December of 1860, South Carolina seceded from the United States; North Carolina on May 20, 1861; and Tennessee on June 8, 1861. On February 7, 1861, the Choctaw Nation announced its intentions to ally itself with the Confederacy. Two days later, Jefferson Davis, who had once been a young lieutenant in the U.S. Army stationed at Fort Gibson, was elected president of the Confederate States of America. On April 12, 1861, Confederate forces under the command of General P. G. T. Beauregard fired a cannon battery across the Charleston, South Carolina, Harbor toward Fort Sumter, and the Civil War had begun. Two days later, Union forces at Fort Sumter surrendered. President Abraham Lincoln responded by authorizing a Union army of seventy-five thousand men to serve for three months.

In April of 1861, the Creek Nation became divided, with mixed-blood leaders announcing for the Confederacy, and traditional, full-bloods, under the leadership of Opothleyahola, declaring themselves to be neutral. In March of that year, Arkansas held a secession convention at which Elias C. Boudinot, son of the slain treaty signer, was elected secretary. Stand Watie and his small private army, calling themselves the "Knights of the Golden Circle," were still holed up near Fort Wayne in Arkansas. They began calling themselves "the Southern Rights Party."

On March 5, the Confederate States of America commissioned Albert Sidney Pike as brigadier general in charge of the Confederate Indian

Brigade and Indian Commissioner of the Lands West of Arkansas. The Confederacy also created a Bureau of Indian Affairs and appointed David Hubbard Indian Commissioner. Texas Confederate General Ben McCulloch was given overall command of the district that included Indian Territory. Watie offered the services of his "company," and his offer was accepted. He was commissioned a colonel in the Army of the Confederate States of America.

Under the influence of Reverend Evan Jones and his son John, full-blood, traditional Cherokees, known as Keetoowahs, devoted to the preservation of Cherokee culture and politically opposed to mixed-bloods in the tribal government, became active abolitionists. They were also called "Pin Indians" because of identifying crossed pins that they wore under the lapels of their coats. The Baptist Board recalled the Joneses, presumably because of their political activities.

"In July, 1861," says Gaines, "a company of pro-Southern Cherokees attempted to raise the Confederate flag over Webbers Falls. William Doublehead, a Canadian District senator, and 150 full-bloods confronted the Confederate Cherokee supporters and a fight appeared imminent.... John Drew played a major part in preventing bloodshed between the two groups, and he cooled the hot tempers of their leaders."

By May of 1861, Texas Confederate troops held all the forts in the territory with the single exception of Fort Gibson, which the Union had abandoned in 1857, turning it over to the Cherokee Nation. By August of 1861, Pike had the Choctaws, Chickasaws, and the Lower Towns Creeks on his side. The Confederacy had won the important Battles of Bull Run in Virginia and Wilson's Creek in Missouri. On the twenty-first, a council was held at Tahlequah on the question of Cherokee neutrality. "About four thousand Cherokee males attended," says Gaines, including "Stand Watie and fifty to sixty armed men."

Most of those who spoke at the meeting favored a treaty with the Confederacy, and Chief John Ross, when he spoke, agreed, shifting suddenly from his previous neutral stance. Why? The Cherokee Nation was in danger of becoming divided once again, and Cherokees would be fighting Cherokees again. He spoke of the importance of unity. At this point, also, the South seemed to be winning the war. If Ross continued to hold out for strict neutrality and the South should win, the Cherokee Nation would find itself in a very precarious position indeed.

The Confederacy offered to buy the strip of land in southern Kansas known as the neutral land, which Ross had been trying unsuccessfully to sell to the United States in order to pay the national debt, and the Confederate treaty which was being offered was favorable in many other ways. Then too, "even northern politicians," says Gaines, "made the Cherokees feel uneasy. William H. Seward, in a speech during the election of 1860, was quoted as saying, 'Indian Territory south of Kansas must be vacated by the Indian.'"

Finally, if Ross continued to refuse to deal with the Confederacy, there was a very real danger that the Confederacy would simply negotiate a treaty with Stand Watie, recognizing him as Chief, and Watie, with the force of the Confederacy behind him, would attempt to overthrow the legitimate government of the Cherokee Nation. The council decision was to pursue the Confederate treaty.

In October of 1861, Chief Ross met with General Pike at Park Hill and signed a treaty with the Confederate States of America. At that same meeting, it is said, he shook hands with Stand Watie. The Cherokee Nation then organized a regiment of "Cherokee Mounted Rifles" under the command of Colonel John Drew, offering their services to the Confederacy. Thus, Watie's plans for taking over the Cherokee government with the backing of the Confederacy were for the time being thwarted. Drew's regiment was loyal to Ross, and it was made up largely of "Pin Indians." Drew's regiment had been organized by John Ross and authorized by the Cherokee Nation. Its rival regiment had been put together by Stand Watie and authorized by the Confederacy. Evan Jones, in Kansas, as soon as he heard about the new Cherokee treaty with the Confederacy, began trying to explain Ross's action to the federal authorities.

On March 6, 7, and 8, the Battle of Pea Ridge, also called the Battle of Elkhorn Tavern, was fought in Arkansas. Both Drew's and Watie's regiments were used, along with Texans led by Ben McCulloch. Losses were heavy on both sides, but in the end, the Confederate forces retreated, and the battle was a Union victory. Cherokees, though, were accused of scalping and mutilating the dead, a practice that seemed to offend the whites more than did the killings. However, as Gaines has pointed out, "participants in the battle on the Union side...said that Texans, not Indians, had mutilated the Union dead." It was also reported that at least some of Drew's regiment turned on other Confederates, rather than fight Union soldiers.

The indecisive but bloody Battle of Shiloh was fought in Tennessee in April 1862, and that summer Union forces, made up of Indians from Kansas, many of them refugees from Indian Territory, moved into the Cherokee Nation. Colonel Weer, a white man, in command, tried to get Ross to repudiate the Confederate treaty, but Ross refused. Drew's regiment, however, was practically nonexistent, most of the soldiers having gone over to the other side. And Reverend Jones kept assuring the Union authorities of the loyalty of Ross in spite of present appearances.

At last Weer sent troops under the command of Captain Greeno into the Cherokee Nation. At Park Hill, Greeno arrested Ross and took him back to Kansas, where Ross came to an agreement with Weer. With the Cherokee Nation back on the Union side, the two thousand Cherokee refugees in Kansas were advised to go home and plant their crops. They did so, but Stand Watie's Confederate Indians came sweeping through the Cherokee Nation, and soon there were seven thousand Cherokee refugees at Fort Gibson.

Chief Ross went to Philadelphia to live for the duration of the war, making frequent trips to Washington on behalf of the Cherokee Nation, pleading with President Lincoln to send troops to relieve the situation in the Cherokee Nation. It should be pointed out here that in the Treaty of New Echota, the United States had promised to protect the Cherokee Nation from both invasion and from domestic strife.

With Union and Confederate troops in the Cherokee Nation, the Union troops withdrew to the extreme northeastern portion of the nation, leaving Fort Gibson, Tahlequah, and Park Hill in Confederate hands. Stand Watie called a council at Tahlequah and was elected Principal Chief of the Cherokee Nation. It is likely that all those present were Confederates. In February of 1863, the legitimate Council of the Cherokee Nation met at Cowskin Prairie where they protested Stand Watie's election to the position of Principal Chief, officially abrogated the treaty with the Confederacy, and deposed all Cherokee officials who were disloyal to the Union. They also abolished slavery in the Cherokee Nation.

Then General Thomas Hindman led Union forces into the heart of the Cherokee Nation, driving out Watie's Confederates. Watie continued to fight, but in the far northern part of the Cherokee Nation, and in Kansas, Missouri, and Arkansas. During the winter of 1862 and 1863, most of the battles resulted in Union victories. Tahlequah and the surrounding area was almost completely abandoned.

In the winter of 1863, President Lincoln assured Ross that the treaty between the Confederacy and the Cherokee Nation would not be held against him personally or against the Cherokee Nation by the government of the United States. In the summer of 1863, the tide of war began to change with major Union victories in the East at Gettysburg and at Vicksburg, and in the West at Honey Springs in the Creek Nation. The Confederate Indians withdrew into the Choctaw and Chickasaw Nations and down into Texas. But in the fall of that year, Stand Watie led raids of vengeance into Tahlequah and vicinity, burning the Cherokee capitol and the home of Chief John Ross, among other things.

In May of 1864, Watie was promoted by the Confederacy to the rank of brigadier general, and in September, at Cabin Creek, he captured a Union wagon train of 250 wagons and 750 mules carrying supplies, mostly food and clothing, for 2,000 soldiers, and valued at $1,500,000. For this action, he received high praise from the Congress of the Confederate States and from President Davis.

On April 9, 1865, General Robert E. Lee surrendered to General Ulysses S. Grant at Appomattox, Virginia. The war was over—sort of. Stand Watie did not surrender until June 23. He became the last Confederate general to surrender, signing his letter, "Stand Watie, Principal Chief of the Cherokee Nation."

The Cherokees in North Carolina had not been left alone during the war either. Back in 1861, Will Thomas, now Colonel Thomas, had begun raising what would become known as "The North Carolina Cherokee Battalion" and later "Thomas's Confederate Legion of Cherokee Indians and Mountaineers." They were active throughout the remainder of the war, mostly in east Tennessee and western North Carolina, though they saw little action. On May 6, 1865, troops of Company F, of Valleytown, known as "Conley's Sharpshooters," under the command of Lieutenant Robert T. Conley, fired the last shot of the war in North Carolina.

SOURCE LIST AND SUGGESTIONS FOR FURTHER READING

Cunningham, Frank H. 1959. *General Stand Watie's Confederate Indians*. San Antonio: Naylor Company.

Duvall, Deborah. 1999. *The Cherokee Nation and Tahlequah*. Charleston, S.C.: Arcadia Publishing.

Fugate, Francis L., and Roberta B. Fugate. 1991. *Roadside History of Oklahoma*. Missoula: Mountain Press Publishing Company.

Halliburton, R., Jr.. 1977. *Red over Black: Black Slavery among the Cherokee Indians*. Westport, Conn.: Greenwood Press.

Perdue, Theda. 1980. *Nations Remembered: An Oral History of the Five Civilized Tribes, 1865–1907*. Westport, Conn.: Greenwood Press.

GLOSSARY

Abolitionist. Before the Civil War in the United States, one who advocated abolishing slavery.

Abrogate. To do away with, legally, as to abrogate a treaty.

Cowskin Prairie. An area north of Honey Creek, near the old Delaware District Court House.

Depose. To remove from office.

Fort Wayne. Military post about forty miles north of Fort Smith, Arkansas.

Knights of the Golden Circle. "Secret" organization under the leadership of Stand Watie, strongly opposed to the government of the Cherokee Nation under the leadership of John Ross. Made up largely of Treaty Party members or their descendants, this group was also known as the Blue Circle and the Southern Rights Party. The ranks of Watie's Cherokee Confederate regiment were largely filled from this group.

Opothleyahola. Full-blood Creek traditional leader. When the mixed-blood Creek Nation government voted to join the Confederacy, Opothleyahola led his followers to Kansas.

Pin Indians. The Keetoowah Society of Cherokees became known as "Pins" or "Pin Indians" during the time just before and during the Civil War, because of the identifying pins they wore beneath their lapels. They were mostly full-blood, traditional, abolitionist, and opposed to the "progressive" politics of many of the mixed-blood Cherokees.

Southern Rights Party. Another name for the Knights of the Golden Circle. See above.

CHAPTER TWENTY-TWO

Indian Territory

At the end of the Civil War, the Cherokee Nation was a wasteland. Mooney says that the Cherokee Nation had been "ravaged alternately by contending factions and armed bodies," and the Cherokees saw "all the prosperous accumulations of twenty years of industry swept off in this guerrilla warfare. In stock alone, their losses were estimated at more than 300,000 head." He says further that the war brought the Cherokees "more desolation and ruin than perhaps . . . any other community." Even so, the United States wasted no time in seizing the opportunity to force yet another treaty on the Cherokee Nation. In 1865, President Andrew Johnson, Lincoln having been assassinated, appointed five commissioners to go to Fort Smith, Arkansas, to draw up a new treaty with all of the "territorial" tribes.

Chief John Ross left Philadelphia and headed for the Cherokee Nation. His plan was to travel to the convention at Fort Smith from Park Hill. He was seventy-five years old and weak. His second wife had died only recently, and he had lost a son in the Civil War. His home had been burned to the ground. At park Hill, Ross stayed with relatives at the Murrell Home, one of the few homes left standing in Park Hill, but when the time came for him to journey to Fort Smith, he was too ill and weak. Deputy Chief Lewis Downing went in his place, accompanied by a dozen or so delegates.

At Fort Smith, Commissioner Cooley presided over the meeting. The Southern Cherokees and other Southern Indians did not appear, as they were holding their own meeting elsewhere, but the neutral or Union representatives of several other tribes were there. In spite of the absence of the Confederate Indians, Cooley began the meeting by chastising those present. He charged them with crimes of secession and called them traitors. He also said that, because of their actions, they had forfeited all their rights to both annuities and lands. In other words, he said, all past treaties had been abrogated.

He then said that the president of the United States did not wish to deal harshly with the Indians, and he outlined the terms of the treaty he wanted them all to sign. They must pledge permanent peace and friendship to the United States and to each other. They must aid the United States in securing peace with other Indian tribes. They must abolish slavery and give rights of citizenship to all former slaves. They must give up some of their lands for tribes in Kansas and elsewhere to be relocated. They must be formed into one territorial government with a white governor appointed by the president. They must agree that no white person could live in their country unless he had authorization from the United States or had been adopted into one of their tribes.

At some point in the negotiations, John Ross had roused himself from his sickbed and made the journey to Fort Smith. Shortly after his arrival, a delegation of Southern Indians arrived, their other meeting having been concluded. They were led by Elias C. Boudinot. Then a very strange alliance was formed. Cooley, head of a commission appointed to punish the Confederate Indians, became friendly with E. C. Boudinot and singled out Chief Ross as the main enemy of the United States. He said publicly that the commission refused to recognize Ross as Principal Chief of the Cherokee Nation and suggested that Ross should be deposed, thus contradicting himself.

E. C. Boudinot joined in the attack on Ross, saying, "I will show you the deep duplicity and falsity that have followed him from his childhood to the present day, when the winters of 65 or 70 years have silvered his head with sin; what can you expect of him now?" However, guided by Ross, the Cherokee delegation refused to sign the treaty unless the commissioners would include the following statement: "We, the loyal Cherokee delegation, acknowledge the execution of the treaty of October 7, 1861; but we solemnly declare that the execution of the treaty was procured by the coercion of the rebel army."

At last the commissioners inserted the clause, and the Cherokees and other tribes signed the treaty. However, they had learned that the treaty would not be considered legal until signed in Washington. The meeting broke up, and the Cherokees called a council at Tahlequah to select delegates to send to Washington. They also prepared a memorial to the president in defense of John Ross. When the council concluded, Ross collapsed. He was taken again to the Murrell home. By the time the Cherokee delegation was ready to go to Washington, Ross had managed to get himself out of bed once more. He went with them.

In Washington, they met with President Johnson. Thomas Pegg, one of the delegates, presented the president with the memorial on behalf of Ross and with a number of documents pertaining to the Cherokee Nation's relationship with the Confederacy. In spite of an argument between Ross and Commissioner Cooley, who was also present, Ross felt that the meeting had gone well. In the meantime, delegates from the Confederate Cherokees showed up in Washington, and they began lobbying once again for a division of the Cherokee Nation into two parts with two separate governments. Ross fell ill again and was confined to bed in his hotel room. He continued to direct the activities of the delegation.

On July 19, 1866, the Cherokee delegation in Washington signed a new treaty with the United States, because, according to its preamble, "existing treaties between the United States and the Cherokee Nation are deemed to be insufficient." It declared the Confederate treaty of 1861 (already abrogated by the Council of the Cherokee Nation) to be void. The Cherokee Nation and the United States declared a general amnesty for all crimes "committed by one Cherokee on the person or property of another Cherokee, or of a citizen of the United States."

Since the Cherokee Nation had passed confiscation laws by which they had seized the property of Confederate Cherokees, the treaty repealed those laws and returned the property to the original owners. Freed slaves were made citizens of the Cherokee Nation. The Cherokee Nation was forced to grant railroad rights-of-way. On the matter of a territorial government, a compromise was reached. Instead of a white governor appointed by the president, the treaty stipulated that a territorial government composed of delegates elected by each "nation or tribe lawfully residing within the Indian Territory may be annually convened."

The United States also forced on the Cherokees its right to establish U.S. courts within the Cherokee Nation, and the right to settle "any civilized Indians, friendly with the Cherokees" on Cherokee lands. The Cherokee Nation ceded to the United States all of its land in Kansas, including the "neutral land" and the "Cherokee Strip." And the United States secured the right "to establish one or more military posts or stations in the Cherokee Nation, as may be deemed necessary."

It has been pointed out that none of the rebellious southern states lost any land as a result of their participation in the war. The Cherokee

Nation did. And that in spite of the fact that the Cherokee Nation would not have taken part in the war at all had the United States lived up to its treaty obligations and sent troops to protect its neutrality.

On August 1, 1866, Principal Chief John Ross died in Washington. He had lived just long enough to negotiate this last crucial treaty for the Cherokee Nation. He had not won all of his points, but then, neither had the United States. Shortly before his death, Ross had said, "I am an old man and have served my people and the government of the United States a long time, over fifty years. My people have kept me in the harness, not of my own seeking, but of their own choice. I have never deceived them; and now I look back, not one act of my public life rises up to upbraid me. I have done the best I could, and today upon this bed of sickness, my heart approves all I have done. And still I am John Ross, the same John Ross of former years. Unchanged! No cause to change!"

SOURCE LIST AND SUGGESTIONS FOR FURTHER READING

Lambert, Paul F. 1973. "The Cherokee Reconstruction Treaty of 1866," in *Journal of the West*. 12, no. 3:471–89.

Parins, James W. 1991. *John Rollin Ridge: His Life and Works*. Lincoln: University of Nebraska Press.

GLOSSARY

Amnesty. A general pardon, or legal act of forgiveness for crimes against a government.

Guerrilla. A type of warfare conducted by small bands that harass the enemy from hiding and attack lines of communication.

Murrell Home. Southern plantation-style home built in Park Hill in 1845 by George Murrell, nephew-in-law of Chief John Ross. Called "Hunter's Home" by Murrell, the house miraculously survived the ravages of the Civil War. It still stands at Park Hill, maintained by the state of Oklahoma.

CHAPTER TWENTY-THREE

Jurisdictional Confusion

In November 1866, the Cherokee Council met at Tahlequah and elect-ed William Potter Ross Principal Chief of the Cherokee Nation. W. P. Ross was the nephew of the late chief, and John Ross had groomed him for the job, having paid for his education at Princeton. The new chief came in at a tough time. There were all the old animosities to deal with, and then there were the three most troublesome articles of the latest treaty: the granting of railroad rights-of-way, the establishment of a ter-ritorial government, and the location of U.S. courts in Indian Territory.

The first of these was seen by W. P. Ross, as it had been by his uncle, as a dangerous nuisance. The railroads would take over a great deal of Cherokee land for their rights-of-way. They would bring large numbers of white people, and they would bring in their wake significant numbers of undesirables: the gamblers, prostitutes, whiskey peddlers, and gener-al troublemakers that always seemed to follow the railroads. The other two items, the territorial government and the U.S. courts in Indian Territory, were both obvious infringements on the sovereignty of the Indian nations and were seen by W. P. Ross as harbingers of worse things to come. He was right, of course.

Having been defeated in war, and with their old enemies in power at home, many of the former Confederate Cherokees remained refugees in Texas, the Choctaw Nation, or the Chickasaw Nation. John Ross was dead, but another Ross was there in his place. But by 1867 a split had developed in the Ross Party, and from that division, a new party known as the Downing Party had developed. Some of the Southern Cherokees returned to the Cherokee Nation and helped to defeat Ross in the election of that year, supporting the new chief, Lewis Downing, simply because he was not a Ross. It was a strange alliance, apparently built on nothing more than hatred of John Ross, for Downing was a full-blood, associated with the Keetoowah Society. He had himself been a "Pin Indian" during the war.

The 1867 election also proved that the unrest in the Cherokee Nation had not come to an end. Fights broke out at polling places in all nine of the Cherokee Nation's voting districts. Then, with Lewis Downing in place as Principal Chief, nearly all of the Southern Cherokees returned to the Cherokee Nation. Most of them, including Stand Watie and E. C. Boudinot, settled in the Canadian District around Webbers Falls. Neutral or Union supporting Cherokees who had been refugees in Kansas also returned to the Cherokee Nation, and almost all Cherokees, no matter which side of the war they had been on, found themselves destitute. Their homes had been burned. Their stock was gone. Their fields had grown up in weeds and bramble. They all had to start over again.

Before the beginning of the Civil War, the population of the Cherokee Nation was estimated at 18,000. At the end of the war it was 13,566. One-third of the women were widows, and one-fourth of the children were orphans. While the people were busy rebuilding their homes and their shattered lives, the government was rebuilding institutions. Money from the sale of the Neutral Land and the Cherokee Strip was a big help, and progress in this area was fast. By 1867 the Cherokee Nation had thirty-two public schools back in operation, two years later, forty-two, and sixty-four by 1870.

Churches came back into the area, invited by the chief and the council: Congregationalists, Presbyterians, Methodists, Baptists, and Moravians. And along with the churches came mission schools. In 1870, *The Cherokee Advocate*, which had suspended publication during the Civil War, began publishing once again, and "by authority of the Nation John B. Jones began the preparation of a series of schoolbooks in the Cherokee language and alphabet" (Mooney).

A new two-story brick capitol was built on the capitol square in Tahlequah in 1870. In 1874 a new national prison was constructed at a cost of six thousand dollars. An orphan's home was established at Salina for all the children orphaned by the war. While the Cherokee Nation was thus "progressing" once again, agents of the U.S. government did not hesitate to act on the advantages the 1866 treaty had given them. In 1867, 987 Kansas Delawares were moved into the Cherokee Nation and incorporated as Cherokee citizens, and in 1870, 770 Shawnees.

The territorial general council called for by the U.S. government in the 1866 treaty did meet, but it turned out to be a far cry from what the government had envisioned. Made up of delegates from each of the five tribes, the council met to discuss ways to resist further incursions by the white man, and in 1875 the general council ceased to exist because Congress cut off its funds. In 1871, the Missouri, Kansas and Texas Railroad (known as the MK and T or the Katy) laid tracks from Chetopa, Kansas, through the Cherokee Nation as far as Chouteau, a few miles from the Creek Nation. The Atlantic and Pacific Railroad came in that same year from Seneca, Missouri, and connected with the Katy's line at Vinita.

It was during this time that E. C. Boudinot showed his true colors. He spent a great deal of his time in Washington working on behalf of railroad interests and encouraging the opening of Indian Territory to white settlement.

In 1873, following the death of Chief Downing, W. P. Ross was once again elected to the office by the Cherokee Council. At that early date, Ross could see what the designs of the United States were. In an address to the General Council in November of that year, he said, "The results anticipated ... are the gradual blending of the Indians under the same form of government ... the allotment of their lands in severalty, the gradual extinction of all civil distinction between them and citizens of the United States, and their ultimate absorption as a portion of their population."

In 1874, the agents assigned to each of the tribes were dismissed from service, and the United States established one agency for all of the "Five Civilized Tribes." Known as Union Agency, it was located at Muskogee, in the Creek Nation, a short distance from the border between the Creek and Cherokee Nations. Thwarted in their attempt to have a territorial government with a white governor over all of the Indian nations, federal authorities saw this move as a step in that direction. U.S. courts were not immediately established in Indian Territory; however, the United States Court for the Western District of Arkansas was moved from Van Buren to Fort Smith in 1871 and given jurisdiction over Indian Territory, "except for crimes committed by one Indian against the person or property of another Indian." In other words, the Cherokee courts had jurisdiction only in cases involving only Indians. In any case where a white man was involved, the federal court at Fort Smith had jurisdiction.

The situation within the Cherokee Nation was already uneasy because of the factionalism that had existed since 1835, and because of the effects of the war. There were some Cherokee outlaws, like Tom Starr and his son Sam, who had been set in opposition to the Cherokee Nation government at least since the killing of James Starr. Having taken to violence and lawlessness initially because of their hatred of John Ross, they simply stayed on that road. Then there were all the destitute people, whose homes had been destroyed during the war. Widespread desperation almost always leads to criminal behavior, for some people will resort to almost anything in order to survive, and some will take to stealing before hard work.

And there were many young men who had grown up knowing nothing but violence and the horrors of war during their adult years. Some men survive such an experience and resume normal lives, but others have difficulties reentering civilian life and normal society. The modern age has come up with names for this problem and ways of treating it, but in the years following the Civil War it was simply seen as bad behavior and was dealt with as such. Finally, because of the jurisdictional situation, white lawbreakers found the Indian Territory a very attractive place to be. Local law enforcement had no jurisdiction over them because they were white. They had only to watch out for federal marshals who rode out of Fort Smith to patrol a vast area, much of it mountainous and thickly wooded.

It seems as if the governments of the Indian nations were deliberately put into a situation by the United States where they could not win. They were not allowed to administer justice to white men. Therefore white outlaws swarmed into their territory. At that point, the United States could say that the Indian governments were incapable of maintaining law and order, and therefore, the United States must do it for them. Of course, the U.S. court in Fort Smith, in having jurisdiction over Indian Territory, was the very source of the worst part of the problem to begin with.

In 1872, Zeke Proctor, a Cherokee, went to a place called either Beck's Mill or Hildebrand's Mill in Delaware District to confront a white man named James Kesterson. Kesterson had married one of Zeke's sisters and moved with her to a place in the country near Sallisaw. Later, with two small children to take care of, he abandoned her there. Zeke heard about it, went to Sallisaw, and picked up his sister and her children. He took them home to care for them himself.

Shortly after that, he heard that Kesterson had moved in with the widow who owned the mill in Delaware District, near Zeke's own home. Zeke went there looking for Kesterson. When he confronted the man and pulled a gun on him, the widow, Polly Beck, a Cherokee, jumped between the two men, and Zeke's shot killed her. Kesterson ran away. Zeke Proctor turned himself in to Cherokee law officers for the killing of Polly Beck. He was to be tried in Cherokee courts. But Kesterson had gone to Fort Smith and had Zeke charged with the attempted murder of himself, a white man.

The Fort Smith authorities decided to wait for the outcome of the Cherokee trial. If the Cherokee court sentenced Zeke to hang for murder, they would be satisfied. If, on the other hand, the Cherokee court should release Zeke, then the federal marshals would arrest him for the attempted murder of Kesterson and have him tried in the federal court at Fort Smith. Two deputy marshals showed up at Zeke's trial in the company of a number of Becks, relatives of the slain woman. The Becks started into the courthouse armed, and when Johnson Proctor, Zeke's brother, unarmed, stepped in front of them, they started shooting. Before the fight was over, "nine men had been killed... and two were mortally wounded. An undetermined number of others received minor wounds" (Steele, p. 45.).

The Cherokee Nation issued warrants for the arrest of the Becks, and the U.S. court at Fort Smith issued warrants for the arrest of Zeke Proctor, the judge, jury, even for Johnson Proctor and some others who had been killed. Zeke Proctor hid out in the woods of the Cherokee Nation, and the Becks moved across the line into Arkansas to be safe from Cherokee authorities. The United States thought that the Cherokee Nation should assist them in capturing Zeke Proctor, but Chief Downing refused to cooperate, believing that the United States had no business interfering with the Cherokee courts. (A further complication was that Kesterson had presumably married Zeke's sister in an effort to gain for himself Cherokee citizenship.)

Authorities at Fort Smith were on the verge of calling for U.S. troops to invade the Cherokee Nation, but cooler heads prevailed, and a general amnesty was at last proclaimed. This led to the legend that Zeke Proctor was the only individual with whom the United States ever signed a treaty. The jurisdictional problems presented by the case were never really resolved.

In 1881, a delegation of Cherokees from the Cherokee Nation went to North Carolina to visit the Cherokees there and invite them to move west to join the majority. Some families of eastern Cherokees did make the move.

In 1883, the Cherokee Nation leased the land known as the Cherokee Outlet to the Cherokee Strip Livestock Association, a corporation formed by Kansas cattlemen, for $100,000 a year, a very prudent use of that asset.

In 1887, Deputy United States Marshal Dan Maples was in Tahlequah with a warrant for the arrest of Wili Woyi, a well known and highly respected Cherokee Indian doctor, or medicine man. The year before, Wili Woyi had killed a man he caught trying to steal from him. Like Zeke Proctor, Wili Woyi had turned himself in to the Cherokee authorities, but before the time of the trial, Fort Smith authorities had determined that the dead man was not a Cherokee citizen. Rather than submit himself to arrest by federal lawmen, Wili Woyi, on his way to the trial, had turned around and gone back home.

He had been arrested once after that, but he had escaped, and from that time on the deputy marshals who had gone looking for him had never even caught sight of him again. It was said that he could make himself invisible or take the form of some animal or bird. Dan Maples had come into the Cherokee Nation to try his luck. Maples had arrived in Tahlequah on the morning of a special Cherokee Council meeting that had been called because the Cherokee Female Seminary had burned.

Early that morning, as he was walking across a footbridge over the creek toward his camp just north of town, someone shot him in the back and killed him. No one had seen the killer, yet Ned Christie was blamed for the crime. Ned Christie was a full-blood Cherokee and a member of the council. Information that came to light later indicates that Ned Christie was a special target of the federal authorities because of the combination of his political stance, his outspoken manner, and the respect that he commanded in the Cherokee Nation (Speer).

Ned Christie was a Keetoowah and a strong advocate of Cherokee rights, Cherokee sovereignty, and Cherokee culture. He spoke out on the things he believed in, and people listened to what he had to say. At a time when the U.S. government was doing everything in its power to move the Cherokees closer and closer to the final dissolution of their own government, Ned Christie was, to say the least, troublesome to them. He was a convenient scapegoat. There were several other suspects in the case, but the shooting of Dan Maples was not investigated further. It was assumed that Ned Christie was the murderer. Posses of deputy marshals rode to his house in attempts to capture or kill him. A posse led by Deputy Marshal Heck Thomas burned Ned Christie's house, shot his son Arch in the chest, and shot Ned Christie in the face, breaking his nose and putting out an eye. Both Christies recovered. They built a new house, and the posses kept coming.

In 1889, the new Cherokee Female Seminary was completed at Tahlequah at a cost of sixty thousand dollars. It was built not far north of where Dan Maples had been shot. Also that year the area known as the Unassigned Lands was opened to white settlement, and on April 22 of that year the first of the famous land runs took place. White people were now settled on both sides and to the north of the Cherokee Nation, and they completely surrounded Indian Territory. On May 2, 1890, an Act of Congress created the Territory of Oklahoma out of land that is today the western part of the state of Oklahoma. Indian Territory, or the land of the so-called Five Civilized Tribes, was now bordered on the west by an organized territory, settled by whites. Just as had happened in Georgia, the Cherokee Nation was being surrounded by white people. History was repeating itself.

In 1889, in an effort calculated to force the Cherokee Nation to sell the Outlet to the United States, President Harrison announced that no livestock would be allowed to graze in the Outlet. That move also deprived the Nation of a substantial part of its operating budget, for it brought to an end the lease with the Cherokee Livestock Association.

In the winter of 1891, a badly decomposed body was discovered three miles southeast of the Illinois courthouse near the Illinois River. Federal authorities were quick to "identify" the body as that of Wili Woyi. Conveniently, they closed that embarrassing case.

In 1892, a posse of twenty-three men headed by Deputy Marshal Paden Tolbert surrounded the Ned Christie home. After firing hundreds of bullets at the house (called Ned Christie's fort), and even trying to set the roof on fire by shooting flaming sticks out of the barrels of muzzle-loading rifles, they fired a cannon at the house, still to no avail. Finally, they planted dynamite under the walls and blew the house up. When Ned Christie came out of the smoke and haze of the explosion, a deputy marshal shot him in the back of the head. It had taken them almost five years, but they finally got him.

Ned Christie had never been wanted for any crime other than the killing of Dan Maples, and that was never proved against him. In fact, later investigations strongly suggest that he was entirely innocent of the shooting. In spite of all that, the white press built up a legend of Ned Christie as a notorious outlaw and accused him of numerous unspecified crimes. Like Dragging Canoe over a hundred years earlier, Ned Christie went down in the history books as a bad outlaw when he was actually a Cherokee patriot.

In 1893, the Cherokee Nation gave in to the pressure and sold the Outlet to the United States, and it too was then opened for white settlement with another land rush following that same year.

Back in North Carolina, the small band of Cherokees who had managed to avoid removal, due to the tireless workings on their behalf by Colonel Will Thomas, had survived precariously in their mountain homes. Originally they had submitted themselves to the laws of North Carolina; however, in 1889, they received federal recognition (Finger, 1984, p. xi), and they have continued as a separate, federally recognized tribe up to this day.

◈

SOURCE LIST AND SUGGESTIONS FOR FURTHER READING

Colbert, Thomas Burnell. 1993. "E. C. Boudinot's Hotel." *The Chronicles of Oklahoma* 71, no. 4:376–91.

Conley, Robert J. 1984. "Cherokees On the Scout." *The Roundup.* 32, no. 10, 11–20.

———. "Cherokee Outlaws." Paper presented at the Cherokee Nation History Conference, September 2, 1993, Tahlequah.

Faulk, Odie B., and Billy M. Jones. 1984. *Tahlequah, NSU, and the Cherokees.* Tahlequah: Northeastern State University Educational Foundation.

Harman, S.W. 1898. *Hell on the Border: History of the Great Court at Fort Smith, Arkansas.* Fort Smith: Hell on the Border Publishing Company. Reprinted, Lincoln: University of Nebraska Press, 1992.

Kilpatrick, Jack F. "The Cherokees Remember Their Badmen." *True West* 16, no. 6:21, 62–64.

Miller, H. Craig. 1993. "Cherokee Sovereignty in the Gilded Age: the Outlet Question." *The Chronicles of Oklahoma* 71, no. 2:118–37.

Payne, Ruth Holt. 1965. "One-Man Peace Treaty." *Frontier Times* 39, no. 5:39, 66. (On Zeke Proctor.)

Savage, William W., Jr. 1973. *The Cherokee Strip Live Stock Association.* Columbia: University of Missouri Press.

———. 1993. "Cattle and Corporations: The Rise, Progress, and Termination of the Cherokee Strip Live Stock Corporation." *The Chronicles of Oklahoma* 71, no. 2:138-153.

Shirley, Glenn. 1968. *Law West of Fort Smith.* Lincoln: University of Nebraska Press.

Speer, Bonnie Stahlman. 1990. *The Killing of Ned Christie.* Norman: Reliance Press.

Steele, Philip. 1974. *The Last Cherokee Warriors.* Gretna, La.: Pelican Publishing Company.

Thrasher, Helen Starr. 1972. "The Blood of a Hundred Men." *True West* 19, no. 5:22–25, 59–60. (On Tom Starr.)

Turner, Alvin O. 1993. "Order and Disorder: The Opening of the Cherokee Outlet." *The Chronicles of Oklahoma* 71, no. 2:154–73.

Wellman, Paul I. 1961. *A Dynasty of Western Outlaws.* New York: Doubleday.

West, C. W. 1974. *Outlaws and Peace Officers of Indian Territory.* Muskogee: Muscogee Publishing Co.

———. 1974. *Persons and Places of Indian Territory.* Muskogee: Muscogee Publishing Co.

◈

GLOSSARY

Downing Party. Split off from the Ross party, which had also been called the National Party, the Downing Party was named for Lewis Downing, who had been a Deputy Principal Chief under John Ross and was later Principal Chief. Downing was a traditional full-blood and a Keetoowah. He had been a "Pin Indian" during the Civil War, serving under the command of Colonel John Drew.

Wili Woyi. Famous Indian doctor (or medicine man), Wili Woyi was known in English as Billy Pigeon. U.S. law enforcement authorities searched for him in vain for years, finally identifying an unidentifiable body as his just so they could close the case.

CHAPTER TWENTY-FOUR

The Dawes Commission and Redbird Smith

In 1887, the first telephone line west of the Mississippi River was strung from Tahlequah to Muskogee by Cherokee E. D. Hicks, with the permission of the Council of the Cherokee Nation. That same year the U.S. Congress passed the General Allotment Act, popularly known as the Dawes Act. (W. P. Ross had foreseen this move since at least 1873.) It was called the Dawes Act because the sponsor of the bill was Senator Henry Dawes of Massachusetts, and its intent was abundantly clear. In 1885, in a speech to the annual Lake Mohonk Conference, Dawes had described the Cherokee Nation, saying, "there was not a family in that whole Nation that had not a home of its own. There is not a pauper in that Nation, and the Nation does not owe a dollar. It built its own capitol... and built its schools and hospitals. Yet the defect of the system was apparent. They have got as far as they can go, because they hold their land in common... there is no selfishness, which is at the bottom of civilization."

The Dawes Act, then, was passed to make the Indians into individual landowners, which in turn would lead to their becoming selfish and then at last civilized. Of course, when the individual allotments for any given tribe were all added up, they would come far short of equaling the total number of acres of tribal land. There would therefore be an excess, or surplus, that would be made available to whites. This scheme marvelously illustrated the correlation between selfishness and "civilization" asserted by Dawes.

It is indeed difficult to believe that a majority of U.S. citizens, even a majority of U.S. congressmen, would see any real logic in the argument presented by Henry Dawes. One would think that any right-thinking human being, presented with Dawes's description of the Cherokee Nation would ask, "How can we achieve that same level of comfort for our citizens?" Since they did not react in that way, one can only assume that the majority simply accepted that argument as a convenient way of disguising their real motive, which was, once again, the theft of tribal land.

Specific provisions of the Dawes Act were to grant 160 acres of land to each head of family, 80 acres to each single person over eighteen years of age and to each orphan, and 40 acres to each other single person under eighteen. A deed for the land would be issued to each owner, but the land would be restricted by the U.S. government for twenty-five years. That meant that the owner could not sell or lease his land without permission of the U.S. government. The Indians would have four years in which to select their allotments, and if any individual failed to select one in that time, the government would select one for him. Finally, the Indian allottee would become a citizen of the United States.

Although the Cherokee Nation and the other four nations of the Indian Territory were exempt from the Dawes Act by treaty, the intent of the United States was clear. As mentioned above, W. P. Ross had seen it coming and articulated it back in 1873. If the United States was breaking up the landholdings of other Indian tribes, it was only a matter of time before it would get around to the Cherokee Nation. Sure enough, by Act of Congress, March 3, 1893, a three-member "Dawes Commission" was created and empowered to deal with each of the Five Civilized Tribes for allotment of their lands in severalty. This was clearly preparation for the final dissolution of their governments in order to clear the way for Oklahoma statehood. Again, W. P. Ross had correctly predicted the scheme and its ultimate intentions twenty years earlier.

The next year, the Dawes Commission arrived in Indian Territory. Since the Indian Territory tribes were exempt from the Dawes Act, the job of the commission was to try to convince them to agree to the breakup of their landholdings, or to try to figure out a way to break the treaties. Traditional Indians of all Five Tribes, mostly full-bloods, resented this movement and resisted it in every possible way short of taking up arms against the United States.

In 1895, the membership of the Dawes Commission was increased to five. Its powers were also increased. Its name was officially changed to the

Commission to the Five Civilized Tribes, and Senator Dawes himself was assigned to it. The commission began to survey Cherokee lands. Reasons for the white man's lust for the Cherokee lands, and those of the other four tribes of Indian Territory, even beyond reasons of simple land lust, become abundantly clear when the accomplishments of those tribes are examined. Mooney describes the Cherokee Nation of 1895 in the following words.

> The general prosperity and advancement of the Cherokee Nation at this time may be judged from the report of the secretary of the Cherokee national board of education to Agent Wisdom. He reports 4,800 children attending two seminaries, male and female, two high schools, and one hundred primary schools, teachers being paid from $35 to $100 per month for nine months in the year. Fourteen primary schools were made for use of the negro citizens of the Nation, besides which they had a fine high school, kept up, like all the others, at the expense of the Cherokee government. Besides the national schools there were twelve mission schools helping to do splendid work for children of both citizens and non citizens. Children of non citizens were not allowed to attend the Cherokee national schools, but had their own subscription schools. The orphan asylum ranked as a high school, in which 150 orphans were boarded and educated, with graduates every year. It was a large brick building of three stories, 80 by 240 feet. The male seminary, accommodating 200 pupils, and the female seminary, accommodating 250 pupils, were also large brick structures, three stories in height and 150 by 240 feet on the ground. Three members, all Cherokees by blood, constituted a board of education. The secretary adds that the Cherokee are proud of their schools and educational institutions, and that no other country under the sun is so blessed with educational advantages at large.
>
> At this time the Cherokee Nation numbered something over 25,000 Indians, white and negro citizens; the total citizen population of the three races in the five civilized tribes numbered about 70,000, while the non citizens had increased to 250,000 and their number was being rapidly augmented.

By this time in history, the U.S. government had a long record of looking the other way while its citizens moved illegally onto Indian land and squatted there. Then, when their numbers were sufficient to allow the government to rationalize that it must do something to protect their interests, it simply looked for ways of getting the land away from the Indians. In the case of the lands of the Five Tribes of Indian Territory of 1895, the prospect was even more inviting, for the Indian nations had already built towns and established institutions in keeping with those the white men would eventually build for themselves. The advantage here was that the work had already been done, and the Indians had done it better. The whites could recognize that, and they wanted it all the more for themselves.

To make matters worse, as Hendrix says, "factionalism was reappearing in the Cherokee Nation. The mixed-bloods were so Americanized most of them could not speak Cherokee. The full-bloods spoke little or no English, and there was no way for the two factions to communicate with each other. The mixed-blood families had become so much like the white frontier families that their value systems were no longer Indian. The two groups would probably have had little to say to each other if they had spoken the same language." And the full-bloods "could feel their nations slipping out from under them."

In 1895, Bird Harris proposed that the Cherokee Nation go ahead and sell all of its land to the United States, use the money to purchase land in Mexico or South America, and then remove the entire Cherokee Nation once more, this time completely beyond the long and greedy reach of the United States. Many of the traditional people believed that the troubles of the Cherokees were a result of the Cherokee people having turned away from their own traditions. It was an argument like the one of Tecumseh, and the one of the prophet Charlie, and later of Whitepath. And in 1896, a stomp dance was held in Illinois District. Cherokee, Creek, and Natchez people took part. It was the beginning of what anthropologists call a "Nativistic Revival." More specifically, it was the beginning of what has been called the Redbird Smith Movement.

According to Hendrix, "The three symbols of the [Redbird Smith Movement] were the White Path, the Sacred Fire, and the Wampums. The White Path was spiritual, and a matter of choice. It was the peaceful way, the way of love and passive resistance.... the Sacred Fire is more than just a symbol of a deity, it is the living manifestation of God.... smoke of the Fire... carries the prayers to heaven and... carries spiritual messages from place to place on earth." The Wampums are actual ancient wampum belts with a special significance. Hendrix says that the "interpretation of the symbols which were woven into the belts... would reveal... what they had lost."

Redbird Smith did succeed in recovering the Wampums, and the movement was underway. The belief was that a return to the ancient ways would ultimately save the Cherokees from the destructive ways of the white man. And so, reviving Cherokee culture and returning to traditional ways, Redbird Smith and the Keetoowahs resisted allotment and refused to cooperate with the Dawes Commission.

In 1896, the power of determining its own citizenship was taken away from the Cherokee Nation and given to the Dawes Commission. U.S. authorities were getting tired of trying to play fair with the Cherokees. In 1898, the Curtis Act was passed, "for the protection of the people of the Indian Territory." It gave the U.S. courts the power to determine the membership of the five tribes in Indian Territory. It declared that when the rolls of the Five Tribes were complete, the Dawes Commission "shall proceed to allot" the lands. It required residency for any individual's name to be placed on the rolls. For example, if any of the Confederate Cherokees or their descendants who had sought refuge in Texas during the war had failed to move back to the Cherokee Nation, they would not be eligible for enrollment. It declared that the tribal laws were terminated, and it abolished the tribal courts.

Hendrix says, "Although the Cherokees tried to fight the Curtis Act in court, claiming it violated treaties, they were forced at last into negotiations with the Dawes Commission. Chief Samuel Houston Mayes appointed seven men to meet with the Commission." On January 7, 1899, the seven Cherokee delegates to the Dawes Commission at last agreed to submit to a vote of the people an agreement on the allotment of lands and the dissolution of the government of the Cherokee Nation. On January 31, 1899, such an election was held, and a majority of Cherokees voted for the agreement, but for some reason, the U.S. Congress failed to ratify it. A new but similar agreement was reached in Washington in 1900. This one was ratified by Congress, and according to the U.S. government, became effective in April of that year.

The agreement required the Principal Chief of the Cherokee Nation to sign deeds of transfer for all the land transactions that would follow. It declared that the rolls compiled by the Dawes Commission would be final rolls, and it called for the sale of *The Cherokee Advocate*. It said further that "the government of the Cherokee Nation shall not continue longer than March 4, 1906, subject to such future legislation as Congress may deem proper." It said that all Cherokee citizens would become citizens of the United States. The Secretary of the Interior then decreed that the work of the Dawes Commission should commence among the Cherokees. Agents of the Dawes Commission began their work in the spring of 1902. Many mixed-bloods cooperated. Many whites attempted to enroll as part Cherokee.

Many full-bloods did everything they could to avoid the enrollment officers. They had several good reasons for doing so. In the first place, traditional Cherokees did not believe in the private ownership of land. They believed that all Cherokees owned all the land. In the second place, far from being the ignorant, backward Indians depicted by many historians, the traditional people knew full well that the ultimate aim of the U.S. government was the destruction of the Cherokee Nation, the Cherokee culture, and eventually the Cherokee people themselves, and they had no intention of cooperating in this diabolical venture.

But somewhere around this time, some of the Keetoowah membership gave up the fight. They decided that it would be best to enroll. Redbird Smith did not agree, and he and about five thousand others withdrew from the original Keetoowah organization, forming their own "Nighthawk Keetoowah Society." The Nighthawks continued to avoid enrollment officers and talk against enrollment and allotment.

On August 7, 1902, Chief Thomas Buffington called for an election, and the Cherokee people approved the last agreement. The enrollment process moved forward in earnest, and Redbird Smith and other Nighthawks were arrested and thrown into jail in Muskogee. Redbird Smith finally registered, but many others did not. Hendrix says, "The Government then became more aggressive and U.S. marshals were sent out with the field parties to force the fullbloods to enroll."

By 1904, Charlie Wickliffe, a full-blood Nighthawk, was wanted for the murder of deputy U.S. marshals. He was not wanted for any other crime. There were rumors of an Indian uprising, and Redbird Smith and other Keetoowah leaders were again arrested and thrown in jail. This time they were questioned and released by U.S. marshals.

An election was held in 1903, and William C. Rogers was elected Principal Chief. Rogers was seen as being too cooperative with the federal government in the dissolution of the Cherokee Nation, and in 1905 he was impeached and removed from office by the National Council. The council appointed Frank Boudinot in his place. However, the U.S. government reinstated Rogers, thus making him the first of a string of presidentially appointed chiefs. The Cherokee Nation was supposed to have been dissolved by March of 1906 (according to the Act of 1902), but the whole business of land transfers was so much more complex and time consuming than the federal government had anticipated that the Cherokee government was "continued in modified and restricted form under an Act of Congress until June 30, 1914, when all business in the division of tribal properties was finished" (Woodward, p. 323). However, the Act of 1906 "continued in full force and effect for all purposes authorized by law" the tribal governments of the "Choctaw, Chickasaw, Cherokee, Creek, and Seminole tribes or nations." Chief Rogers remained in office signing deeds of transfer until his death in 1917.

SOURCE LIST AND SUGGESTIONS FOR FURTHER READING

Cohen, Felix S. 1942. *Handbook of Federal Indian Law*. Albuquerque: University of New Mexico Press.

DeVine, John W. 1968. "Last Chief of the Cherokees." *True West* 42, no. 3:22–23, 69. (On Chief Thomas Buffington.)

Girdley, Allan. 1968. "It Spoke Cherokee." *True West* 42, no. 2:36–37. (On E. D. Hicks and the first telephone line.)

Hendrix, Janey B. 1983. *Redbird Smith and the Nighthawk Keetoowahs*. Park Hill, Okla.: Cross Cultural Education Center.

Newberry, Howard. 1967. "Manhunt in the Spavinaws." *Frontier Times* 41, no. 6:34–35, 59–60. (On Charlie Wickliffe.)

Price, Monroe E. 1970. *Native American Law Manual*. California Indian Legal Services.

Smith, Chad. 1992. "Cherokee Nation Legal History Course." Presented February 1992, Tahlequah.

Smith, Rhoda Anderson. 1973. "Deputized Sawmill Man." *Frontier Times* 47, no. 6:28–30, 4547. (Charlie Wickliffe mentioned.)

Thomas, Robert K. 1953. *The Origin and Development of the Redbird Smith Movement*. Master's thesis: University of Arizona, Tucson.

GLOSSARY

Nighthawk. A member of the Nighthawk Keetoowahs, a branch of the Keetoowah Society that split off when the Society decided to cooperate with the enrollment officers of the Dawes Commission.

CHAPTER TWENTY-FIVE

Oklahoma

"The citizens of Indian Territory," Littlefield says, "made one last effort to secure their Indian state.... Four of the five tribes, the Chickasaws excepted, met in a convention in July, 1905, at which time they drew up a constitution for the state of Sequoyah, a separate and distinct state from that of Oklahoma Territory which was at the same time seeking statehood. The people of Indian Territory who voted on the measure ratified the constitution by an overwhelming majority, but the number of people voting represented less than one-half of the qualified voters. Nevertheless, the measure was presented to Congress where it received little attention."

In 1906 the U.S. Congress passed an Act to Provide for the Final Disposition of the Affairs of the Five Civilized Tribes. By means of that law, the Department of Interior took over the Indian schools and school funds, and all government buildings and furniture. The law declared that the tribal governments would continue "in full force and effect for all purposes authorized by law." The law further provided that the office of Principal Chief "may be declared vacant by the President of the United States, who may fill any vacancy arising from removal, disability, or death of the incumbent, by appointment of a citizen by blood of the tribe." It further explained that if a chief failed to sign a document presented to him by U.S. authorities at the time and place called for, he could be removed from office and replaced, or "such instrument may be approved by the Secretary of Interior."

On November 16, 1907, Oklahoma Territory and Indian Territory were combined to create the new state of Oklahoma. President Theodore Roosevelt signed the proclamation bringing the forty-sixth state into the Union. At Guthrie, the temporary capital, there was much celebrating, including a mock marriage between Miss Indian Territory (a white girl dressed up as an Indian "maiden") and Mr. Oklahoma Territory (a white cowboy).

Although nothing in the law prohibited Cherokees from electing their chief and council, a regime of bureaucratic imperialism had begun. For all practical purposes, the Cherokee Nation had become dormant. Chief Rogers was still signing land transfers, and the Dawes Commission was still at work. Many mixed-blood Cherokee politicians simply became prominent Oklahoma state politicians, among them Clem Rogers (father of the later famous Will Rogers), Oliver Hazard Perry Brewer, W. W. Hastings, and Robert Latham Owen. Hendrix says, "There were hundreds of fullbloods who refused to claim their allotments as a matter of principle. Most of them did not even know where their allotments were. Much of the lands just grew up in jimson weed and scrub oak through neglect, but many acres were tilled or used as pasture by white trespassers who asked no questions and were seldom challenged."

In 1910, Redbird Smith made the following speech to the Council of the Nighthawk Keetoowahs:

> After my selection as chief [of the Nighthawk Keetoowahs],
> I awakened to the grave and great responsibilities of the
> leader of men. I looked about and saw that I had led my
> people down a long and steep mountainside, now it was
> my duty to turn and lead them back upward to save them.
> The unfortunate thing in the mistakes and errors of leaders
> or of governments is the penalty the innocent and loyal fol-
> lowers have to pay. My greatest ambition has always been
> to think right and do right. It is my belief this is the
> fulfilling of the law of the Great Creator. In the upbuilding
> of my people it is my purpose that we shall be spiritually
> right and industriously strong.
>
> Our pride in our ancestral heritage is our great incen-
> tive for handing something worthwhile to our posterity. It is
> this pride in ancestry that makes men strong and loyal for
> their principle in life. It is this same pride that makes men
> give up their all for their government.

That same year Redbird Smith and other Nighthawks went to Mexico with a document dating from 1820 hoping to prove a claim to land under that government, but nothing ever came of it. They then appealed to President Woodrow Wilson in 1914 for a reservation where Keetoowahs could live together. The government rejected that as a backward step. "But," says Littlefield, "the Cherokee fullbloods did not give up their dreams of an Indian commonwealth, and they revived the 'Plan for preserving in effect the Continuity of Tribal Relations of the full-blood Indian.'" In 1921, one hundred Cherokees, members of thirty-five families of the Brush Creek and Yellow Locust Fire of the Keetoowah Society left their homes in Mayes and Delaware Counties to locate together in the extreme southeastern corner of Cherokee County. "The brainchild of Redbird Smith," according to Littlefield, the community, with the aid of a white philanthropist, flourished for a few years, then faded away.

William C. Rogers died in 1917, and the U.S. government apparently saw no need for a Cherokee chief again until 1919, when A. B. Cunningham was appointed chief by the president of the United States. Cunningham, the first of six men who would go down in history as "chiefs for a day," actually served from November 8 until November 25. Presumably he had signed all the necessary documents during those seventeen days.

These early days of Oklahoma statehood were also marked by theft of Indian land on a grand scale. Debo says, "The orgy of exploitation . . . is almost beyond belief. Within a generation these Indians, who had owned and governed a region greater in area and potential wealth than many an American state, were almost stripped of their holdings, and were rescued from starvation only through public charity." She says further, "The plunder of Indians was so closely joined with pride in the creation of a great new commonwealth that it received little condemnation. The term 'grafter' was applied as a matter of course to dealers in Indian land, and was frankly accepted by them."

Ed M. Frye was appointed "Chief for a Day" on June 23, 1923. Then Richard B. Choate was appointed on October 15, 1925, to serve one day on or before December 31, 1925. The U.S. government treated the Cherokee Nation as nothing more than a convenient tool. "To fill the void," Merideth says, "the Cherokee people began to meet in National Council during the decades of the twenties and thirties. In between the large conventions, a loose coalition grew up known as the Cherokee Executive Council. It was made up of representatives from four local groups—Eastern Cherokee Council [immigrant Indians]; Western Cherokee Council [Old Settlers]; Tulsa Cherokees, also known as the Cherokee Executive Committee; and the Kee-too-wah Society, Inc. Levi Gritts of the

Kee-too-wah Society, Inc., acted as the Principal Chief of the united organization upon his selection at the convention of 1925."

The U.S. government, of course, did not recognize the Cherokee Executive Council, but its leaders were occasionally able to get government officials to listen to their grievances. And by this time, more enlightened white people and even some government officials were beginning to see the error of government policy in its dealings with Indians. In 1928, the Meriam Report was published, and it declared that the allotment process had been a failure and a disaster. The mood of the country and of the government toward Indians was changing. In 1934, under the administration of President Franklin Roosevelt and his Commissioner of Indian Affairs, John Collier, the Wheeler-Howard Act, or Indian Reorganization Act (IRA), was passed, and it signaled an almost complete reversal of federal Indian policy.

The purposes of the IRA were to stop the process of allotment of Indian lands, to provide ways for Indians to acquire more land, to strengthen tribal governments, to assist Indian tribes in developing business enterprises, to establish a system of credit for Indian tribes, to provide for higher education for Indians, and to situate Indians in positions in the Federal Indian Service. Indian tribes in Oklahoma were excluded from some of the articles in the IRA, specifically those involving self-government; however, in 1936, another law was passed called the Oklahoma Indian General Welfare Act (OIGWA). This law gave the rights of self-government to tribes in Oklahoma. Sort of. It allowed any ten Indians in the state to form a corporation and seek a federal charter. It stated that any organization chartered under the law would have "all the rights and responsibilities of any federally recognized Indian tribe."

The Great Depression of the 1930s hit Cherokees hard, as it did other Americans. Hundreds of Cherokees, along with other "Okies," migrated to California, Washington, and Oregon, in search of better jobs and a better living for their families. So many Cherokees made the difficult move that the period of the Depression might be termed a second Trail of Tears, this one an economic trail. Descendants of many of the people who made this historic move still live on the West Coast. In 1930, according the census, there had been forty thousand Cherokee citizens living in Oklahoma. By 1940, there were but twenty thousand. Twelve thousand of the twenty thousand who left stopped at Bakersfield, California, on U.S. Route 66.

Charles J. Hunt had been appointed "Chief for a Day" of the Cherokee Nation for December 27, 1928. Oliver H. P. Brewer was Chief on May 26, 1931. And W. W. Hastings was Chief on January 22 of the very year in which the OIGWA was passed. The Cherokee Nation seemed to have no government to take advantage of the new law. In 1938, the National Council met again and was attended by three hundred Cherokee men and women, and Jesse Bartley Milam, a mixed-blood Cherokee banker from Chelsea, was elected Principal Chief. On April 21, 1941, acting in the spirit of his "New Deal," President Roosevelt appointed Milam Principal Chief of the Cherokee Nation. And the appointment was not just for a day.

Once Milam was in place as Principal Chief, he still did not apply for a charter under the OIGWA. He was certainly familiar with the law, for in 1936 he had been instrumental in establishing the Indian Credit Association under that law. Rather, he saw before him a "better means to represent" the interests of the Cherokee people. He was "leading the Nation to bring about the foundation for their self-determination. It was seen clearly... that the United States government could not be expected to act responsibly as a trustee for the Cherokee Nation or its people. The only entity that could do that was a government of the Cherokee people, acting as a 'domestic dependent nation,' as prescribed by the Supreme Court of the United States" (Meredith, p. 107). The Cherokee Nation was already in possession of its inherent sovereignty.

So technically, the Chief was still a presidential appointee, but this time he was also a Chief who had been elected by the Cherokee people, even though the U.S. government did not recognize the validity of that election. The president of the United States had, in effect, "rubber stamped" the election. It was a very significant day in Cherokee history, for it marked a major step in the direction of a return of self-government for the Cherokee people.

SOURCE LIST AND SUGGESTIONS FOR FURTHER READING

Debo, Angie. 1940. *And Still the Waters Run: The Betrayal of the Five Civilized Tribes.* Princton, N.J.: Princeton University Press.

Littlefield, Daniel F., Jr. 1971. "Utopian Dreams of the Cherokee Fullbloods, 1890–1934." *Journal of the West* 10, no. 3:404–27.

Merideth, Howard L. 1985. *Bartley Milam: Principal Chief of the Cherokee Nation.* Muskogee, Okla.: Indian University Press.

GLOSSARY

Chiefs for a Day. Succession of six Principal Chiefs of the Cherokee Nation

appointed by the president of the United States between the years 1919
and 1936. Often they were actually appointed just for a day.

Depression. A period marked by high unemployment, low wages, low prices,
and a general slackening of business activity.

Meriam Report. An extensive report on the problem of the administration
of Indian affairs, authorized by the Coolidge administration and conducted by the Institute for Government Research. Lewis Meriam was
the supervisor of the study, and its official title is *The Problem of
Indian Administration*.

CHAPTER TWENTY-SIX

World War II

A ccording to biographer Howard Merideth, Bartley Milam, as soon as he became chief, began to pursue two important issues. The first was ownership of the riverbed of the Grand River, and the second was the Cherokee language. Milam believed that the riverbed belonged to the Cherokee Nation, because the Cherokee Nation had originally been issued its title to the land in fee simple. When the land had been surveyed and the allotments given out, the riverbed had not been dealt with. Therefore, the Cherokee Nation would still be the owner. Milam's reason for pursuing this matter was that the riverbed could be a source of income for the Cherokee Nation, and the income could be used for per-capita payments to individual Cherokees, many of whom were living in abject poverty, or it could be used for programs that would benefit the Cherokee people.

His concern for language was because of a belief that the language "gave the people their identity and world view." He searched for, located, and secured the original matrices of the Cherokee syllabary with the aim of having type made and starting to print the syllabary once more. He was also instrumental in causing two university-level courses in the Cherokee language to be offered and taught, one at the University of Oklahoma and the other at the American Business College in Tulsa. Milam's interest in language, culture, and history also led him to investigate the possibility of purchasing the original site of the Cherokee Female Seminary at Park Hill "to be developed as a national heritage center for the Cherokee people."

He also pursued other claims against the U.S. government, claims for ownership to land that was never allotted, claims for money that was owed. He worked for better roads and better postal service in the rural areas of Delaware, Mayes, Cherokee, Adair, and Sequoyah counties. And he planned a Cherokee cattle association in the Kenwood area.

But the outbreak of and the entry of the United States into World War II took the minds of the citizens and the government of the United States off of matters of interest to Indian tribes, and many of Chief Milam's projects remained dreams for the time being. And then, says Merideth, "The most tragic event that affected the principal chief was the Cherokee Removal of 1942." He goes on to describe this event as follows:

> Once more the United States demanded the lands of Cherokee families for what it perceived as the greater good. Early in 1942, the United States Army thought that it needed to expand Camp Gruber in the Green Leaf Hills and the Cookson backcountry. It required the immediate necessity of relocation with very little forethought. There were eighty tracts of restricted Cherokee land in a fifty square mile area in Cherokee County that was condemned. These tracts were all allotted lands held in trust by the United States Secretary of the Interior for the Cherokee people who lived there in the hills. There were forty-five Cherokee families of one-half degree of blood or more living within the area. Sixteen families were engaged in farming and stockraising. They were entirely self-supporting through their farming efforts. . . . A majority of the other families had cattle, hogs, and poultry. All of the families had good gardens. Where they needed extra funds to support the family, they supplemented their income by day labor, tie hacking, or work in various public works' programs.
>
> All of the Cherokee families were making crops. They had started their gardens and if abandoned, they would not have the winter food supplies for the year. In addition, the people had no means of travel except on foot or riding a work horse. Army officials made it very clear that they could not spare trucks to aid in relocation. Only two of the forty-five Cherokee families living in the area had moving funds. As a result very few had a place to live. The Bureau of Indian Affairs patched a few old houses together for temporary occupancy in addition to some Civilian Conservation Corps

barracks. This problem was compounded by the fact that the
Cherokees did not receive enough payment for their land.
Soon they were without food or homes.

Chief Milam worked diligently with agents of the Bureau of Indian
Affairs (BIA) to acquire decent housing for these dislocated people, and
he used the newspapers in an attempt to gain public support. He also
encouraged the displaced landowners to go to court, and those who took
his advice did receive more compensation for their lost lands. Milam's
hope was that the land would be returned at the end of the war.

In spite of the U.S. Army's callous treatment of Cherokees, Cherokees
did join the U.S. military and fight in World War II. Records are not com-
plete for Cherokees who served in World War II, so the following list does
not include everyone. Best known, perhaps, is Admiral Joseph James
"Jocko" Clark from Rogers County, but there were many others. Lieutenant
Jack Montgomery was awarded the Congressional Medal of Honor.
Lieutenant William Sixkiller, Lieutenant Richard Griffin, Captain Joseph
Woody Cochran, and Lieutenant Jack C. Montgomery were all Silver Star
recipients. Staff Sergeant William Comfort and Captain Joseph Woody
Cochran received the Distinguished Flying Cross. Staff Sergeant William
Comfort, Lieutenant Earl Bradley, and Captain Joseph Woody Cochran
each received the Air Medal. The Purple Heart was awarded to many,
including Franklin Gritts, Jack Montgomery, Noah Falling, Jim Hair, Bill
Hummingbird, Ben Parris, Bennie Quinton, and Joseph Woody Cochran.

Thomas Bearpaw, Franklin B. (Bob) Crittenden, James Hornett, Lewis
West, Edwin Mathison, and Soldier Sanders were all prisoners of war. Jim
Chuculate, William Sixkiller, Jr., Quanah Fields, James Willis Bench,
Sequoyah Downing, Wirtner Ward, James Kingfisher, Earl Bradley, Hiawatha
Tuggle, and William Hanks, Jr., and many others all gave their lives.

And the women did not all stay at home. Lieutenant Elsie Hogner was
a nurse in the U.S. Army. First Lieutenant Marian Brown (later Mrs. Martin
Hagerstrand) was an army mess officer, spending time in two war zones
and returning home with a Battle Star. Susanna Owens was in the army.

In the meantime, Bartley Milam was still busy making the office of
Principal Chief of the Cherokee Nation into a much more serious position than it had been since before Oklahoma statehood. Merideth says,
"The preservation of Cherokee property, historical manuscripts, and justice became Milam's watchwords."

World War II brought several important and far-reaching changes
to Indians in general. Of course, it had redirected the entire budget of
the United States, and many of the programs instituted by the Collier

administration of the BIA were abandoned. During the war, many Indians had moved from their reservations or rural homes into cities where wartime jobs were plentiful. At the war's end, many stayed in their new locations. The Indian population began to shift to an urban population. More Indians went to college because of the GI Bill. And all of these changes gave rise to a new phenomenon, the national Indian organizations. Women stayed in the workforce, and the family dynamic changed.

For the first time in history, Indians from different tribes all over the country banded together in common causes to form organizations of national scope. Chief Bartley Milam saw the value of these organizations and saw the need for Cherokee participation. The National Congress of American Indians (NCAI) was founded in 1944. Sixty years old, Chief Milam was at the organizational meeting in Denver. Merideth says the Indian delegates "adopted a constitution and established the organization to bring tribes together for the purpose of enlightening the general public, preserving American Indian cultural values, seeking equitable adjustment of tribal affairs, securing and preserving tribal rights under treaties with the United States, and reform the administration of Indian Affairs." N. B. Johnson, Cherokee and District Judge of the Twelfth Judicial District of Oklahoma, was the first elected president of the NCAI. "Everybody else," he said, "has taken a hand in determining Indian welfare and Indian destiny—why should not the Indians themselves?"

Following the Denver meeting, Milam, with the cooperation and approval of the BIA, began working toward organizing a committee or council of two representatives from each of the nine districts of the Cherokee Nation to be an advisory group to the Chief. In order to accomplish this goal, he had to deal with various groups or factions of Cherokees: the Cherokee Seminaries Students Association, the Seven Clan Society, the Keetoowah Society, Incorporated, the Nighthawk Keetoowah Society.

In 1946, Milam reported that of the original 4,420,068 acres of the Cherokee Nation, 4,346,145 acres had been allotted. The "surplus" land had been sold. Of the allotted land, only 425,000 acres remained restricted and owned by the allottees. An incredible nine-tenths of the allotted lands had been lost.

Also in 1946, a group of full-blood Cherokees, under the authority of the Oklahoma Indian General Welfare Act, organized the United Keetoowah Band of Cherokee Indians in Oklahoma (UKB). Their application was approved, and they received a federal charter and corporate papers. They were also added to the list of federally recognized Indian tribes. Their constitution called for an elected chief, assistant chief and council. The first chief of the UKB was Levi Gritts.

And in 1946, in response to the urgings of the NCAI, the U.S. Congress created an Indian Claims Court. Indian tribes could take their claims directly to this court and not have to petition Congress as in the past.

At the NCAI convention held in Oklahoma City in 1946, Chief Milam was elected treasurer of that organization.

In 1948, Milam called a national convention at Tahlequah for the purpose of organizing the Executive Committee of the Cherokee Nation. After much discussion, the committee was formed and members were selected. It was made up of W.H. Sunday of Cooweescoowee District, Ben Smith of Delaware District, Eldee Starr of Tahlequah District, J. B. Sixkiller of Flint District, Hill Stansill of Goingsnake District, William Peak of Sequoyah District, Dan Coodey of Illinois District, O. H. P. Brewer of Canadian District, Amanda Bell of Saline District, C. C. Victory, a member at large, and W. W. Keeler, representing the Texas Cherokees.

In 1949, on May 8, Principal Chief Bartley Milam died at St. Luke's Hospital in Kansas City, Missouri. Much of what he had wanted to accomplish was left undone, yet he had brought the Cherokee Nation a long way on the road back to self-determination.

SOURCE LIST AND SUGGESTIONS FOR FURTHER READING

Hale, Duane K. 1992. "Uncle Sam's Warriors: American Indians in World War II." *Chronicles of Oklahoma* 69, no. 4:408–29.

GLOSSARY

BIA. The Bureau of Indian Affairs. Originally established under the War Department, this federal agency, which deals directly with federally recognized Indian tribes, is now located in the Department of Interior.

Camp Gruber. United States Army base in Cherokee County, Oklahoma.

Cherokee Seminaries Students Association. An organization made up of former students of the Cherokee Male and Female Seminaries.

Civilian Conservation Corps. A federal program under the Franklin Roosevelt administration's "New Deal."

Condemn. Legally, regarding property, to acquire ownership of for a public purpose.

Cookson. Area in eastern Oklahoma, so-called because of the Cookson Hills.

Cooweescoowee. The Cherokee name of a bird, possibly a white water fowl, presumed to be extinct. Also the Cherokee name of Chief John Ross. One of the nine voting districts of the Cherokee Nation was named this for Chief Ross.

Green Leaf Hills. An area of the Cookson Hills near the border between the Cherokee Nation and the Creek Nation.

Kenwood. A Cherokee town in Delaware County, Oklahoma; also the area around that town.

Matrices. Plural of matrix, a mold for casting typefaces.

NCAI. National Congress of American Indians.

OIGWA. Oklahoma Indian General Welfare Act.

Per capita. By or for the individual person.

Seven Clan Society. Cherokee traditionalist group with a stomp ground near Proctor, Oklahoma.

Tie hacking. Cutting railroad ties.

United Keetoowah Band of Cherokee Indians in Oklahoma. (UKB) Band of Cherokees organized under the OIGWA, with an elected chief, deputy chief and council, and a tribal roll. The UKB is on the list of federally recognized Indian tribes and is headquartered in Tahlequah.

CHAPTER TWENTY-SEVEN

Renaissance

In 1947, the Hoover Commission on postwar governmental reorganization, signaling yet another reversal in federal Indian policy, had recommended in its Task Force Report that American Indians be integrated "into the mass of the population as full, tax-paying citizens." Two years later, in 1949, President Harry Truman appointed W. W. Keeler Principal Chief of the Cherokee Nation. The former member of Chief Milam's Executive Committee representing the Texas Cherokees, Keeler was also, by 1949, manager of the refining department of Phillips Petroleum Corporation with headquarters in Bartlesville, Oklahoma. In 1951, he was elected vice president of the executive department and to the board of directors.

In 1953, the official Indian policy of the U.S. government became the termination of the special relationship of the federal government with American Indian tribes. That meant that the government would cease to recognize Indian tribes and cease to deal with them as separate, "domestic" and "dependent" or otherwise. It would mean an end to the treaty rights of the tribes and to the treaty obligations of the United States. It would mean, as the supporters of the policy were fond of saying, "an end to the Indian problem."

In 1954, Chief Keeler became a member of the executive committee of Phillips.

As a part of its termination policy, the federal government came up with what it called the "Relocation Program" for Indians. The theory was that in order to get Indians ready for the termination of their own tribal governments and for their own individual roles as assimilated U.S. citizens, they needed to be moved out of their rural enclaves, reservations or otherwise, and settled in cities across the United States. One of the many Cherokee families relocated during this period was that of Wilma Mankiller, later to become Principal Chief, from the Rocky Mountain community in Adair County, Oklahoma. Like many other Cherokee families, they were relocated to the West Coast, adding to the already significant Cherokee population there.

The federal government went at termination with a vengeance, terminating its relationship with over one hundred tribes over the next thirteen years. In the process, over a million acres of Indian land were lost.

Milligan says, based on an interview with Keeler, "Duties with Phillips took Keeler out of the country for increasing periods, so in 1954 Keeler resigned as chief, suggesting to the Secretary of the Interior who made the appointments that he 'Get a full-blood chief,' one who speaks Cherokee fluently.'

"Much to his surprise the full-bloods of the Cherokee Nation petitioned the Dept. of the Interior to keep Keeler as chief. He agreed, promising to stay until the Cherokees attained the right to vote for their leader." But the actual relationship of Chief Keeler and the full-bloods remains a subject of much controversy.

In 1956, Chief Keeler became executive vice president of Phillips, and in 1962, chairman of the executive committee. The year 1962 also revealed the beginnings of another shift in the direction of federal Indian policy, for under the administration of President John F. Kennedy, Indian tribes became eligible for funds under the Manpower Development and Training Act.

In 1966, a Cherokee hunter named John Chewie appeared in court in Jay, Oklahoma, to defend himself against charges of hunting out of season and without a license. The case attracted a great deal of attention, so much so that, according to Steiner, John Chewie "had, by killing a deer, become the symbol of the Red nationalist rebellion." Chewie did not deny the charges. "He was a full-blooded Cherokee and he would not apologize for hunting on land that rightfully belonged to his people; nor did he have to be licensed like a dog by the state. He had hunted because he was hungry, he told the court; to feed himself and his family."

Four hundred armed Cherokees showed up in Jay on the morning of Chewie's court appearance, waiting to see how the case would turn out. It was held over for federal court, and there was no violence in Jay that day. There had been a public display of Cherokees' insistence on Cherokee rights, a short prelude to a national demand for Indian rights just ahead.

In 1967, Chief Keeler became president and chief executive officer of Phillips. On June 1 of that year, he hired Ralph Keen, a Cherokee, as Business Manager of the Cherokee Nation. Keen says, "In 1967, Indian tribes all over the country were beginning to take charge of their own affairs once more." Other tribes were receiving funds from the Economic Opportunity Act of 1964, but the tribes in eastern Oklahoma were not eligible for those funds. The Cherokee Nation had, however, won a four-teen-million-dollar judgment in the Indian Claims Court.

The fourteen million dollars was to be paid out on a per-capita basis to all of the "original enrollees" on the Dawes Roll or to their heirs, but while this process was underway the money was earning interest. The interest and any unclaimed shares were to be used for tribal programs. With one million dollars in the bank, Chief Keeler and Business Manager Keen set about pursuing some of the unfulfilled dreams of Chief Bartley Milam. The Cherokee National Historical Society was established, inde-pendent from the tribal government, and it acquired the site of the orig-inal Cherokee Female Seminary. Colonel Martin Hagerstrand, a white man married to a Cherokee, was hired as Executive Director, and work was begun on the Cherokee Heritage Center, which would eventually include a museum, an outdoor theater, an ancient village, and other attractions for tourists.

Land owned by the federal government outside of Tahlequah was declared surplus and given to the Cherokee Nation, and on that land the construction of tribal office buildings was begun. At that time, Keeler and Keen also came up with another source of income for the Cherokee Nation. The first building they had constructed was rented to the BIA for its Tahlequah offices.

In 1968, Chief Keeler became chairman of the board and chief exec-utive officer of Phillips. The year 1968 also saw passage in the U.S. Congress of the Indian Civil Rights Act, which imposed most of the pro-visions of the Bill of Rights upon the tribal governments. And in 1968 the Cherokee Nation began publishing *The Cherokee Nation News*, with Ralph Keen as editor. Chief Keeler said that it would "greatly assist in avoiding misunderstanding, misinformation, and often times opposi-tion, because of this communication problem with which I have been concerned ever since I became principal chief."

The year 1968 marked the beginning of a period that has been called an American Indian Renaissance and a time of Indian activism. Cherokee activities in this vein had not been confined to the John Chewie case. The Five County Cherokee Movement had been formed in 1966 with a Declaration that read in part, "We meet in a time of darkness to seek the path to the light. We come together, just as our fathers have always done, to do these things. . . . We offer ourselves as the voice of the Cherokee people. For many years our people have not spoken and have not been heard. Now we gather as brothers and sisters."

"With the help of a few white university researchers," Collier says, "the Cherokees set up a newspaper, began to print Cherokee literature again, and even started a local radio program. . . . By 1967, the spontaneous outrage that had led to the formation of the Five County Cherokee Movement had swept through all the full-blood settlements, and the Original Cherokee Community Organization (OCCO) was organized."

Working out of a rented office in Tahlequah, the OCCO put out a monthly newsletter using a mimeograph machine, filed suits on behalf of Cherokee people whose land was being lost or whose welfare checks were being swindled away from them, and held regular monthly meetings to discuss ways in which to continue their work of standing up for the rights of Cherokees and improving the lot of the Cherokee full-bloods. Questioned about the OCCO, Chief Keeler said, "Oh, I suppose this OCCO group has managed to mislead a few Indians, but it doesn't have but a few people behind it now, this white civil rights man named Trapp and a few others. Anyway, it is just another case of outsiders trying to direct the Indian. It first got started when some university people came down here to teach our Indians their language. I was all for that. But then the first thing you know, I started getting these phone calls saying that these outsiders were telling Indian people to be militant and carry guns" (Collier, "Theft").

In 1969, Indians seized Alcatraz Island, claiming it in the name of "Indians of all tribes." Twenty-four-year-old Wilma Mankiller, who was involved, said later, "They declared it Indian property under the terms of the Fort Laramie Treaty of 1868. That document contained a provision allowing any male Native American older than eighteen whose tribe was party to the treaty to file for a homestead on abandoned or unused federal property."

Vine Deloria, Jr., a Sioux from the Standing Rock Reservation in South Dakota, published *Custer Died for Your Sins: An Indian Manifesto* in 1969 and became an instant celebrity. The book was widely read.

Then, in 1970, the termination policy of the United States was at last replaced "when President Nixon issued a statement on Indian affairs. . . . He declared termination to have been a failure, and called upon Congress to repudiate it as a policy. He stressed the continuing importance of the trust relationship between the federal government and the tribes. Finally he urged a program of legislation to permit the tribes to manage their affairs with a maximum degree of autonomy" (Canby).

Also in 1970, the U.S. Congress, acting in the spirit of the president's message and in response to requests from the five Indian Territory tribes, passed a law that included the following statement: "the principal chiefs of the Cherokee, Choctaw, Creek, and Seminole Tribes of Oklahoma and the governor of the Chickasaw tribe of Oklahoma shall be popularly selected by the respective tribes in accordance with procedures established by the officially recognized tribal spokesman and or governing entity. Such established procedures shall be subject to approval by the Secretary of the Interior." Thus elections were returned to the Cherokee people.

And a U.S. Supreme Court ruling that year confirmed Cherokee, Choctaw, and Chickasaw ownership to ninety-six miles of the bed and banks of the Arkansas River.

In 1971, the Cherokee Nation held its first election for Principal Chief since before Oklahoma statehood in 1907. W. W. Keeler was elected by an overwhelming majority of the voters. Voter eligibility was determined by the Dawes Roll.

SOURCE LIST AND SUGGESTIONS FOR FURTHER READING

Canby, William C., Jr. 1981. *American Indian Law in a Nutshell*. St. Paul: West Publishing Company.

Collier, Peter. 1972. "The Theft of a Nation." *Ramparts*, 36–45.

Deloria, Vine, Jr. 1969. *Custer Died for Your Sins: An Indian Manifesto*. New York: Macmillan.

Gridley, Marion E. 1971. *Indians of Today*. I.C.F.P.

Keen, Ralph. 1993. Statement made at the Cherokee Nation Legal History Class in Tahlequah, transcribed and included in materials for the class.

Littlefield, Daniel F., Jr. and James W. Parins, eds. 1986. *American Indian and Alaska Native Newspapers and Periodicals*, 1925–1970. New York: Greenwood Press.

Mankiller, Wilma P., and Michael Wallis. 1993. *Mankiller: A Chief and Her People*. New York: St. Martin's Press.

Milligan, Dorothy. 1977. *The Indian Way: Cherokees*. Nortex Press.

Steiner, Stan. 1968. *The New Indians*. New York: Harper and Row.

GLOSSARY

Alcatraz. An island off the coast of California in San Francisco Bay. A federal
        prison by the same name was established there and later abandoned.

Assimilation. The act or process of being absorbed or brought into conformity.

Enclave. A country or a portion of a country entirely or almost completely sur-
        rounded by another country.

Five County Cherokee Movement. Grass-roots Cherokee organization of the
        1960s with a goal of asserting Cherokee rights. It led directly to the
        OCCO (see below).

Indian land. Land owned by Indian tribes or individuals for which the U.S. gov-
        ernment holds the title in trust for the owner. Also called restricted land.

OCCO. The Original Cherokee Community Organization. Developed from the
        Five County Cherokee Movement, it had the same goals but was wider
        reaching, partly because of help from university researchers.

Relocation. Government program of the 1950s by which Indians were moved
        from their homes to cities so as to blend in with the general population.

Termination. Federal government policy of ending or terminating the rela-
        tionship between the federal government and Indian tribes. In other
        words, the federal government would simply stop recognizing and deal-
        ing with Indian tribes at all. Legally, Indians would not exist any more.

CHAPTER TWENTY-EIGHT

Self-Determination

Chief Keeler served one four-year term as elected Principal Chief before he retired in 1975. The new tribal headquarters south of Tahlequah, now known as the Keeler Complex, consisted of the BIA building; a tribal office building; a smaller office building that had been rented out to the Cherokee Bilingual Education Program, a private and not a tribal program; a motel with restaurant, bar, swimming pool, and gift shop; a service station (Phillips, of course); and several metal buildings on the back side of the property in which various programs were housed. The Cherokee Heritage Center under the leadership of Colonel Hagerstrand was in full operation, drawing thousands of tourists to Tahlequah each summer to attend the outdoor drama *The Trail of Tears*, or to visit the ancient village and museum. Visitors to Tahlequah often said, "The Cherokees are doing very well indeed."

But the 1970 census figures told a very different tale. Many Cherokee families were still living in abject poverty. Many homes had no running water and no electricity. The average adult Cherokee had five and one-half years of school. And all this in sharp contrast to the description of the Cherokee Nation given by Senator Henry Dawes back in 1887. Sixty-three years of statehood had not been good for the Cherokees. Will Rogers, world famous and universally loved Cherokee humorist, once said, in a seldom quoted comment, "We spoiled the best Territory in the World to make a state."

Keeler decided not to run for reelection in 1975. During his four-year term as an elected chief, he and Phillips Petroleum Corporation had been indicted, tried, and found guilty of having made illegal campaign contributions to Richard Nixon.

More than a dozen candidates filed to run for the office of Principal Chief, but when the time for the election arrived, Keeler postponed it. Well after the filing deadline and even well after the first announced date for the election, Ross O. Swimmer, Oklahoma City attorney, filed for office with a strong endorsement from Chief Keeler. Keeler changed the filing deadline and changed the age requirement. (Swimmer was too young.) Keeler had found the man he wanted to replace him as chief, and Ross Swimmer was elected. The new deputy chief was Perry Wheeler, a funeral director from Sallisaw.

Later that year a constitution was drawn up to supercede the 1839 constitution. It called for elections every four years for Principal Chief, Deputy Principal Chief, and a fifteen-member tribal council. All positions were to be elected at large. The constitution also called for a three-member judicial tribunal to serve as the Cherokee Nation's highest court. The revitalized government of the Cherokee Nation was therefore much like the one that had existed before Oklahoma statehood. It was again a tripartite system with executive, legislative, and judicial branches. The new legislative branch, though, unlike the old one, was not bicameral and was not made up of members elected from different districts. The Department of Interior approved the new constitution, and it was ratified by vote of the Cherokee people in June of 1976.

In 1975, the U.S. Congress had passed the Indian Self-Determination and Education Assistance Act. Under this new law, Indian tribes could contract with either the BIA or the Indian Health Service (IHS) to begin operating for themselves programs that those two federal agencies had been operating for them. The revitalized Cherokee Nation was ready to begin taking advantage of this new law.

In 1976, an important case was decided by the United States District Court, District of Columbia. Known as *Harjo* v. *Kleppe*, the case was heard when "four members of Creek Nation brought action" against the Interior Department for dealing with the Creek Nation only through the principal chief. The Court held that, in spite of the intentions of Congress to "terminate the tribal government of the Creeks," the final termination of the Creek government was never accomplished. "Nothing in the Acts of 1898, 1901 and 1906 or any other legislation abolished the Creek National Council." In other words, in spite of the loss of a tremendous amount of land, the government of the Creek Nation continued in full force. The laws cited were the same laws that were applicable to the Cherokee Nation.

In 1977, the last issue of *The Cherokee Nation News* was published. It was replaced as the official publication of the Cherokee Nation by a new, monthly *Cherokee Advocate*. The first editor of the new *Advocate* was Helen Bennett, a Creek.

That same year, Wilma Mankiller, having returned home from California, went to work for the Cherokee Nation as a program development specialist. It was another election year, and Chief Swimmer was reelected. In 1981, Mankiller was named Director of the new Cherokee Nation Community Development Department. The Bell Community self-help project, which resulted in several rehabilitated homes and a new sixteen-mile water line for the community, received national attention.

In 1978, the American Indian Religious Freedom Act was passed, guaranteeing to Indians the right to practice their traditional religions.

In 1983, Chief Swimmer was once again elected. This time his running mate was Wilma Mankiller, and she became the Deputy Principal Chief of the Cherokee Nation, in spite of considerable opposition to the idea of having a woman in that position. Chief Mankiller recalls, "Although Swimmer had chosen me as deputy and had stuck with me through the rough campaign, there were major differences between us. He was a republican banker with a very conservative viewpoint, and I was a democratic social worker and community planner who had organized and worked for Indian civil and treaty rights. Also, I had been elected along with a fifteen member tribal council that, for the most part, did not support me."

In 1984, the tribal councils of the Cherokee Nation and of the Eastern Band of Cherokees met together for the first time in 146 years in a joint session at Red Clay, Tennessee, the site of the last Cherokee Council meetings before the Trail of Tears.

In 1985, Chief Swimmer was nominated by President Ronald Reagan for the post of Assistant Secretary of the Interior for Indian Affairs, the position formerly called Commissioner of Indian Affairs. The nomination was confirmed by the U.S. Senate, and Swimmer accepted the position. He was two years into his third term as Principal Chief, having held the position for ten years. Therefore, on December 5, 1985, in accordance with the Constitution of the Cherokee Nation, Deputy Chief Wilma Mankiller became Principal Chief of the Cherokee Nation, the first woman ever to hold that constitutional office.

◆

SOURCE LIST AND SUGGESTIONS FOR FURTHER READING

Cherokee Nation, The. 1975. *Constitution of the Cherokee Nation of Oklahoma.* Tahlequah: The Cherokee Nation.

Littlefield, Daniel F., Jr. and James W. Parins. 1986. *American Indian and Alaska Native Newspapers and Periodicals,* 1971–1985. New York: Greenwood Press.

GLOSSARY

Contracting. A process by which an Indian tribe is allowed to take over programs that have been operated for the tribe by a federal agency.

Self-Determination Act. Law passed by the U.S. Congress in 1975. It allowed the contracting by tribes of programs from both the BIA and IHS, and it provided money for Indian education programs.

CHAPTER TWENTY-NINE

The First Woman Chief

When Wilma Mankiller became Principal Chief of the Cherokee Nation there was mixed reaction. On the one hand, there was much praise and acclaim, including a great deal of national attention, for the first woman chief of the second largest Indian tribe in the country. On the other hand, there were complaints, mostly local, about having a woman in that office. There were also many jokes made, mostly outside the Cherokee Nation, about a woman chief with the name of Mankiller.

In 1987, after having fulfilled the balance of Chief Swimmer's term, Chief Mankiller decided to run on her own for reelection. When she had taken over the office from Chief Swimmer, the council had selected from its own ranks, according to the constitution, John A. Ketcher to be the new Deputy Chief, and Chief Mankiller also chose Ketcher as her running mate in 1987. She won the office in a run-off against her opponent, Sallisaw funeral director and one-time Deputy Chief under Ross Swimmer, Perry Wheeler.

In 1988, the Creeks brought another important action to federal court. In *Muskogee (Creek) Nation* v. *Donald Hodel, Secretary, U.S. Department of Interior*, heard by the United States Court of Appeals, District of Columbia, the court stated that the OIWA had repealed the Curtis Act and permitted the establishment of tribal courts. The applicability of this case to the Cherokee Nation was the same as in *Harjo* v. *Kleppe*.

In 1990, in *Ross* v. *Neff*, the United States Court of Appeals, Tenth Circuit, determined that the state of Oklahoma does not have jurisdiction on Indian land.

Also in 1990, Chief Mankiller signed "the historic self-governance agreement authorizing the Cherokee Nation to assume responsibility for funds formerly administered by the BIA" (Mankiller). The Cherokee Nation's new Justice Department was established in 1991, including a Cherokee Nation marshals service, and a new Cherokee Nation court with a tribal prosecutor. Chad Smith, former tribal planner in the Swimmer administration, was hired as prosecutor, and under his direction the Cherokee Nation Tax Commission was established. Because of jurisdictional confusion (a longtime problem) resulting from the land situation in eastern Oklahoma, a cross-deputization agreement was reached between the Cherokee Nation marshals and county sheriffs of Cherokee County, and a Cherokee Nation Code conforming with Oklahoma statutes was adopted.

The Cherokee Nation imposed a tax on tobacco products sold from Indian Smoke Shops, and when the United Keetoowah Band licensed some Smoke Shops of its own, the Cherokee Nation marshals raided the UKB Smoke Shops, confiscating funds and cigarettes. The UKB took the case to court and lost. The courts determined that, though the UKB is a federally recognized Indian tribe, it does not have jurisdiction over any "Indian land." Cherokee Nation licensing and taxing of Smoke Shops was upheld.

Also in 1990, the Cherokee tribal membership reached 100,000. Voting districts were established once again, and, in 1991, the first election making use of these newly established districts took place. Chief Mankiller ran again for reelection. This time she won a landslide victory, receiving 82.7 percent of the votes. At her inauguration ceremony, Chief Mankiller said, "It's a fine time for celebration because as we approach the twenty-first century, the Cherokee Nation still has a strong, viable tribal government. Not only do we have a government that has continued to exist, we have a tribal government that's growing and progressing and getting stronger. We've managed not to just barely hang on, we've managed to move forward in a very strong, very affirmative way. Given our history of adversity I think it's a testament to our tenacity, both individually and collectively as a people, that we've been able to keep the Cherokee Nation government going since time immemorial."

In that same election, a record six women were elected to positions on the Cherokee Nation's tribal council.

In 1993, the Cherokee Nation hosted two historic conferences, both orchestrated by Chad Smith. On September 1, 2, and 3, following a call for papers, twenty-five nationally known scholars gathered at Park Hill on the grounds of the Cherokee Heritage Center to take part in the Cherokee Nation History Convention. And on September 13, 14, and 15, the Cherokee Nation hosted the "1843–1993 International Indian Council." It was 150 years after the council called by Chief Ross in Tahlequah to establish friendly relations with all neighboring tribes.

At that first international council, Chief Ross had said, "Brothers, it is for renewing in the West the ancient talk of our forefathers, and of perpetuating forever the old pipe of peace, and of extending them from nation to nation, and of adopting such international laws as may redress the wrongs done by the people of our respective tribes to each other, that you have been invited to attend the present Council. Let us, therefore, so act that the peace which existed between our forefathers may be pursued, and that we may always live as members of the same family."

The Cherokee Nation's invitation to the 1993 Council reads, in part, "It is in that same spirit of peace, friendship and unity that again, 150 years later, we invite you to this present International Council of American Indian Nations." Three hundred Indians representing 109 Indian tribes showed up to take part in the historic event and to sign a "Resolution of Peace and Friendship."

In 1995, toward the end of Chief Mankiller's ten-year administration and another election year, Chief Mankiller announced that she would not seek reelection for another term. According to *The Tahlequah Daily Press*, she would leave behind a Cherokee Nation with over thirteen hundred employees, 85 percent of whom were Cherokees, with a monthly payroll of 1.6 million dollars; a Cherokee Nation that operates dozens of service programs in housing, employment, health education, and other areas; a Cherokee Nation with over twenty business enterprises in full operation, including Cherokee Nation Industries in Stilwell, Oklahoma; a Cherokee Nation in control of its own finances; a Cherokee Nation with a rejuvenated and fully operable justice system; a Cherokee Nation that is the second largest federally recognized Indian tribe in the United States, with over 150,000 tribal members, a figure that is growing each day; a Cherokee Nation with five rural health clinics and a number of other health programs; a Cherokee Nation with an annual total budget of over 42 million dollars; and a Cherokee Nation in which traditional tribal culture, including the language, is still strong.

When she decided that she would not seek reelection in 1995, Chief Mankiller, like her two immediate predecessors, selected the person she wanted to follow her in office. Her choice was George Bearpaw, a full-blood accountant who had been working quietly for the Cherokee Nation for a number of years. Known by local Cherokees, Bearpaw had never been in the limelight. He seemed an unlikely choice. However, Chief Mankiller put all her energies and resources behind his campaign. Bearpaw's two most serious challengers were Joe Byrd, a full-blood, bilingual, high school counselor and coach and member of the Cherokee Nation Council; and Chad Smith, attorney, former tribal prosecutor, former tribal planner, and direct descendant of Redbird Smith, the great Cherokee nationalist and traditionalist.

The campaign was hard fought and bitter, with accusations being flung in every direction. Even so, with all the power of the previous administration behind him, it looked like Bearpaw would win hands down, and he did come out ahead in the primary, but he failed to receive enough votes to avoid a runoff. The second highest vote getter was Joe Byrd. Chad Smith was third. So the runoff ballots would be prepared with the names of Bearpaw and Byrd on them. Smith was out of the race. As soon as the news of the count was out on election day, Joe Byrd approached Chad Smith immediately, asking for his support in the coming runoff. Standing in the yard behind the Smith campaign headquarters in Tahlequah, Smith looked Byrd in the eyes and said, "Joe, I have a problem with your honesty." Earlier in the day, Bearpaw had dropped by the Smith headquarters to ask Smith how he had spent the day. Smith said that he had been out greeting voters. Bearpaw smiled and said that he had spent the day swimming. It did look very much like George Bearpaw would be the next Principal Chief of the Cherokee Nation.

Then someone broke the news that Bearpaw, a Viet Nam war veteran, had pled guilty to a felony twenty years earlier, thus making him, according to the Constitution of the Cherokee Nation, ineligible to run for office. He had shot a man in the stomach. He had served a period of probation, and then the record had been expunged. Bearpaw maintained that he believed that he was not required to reveal that information because of the expungement. The case was referred to the Judicial Appeals Tribunal, the highest court in the Cherokee Nation. Chief Justice Dwight Birdwell and Justices Ralph Keen (formerly tribal business manager under Chief Keeler) and Philip Viles, a grandson of Chief Milam, declared on the basis of the Cherokee Constitution that Bearpaw was ineligible to run because he had failed to disclose that he had in fact pled guilty to a felony when he had filed to run for office.

In a desperate move to salvage the campaign and her candidate, Chief Mankiller issued a pardon to Bearpaw, but the Tribunal ruled that a Cherokee Nation pardon had no effect as Bearpaw's crime had not been committed under the jurisdiction of the Cherokee Nation. The next morning, a local Cherokee-owned doughnut shop displayed a sign with the following message: "TODAY'S SPECIAL: BEARCLAWS. BUY ONE AND GET A PARDON FREE." Mankiller and Bearpaw had tried everything to no avail. Bearpaw was out.

The Chad Smith camp then petitioned the Tribunal to order that the runoff be postponed and new ballots printed with the names of Joe Byrd and Chad Smith on them, but in the end the justices ruled that the runoff would proceed as scheduled with the ballots as printed, but "no votes for Bearpaw would count." Justice Viles dissented. The other two had handed the election to Joe Byrd by default, but they would live to regret their action.

SOURCE LIST AND SUGGESTIONS FOR FURTHER READING

"Faces of Progress in Cherokees." 1994. *The Tahlequah Daily Press,* April 24.
Mankiller, Wilma, and Michael Wallis. 2000. *Mankiller: A Chief and Her People, Revised Edition.* New York: St. Martin's Press. (A new chapter covering the Joe Byrd years has been added.)

GLOSSARY

Smoke Shops. Shops that sell tobacco products on Indian land and may therefore be exempt from state tobacco taxes.

CHAPTER THIRTY

"What Do They Want with This Old Building?"

The first two years of Chief Byrd's administration were relatively calm and uneventful. There were complaints, but there always were. People said Byrd was not doing anything. People said that he would promise anything and then not follow up. The biggest public controversy came when the term of Chief Justice Birdwell expired. Chief Byrd was expected to reappoint Birdwell, but he dragged his heels on the issue making various excuses. It seemed strange. After all, Birdwell and Keen had made him Chief. (And Birdwell and Byrd were related to one another.) At last Byrd made the reappointment, but he did not reappoint Birdwell Chief Justice. He appointed Birdwell back to the Tribunal but made Ralph Keen Chief Justice. Another strange move. Joe Byrd was beginning to display his main characteristic: strange, seemingly inexplicable behavior.

But Council member Barbara Starr Scott suspected more. She suspected financial wrongdoing and requested some financial records. Her request was denied. The records, she maintained, were supposed to be public access records, and certainly, she, as a member of the Cherokee Nation's legislative body, should be able to examine them. Still she was denied access to the records. Frustrated, she went to Tribal Prosecutor Diane Blalock. (Chad Smith had resigned from the position in order to

run for office.) Blalock asked Ralph Keen to issue a search warrant for the
records in Byrd's office. On February 24, 1997, Keen, Chief Justice of the
Cherokee Nation's Judicial Appeals Tribunal, the highest Cherokee court,
with the final word on interpreting the Constitution, still made up of
Justices Keen, Dwight Birdwell, and Philip Viles, issued the warrant and
gave it to Pat Ragsdale, head of the Cherokee Nation's Marshal Service.

On the morning of February 25, acting under orders from the
Nation's highest court, the marshals carried out a search of the tribal
administrative offices and seized the records under question long
enough to make copies, leaving the originals in place. Chief Byrd reacted by firing Ragsdale and Lt. Sharon Wright. The Judicial Tribunal
declared the firing to be illegal, in effect reinstating the marshals, and
declaring that anyone interfering with the Court's orders and/or the
investigation would be charged with contempt of court. At a press conference called by Byrd on February 26, Byrd declared, "There is no need
for an investigation because absolutely no money has been misused." He
said further, "I can decide which orders of the court are constitutional."
Phone service to the marshals' headquarters was cut off and locks were
changed, so the marshals relocated to the Cherokee Court House in
downtown Tahlequah. The court house had been built originally back in
1873 as a national capitol for the Cherokee Nation. At statehood it had
been taken over and used as the court house of the new Cherokee
County, Oklahoma. Under the Swimmer administration, ownership of
the building and the square block on which it sits was returned to the
Cherokee Nation, the government of which had by then far outgrown
the building. The new "Tribal Complex" was four miles south of
Tahlequah, so the Cherokee Nation chose to house its newly activated
judicial branch in the old capitol building. It was put under the control
of the Judicial Appeals Tribunal and the justices and the tribal prosecutor set up their offices there.

So with a standoff between the two branches of government shap-
ing up, the justices and the marshals were holding on to the old capitol,
now being called the Court House. The administration was still firmly in
control at the Tribal Complex. The justices ordered Chief Byrd to appear
in court. He failed to show. They cited him for contempt of court and set
a new court date. Still he refused to appear. They issued warrants for his
arrest for contempt of court and for obstructing justice.

Byrd, with eight of fifteen council members siding him, formed a
"court of impeachment" to have the justices impeached. The Tribal
Council met on May 3, 1997. Deputy Chief Garland Eagle declared the
meeting to be in session. He further declared that it was not a council

meeting but a court of impeachment, and as he was presiding over the "court," he was the highest judge in the Cherokee Nation. Chad Smith, representing six of the boycotting council members, stood up from the crowd and called, "Point of order." Eagle declared Smith out of order and had him forcibly removed from the Council chambers. The "court" impeached the justices, found them guilty, and removed them from office.

The Cherokee Constitution required that ten council members be present before any meeting could take place, and only eight members, known as the Byrd "loyalists," were present for the "impeachment court," so both the meeting and the impeachment were illegal. Nevertheless, the Byrd administration proceeded as if the impeachment had been valid. When asked later about this illegal meeting, Byrd said that the Constitution was outdated and needed to be revised. He also stated publicly that he would obey the Constitution when he believed it to be right. He hired new "marshals," bought new police cars and new weapons. He set up a new "court" at the Tribal Complex.

The justices and the marshals, taking directions from the justices, still held the Cherokee Court House in downtown Tahlequah, still pursued legal avenues, still stayed on the job—without pay. With two rival marshal services, both armed, people began to fear an explosion of violence. Apparently Chief Byrd had the same fear. He called the Bureau of Indian Affairs and requested that they send BIA police to protect the Cherokee Nation. He said that a "renegade marshal" was planning a "Rwandan type coup" against his administration. The BIA responded to his request without bothering to investigate the situation or question his claims. BIA police moved into the Tahlequah Holiday Inn Express and took over law enforcement for the Cherokee Nation. Neither the original marshals nor Byrd's new marshal service were allowed to carry weapons. Byrd's new marshals became "security guards."

On June 20, 1997, in the predawn hours, while one female deputy marshal was on duty in the Cherokee Court House, Byrd's security guards, "apparently aided by the BIA and local law enforcement" staged a surprise raid and took over the Court House. A crowd of concerned Cherokees gathered across the street from the square. Police tape was stretched around the entire square, declaring it "off-limits." Chad Smith, in front of the crowd, looked over his shoulder and asked, "Whose Court House is this anyway?" The crowd answered him with calls of "It's ours," and "It's the Cherokee people's." Then Smith said, "Well, let's go and ask for it back." He broke the tape and led the crowd onto the square. An officer ran up and tackled Smith from behind, taking him to the ground. Four other officers joined him. They handcuffed Smith, arrested him, and took him to jail where he was charged with assaulting an officer and inciting a riot. (Cherokee artist Wendell Cochran commented, "Obviously Chad's guilty. He attacked that man with his back.") On July 9, Byrd fired tribal prosecutor Blalock.

The May-June issue of the *Cherokee Advocate* came out with a front-page story entitled "Constitutional Crisis Continues, Issue Moves to Federal Court." The article read, in part, as follows:

> In a May 3 court proceeding held by eight members of the tribal council, the three member judicial branch was impeached. The next day the justices said the court proceeding was illegal because the council failed to meet a quorum as called for by the tribe's constitution. The justices have vowed to stay in office.
>
> But Principal Chief Joe Byrd and the majority of the tribal council called the impeachments final, and say they are not recognizing orders or decisions coming from the former tribunal members....
>
> The tribunal issued arrest warrants on May 27 for Chief Byrd and Deputy Chief J. Garland Eagle because they did not appear for a court hearing that morning....
>
> Because the Cherokee marshals were under a restraining order, the tribunal requested the BIA carry out the arrests, but the BIA officers informed the tribunal they would submit the order to the solicitor's office of the Department of Interior to determine if the orders are valid.... The solicitor's office has yet to reach a decision.

In spite of the fact that the reporting seemed fair and balanced, *Advocate* editor Dan Agent had just time to get out one more issue of the paper before Chief Byrd fired him and all of his staff except the department's clerk typist. "The layoffs followed months of tension," Agent said, "between the *Advocate* staff and Principal Chief Joe Byrd, whose administration has been marked by allegations of financial misconduct, a federal investigation, lawsuits, and outrage from many Cherokees over Byrd's attempted removal of the Cherokee Nation Judicial Appeals Tribunal—which is comparable to President Clinton attempting to impeach the U.S. Supreme Court. In addition, Byrd fired the tribal prosecutor and the entire tribal marshal service, representing virtually every Cherokee official charged with enforcing Cherokee law."

On August 10, the Judicial Appeals Tribunal ordered the "fired" marshals to take back the Cherokee Court House at noon on August 13, 1997. Apparently reacting to that news, Chief Byrd swore in ten new marshals on August 12. Although the U.S. Department of Justice and the U.S. Department of Interior had both recognized the Tribunal as the legal Cherokee high court, the BIA police continued to refuse to enforce the Tribunal's orders. On August 13, Pat Ragsdale and the remaining legitimate marshals were sworn in as bailiffs of the court to serve a legal court eviction requiring Byrd's security forces to vacate the Cherokee Court House.

Possibly anticipating an unpleasant confrontation, Michael Anderson, signing for Ada Deer, Assistant Secretary of the Interior for Indian Affairs, issued a statement of the Bureau's position. The BIA, he said, "has assumed exclusive responsibility for tribal law enforcement for the Cherokee Nation . . . no one other than BIA law enforcement officials is authorized to enforce tribal law. Persons other than BIA officers who purport to have such law enforcement responsibility could expose themselves to legal liability." He went on to say that the Court House in downtown Tahlequah was under the jurisdiction of the Tahlequah City Police and the Cherokee County Sheriff's Department. Copies of the statement were sent to Chief Joe Byrd; Cherokee County Sheriff Delena Goss; Tahlequah Police Chief Norman Fisher; Mr. Charles W. (Chuck) Shipley, Attorney for the Judicial Appeals Tribunal; Pat Ragsdale, Head of the Cherokee Nation Marshal Service; and Jim Fields, Area Director, Bureau of Indian Affairs, Muskogee Office. Then followed the confrontation of August 13, 1997.

Rob Martindale of the *Tulsa World* called it "perhaps the darkest day in the modern history of the Cherokee Nation." Knowing that the Cherokee Nation marshals were going to attempt to retake the Cherokee Court House, believing that they would be met by resistance by the Chief's men, and having heard the position of the BIA, around three hundred Cherokee people gathered on the Court House square on the morning of the thirteenth in anticipation of the expected events. Chad Smith and Dan Agent were there. It was not a crowd of rabble rousers. Rather, it was a crowd of concerned Cherokee citizens, including such respected Cherokees as Bridge Chuckluck, Cherokee Baptist minister and former Director of the Cherokee Baptist Association. Barbara McAlister, internationally known Cherokee opera singer, was in the crowd. There were men and women of all ages.

As the crowd waited anxiously for the appointed time, there was no sign of the Cherokee Nation marshals, although there was plenty of other police presence. A large number of Oklahoma state highway patrolmen stood in line on the other side of Water Street across from the south side of the Cherokee Court House. At the back door of the building on the concrete porch were Cherokee County sheriff's deputies. Deputy sheriffs from Sequoyah County, Tahlequah City Police, and Bureau of Indian Affairs police were also very much in evidence. Altogether there were at least fifty police officers of various kinds.

People milled around visiting with one another, speculating on what might happen when twelve o'clock arrived. "Where's Pat and the marshals?" someone asked, referring to Pat Ragsdale, Head of the Cherokee Nation Marshal Service. Someone guessed that they were in a small house across Keetoowah Street, the former campaign headquarters of Chad Smith, occupied by Linda Turnbull-Lewis, Smith's former campaign manager. "Where are the justices?" someone asked, and the response was, "Maybe they're over there too."

The tension mounted as noon drew closer. No gunplay was anticipated, as the BIA had sent down word that anyone showing up with weapons would be liable for prosecution. The only weapons showing were in the hands of city, county, state, and federal police officers. In addition, over the last several months, Ragsdale and the marshals had shown remarkable restraint, too much, some had said, demonstrating on more than one occasion their tendency to avoid any violent confrontation with the forces of the administration.

Then, a few minutes after noon, Ragsdale and the other nine marshals at last made their appearance, uniformed but unarmed. They came out the front door of Turnbull-Lewis's home-office and crossed the street walking onto the square. The crowd gathered around them. Ragsdale stopped long enough to talk to some of the crowd. He urged them to move back and remain calm. Above all, he said, they should avoid any physical confrontation. "We don't want anyone to get hurt or go to jail," he said. He had said that before on more than one occasion since the beginning of this thing the newspapers had been calling a "constitutional crisis."

The crowd was thick around the marshals as they moved to the back door of the Cherokee Court House and Ragsdale went inside alone. The other marshals remained outside on the lawn. Someone said, "They're probably in there trying to cut a deal." When Ragsdale came out the back door, he was followed by a BIA police officer. He stopped on the porch, turned, and shook hands with the officer. Both were smiling and seemed friendly. Ragsdale then went down the steps and back out on the lawn to rejoin the other marshals. Then he more or less confirmed the latest speculation in the crowd.

"We've been talking inside," he said. "We're going to take a thirty minute break and then talk some more." People in the crowd speculated about the purpose of the thirty-minute break. Someone suggested that perhaps those inside the building had made a proposal that Ragsdale lacked the authority to answer. He would have to talk to the justices. At any rate, the thirty minutes dragged on to an hour. Then the word went around the crowd that the Chief's men inside the building had said that Ragsdale and the marshals could come inside. A few minutes later, Ragsdale once again headed for the back door, this time followed by the rest of the marshals.

As Ragsdale walked up the steps to the back porch, the other marshals close behind him, the crowd pressed around the porch. Reporters with cameras followed close behind. Others from the crowd pressed against them, moving up the steps. Ragsdale knocked on the back door. Suddenly the Chief's men began pushing from inside the building, and the crowd pressed from outside on the porch. Ragsdale went down. Cameramen stretched their arms high, aiming their cameras down to gets shots of the doorway. The fight was on.

There was sudden and violent jostling, shoving, scuffling, and a few fists flying. Policemen flung women and men alike backward off the porch and down the concrete stairs onto the paved parking lot below. There was screaming and shouting. Unarmed Cherokee Nation marshals who had just been standing there waiting to go peacefully into the building were grabbed from behind by sheriff's deputies and dragged backward down the stairs. People farther back in the crowd, down on the parking lot, were screaming desperately at the police to stop. One young woman, near hysterics, was shouting and crying at the same time. One policeman reached for the gun at his side, but fortunately restrained himself from actually pulling it out.

Cherokee Nation Marshals, those who had been flung bodily from the porch, far from entering the fray to fight back or urging the crowd on, turned to face the crowd behind them, held up their arms, and called for restraint. "Back off," they shouted. "Please. Calm down." At last a degree of calm was restored, but not before at least six people had been injured, one taken to the hospital. The police were on the porch. The crowd was down in the parking lot shouting at the police. "This is a tribal matter," they said. "What are you doing here. You have no business here."

Paul Thomas, head of the Cherokee Elders Council, an advisory group to the tribal government, got on the steps between the police and the crowd. He tried to quiet the crowd, but they shouted him down. "You haven't done anything in all this time," someone shouted at him. Jess Bryant, former candidate for the office of Deputy Principal Chief and owner of Bryant's Donut Delight in Tahlequah, joined Thomas. In a forceful and commanding voice, Bryant tried to quiet the crowd—to no avail. "Let's go over to the gazebo and talk," he said. The gazebo was in front of the square toward Keetoowah Street. It would have been well away from the back porch. So few took his advice that Bryant didn't even bother going to the gazebo himself. Reverend Chuckluck, whose son was one of the marshals thrown from the porch, climbed up the stairs and faced the crowd. "We are a peaceful people," he cried, and then sweeping his arm toward the police behind him, he added, "These are men of violence." He urged the crowd not to fight, because it would be "billy clubs and guns against flesh and bones."

At last the crowd broke up into smaller groups, some few going on toward the gazebo, some going around to the front of the building, most staying in the back parking lot. At the front of the building, the door was guarded by Cherokee County and Sequoyah County deputies, BIA police, and Oklahoma highway patrol. Reverend Chuckluck moved around to the front of the building, carefully leading his nearly blind wife. He said he wanted to talk to those policemen. He accused them of police brutality, and told them that he had seen a policeman throw a woman backward down the stairs.

"Who was it?" a deputy said.

"I don't know," said Chuckluck.

"Find out and file a complaint," the deputy said.

When asked why they were even there interfering in tribal affairs, the deputies responded, "You'll have to ask our boss. We're just doing what we were told to do." Someone in the crowd compared that to what the Germans said after World War II. Then the word circulated among the crowd that Pat Ragsdale and Diane Blalock had both been injured and arrested. Ragsdale was charged with assaulting an officer, presumably at the back door when the fighting broke out and he went down under the feet of the pressing crowd. Blalock had sometime during the fray gone to the front of the building and attempted to gain entry there. Finding the door locked, she had broken a window but had been stopped by officers before she could climb through. She was charged with "willfully damaging property."

It was two o'clock in the afternoon before it was all over and quiet. Richard Mankiller, brother of former Principal Chief Wilma Mankiller, looked on the Cherokee Court House with a long face. "I want you to take a good look at that," he said. "That's our capitol building. This is what it's come to." A young woman wandered onto the square a few minutes later, and she said, "What's this all about? What do they want with this old building anyway? Why is it so important?"

◈

SOURCE LIST AND SUGGESTIONS FOR FURTHER READING

Agent, Dan, 1998. "Cherokee Removal: News Staff Let Go in Crisis." In *From the Front Lines: Free Press Struggles in Native America*, ed. Karen Lincoln Michel. Minneapolis: Native American Journalists Association.

Cherokee Advocate. 1997. "Constitutional Crisis Continues, Issue Moves to Federal Court." May-June. Tahlequah: The Cherokee Nation.

Martindale, Rob. 1997. "Cherokee Dispute Erupts in Violence." *Tulsa World*, August 14.

GLOSSARY

Assistant Secretary of the Interior for Indian Affairs. Position in the federal government appointed by the president of the United States. Head of the Bureau of Indian Affairs, formerly called Commissioner of Indian Affairs.

Cherokee Baptist Association. Full name, Cherokee Indian Baptist Association, an organization of Indian Baptist churches (at one time with as many as one hundred member churches) founded in 1869, almost certainly with the involvement, perhaps at the instigation of, Rev. John B. Jones. It is still active and has held annual meetings at the Cherokee Indian Baptist Assembly Grounds near Tahlequah for over 130 years.

Cherokee Elders Council. An advisory group of Cherokee elders, organized under the administration of Chief Wilma Mankiller.

Coup. A blow or stroke, sometimes short for coup d'etat, a sudden action in politics, usually resulting in a change of government. From the French, lit., cut, or cut of state.

Impeach. To accuse a public official of misconduct before an appropriate tribunal. Impeachment is not removal from office. If one is found guilty at an impeachment trial, then he may be removed from office.

Point of order. A question raised as to whether proceedings are going according to parliamentary law.

Quorum. The number of members of a group required to be present in order to transact business.

Rwandan. Of or pertaining to Rwanda, a republic in Central Africa, much in the news in recent years for violent civil unrest.

CHAPTER THIRTY-ONE

"What Greater Gift Can We Give Our Children?"

The rest of the Joe Byrd years were marked by suits and countersuits, charges and countercharges. The BIA police remained in Tahlequah and protected Byrd effectively from the Cherokee Nation's judicial system. Some people were saying, as had others back in the Indian Territory days, that the Cherokee Nation was incapable of taking care of its own problems. The proper answer to that accusation in both cases was that the Cherokee Nation could have managed its affairs right well if the federal government had not interfered.

One result of all the turmoil in the Cherokee Nation was that widespread media attention was focused on the Cherokees for the first time in years. There were stories in the newspapers in Washington, D.C., and in New York City. Secretary of Interior Bruce Babbitt and Attorney General Janet Reno were both drawn into the conflict.

In an attempt to keep Joe Byrd and his eight "loyalists" on the tribal council from passing more illegal acts and resolutions, six other council members began boycotting council meetings to prevent the council from having a quorum and thereby being able to conduct business.

But the Cherokee people had to wait until the next election for any relief from the Byrd administration. Byrd served his full four-year term.

As the time for the election drew nearer, as usual several candidates for the office of Principal Chief emerged. Joe Byrd chose to run for reelection. Chad Smith filed, and selected as his running mate Hastings Shade, full-blood, bilingual, highly respected local teacher, craftsman. and traditionalist. Former Principal Chief Ross Swimmer backed his niece, Meredith Fraley, for the office. And former Chief Wilma Mankiller got behind Pat Ragsdale, the illegally fired Director of the Cherokee Nation Marshals Service.

There was widespread fear that the election would not be honest, and so the Carter Foundation was contacted and agreed to oversee the entire election process. On election day, May 22, 1999, with Carter Foundation people present and visible, voters turned out. No one received the required 51 percent of the votes to win hands down. A runoff was called between Joe Byrd and Chad Smith. The Fraley supporters came over to the Smith campaign that same evening, although Fraley herself, in a surprise move that baffled even her supporters, jumped the fence later to join the Byrd camp. The Ragsdale camp, still backed by Wilma Mankiller, shifted support to Smith, as did Ross Swimmer himself. On July 24, Chad Smith won the runoff with 58 percent of the votes. Hastings Shade defeated his opponent with nearly 60 percent. There was actual dancing in the streets that night.

Smith's inauguration, on August 15, was in itself a historic event. Conducted outside on the square in front of the historic capitol building and open to all, it incorporated the Cherokee language and ceremonials. Chad Smith himself appeared, not in a business suit, but in a traditional Cherokee hunting jacket. The event was attended by a large number of people, and the mood was celebratory, sometimes solemn, and overall jubilant. The following Monday, August 17, 1999, Principal Chief Chad "Corntassel" Smith moved into the offices in the Cherokee Nation's administrative complex. Locks came off of doors and walls came down. The special parking places for the chief and deputy chief were painted over and turned into handicapped parking. Books were opened to the general Cherokee public, and a new open-door policy was established.

On November 12, 1999, Chief Smith issued a progress report to the Cherokee People. It reads, in part, "there were a number of very severe problems in the Cherokee Nation when we took office. Finances were in a mess, there was excessive administration, the Council had been denied financial information, and there was no plan for the future of the Cherokee Nation. We had been in the press almost daily with scandals from an unconstitutional take-over of various departments of the government to illegal wiretapping."

Smith described his "approach to build a better Cherokee Nation" as "thoughtful not reactive," and stated that "our entire administration is to put the Cherokee People FIRST." Smith's report went on to outline accomplishments to date, which included the approval by the Council of a year 2000 budget, the reestablishment of the Cherokee Nation Marshal Service, the conducting of a two-day cultural conference "to plan and address the needs of the citizens," and other items. The thirty-seven-page report went on from there to outline specific plans for the future. Included in those plans was a message from Chief Smith regarding the importance of culture. The following is excerpted from that message:

> What greater gift can we give our children than the sense of identity, the knowledge and strength of our ancestors and the inspiration to live good lives? What greater service can we provide to our citizens than cultural education? It is such an important duty that our elected officials are obligated by the constitution to swear an oath to do everything within their power to promote the language and culture.
>
> The principles and wisdom of our culture, clearly, are the driving forces that have allowed us, as a people, to face adversity, survive, adapt, prosper and excel. It is equally clear that these same principles, wisdom and sense of identity will keep our children in school, off drugs and alcohol, and make them resilient as they grow into happy, productive adults.
>
> The power and spirit of our tribe is its culture. It is the richness of that culture that will allow our children to be strong, proud and fulfilled.

Four years later, Smith again defeated Byrd. In 2003, the marshals who had been opposed to the Byrd administration were awarded Cherokee Medals of Patriotism. The Cherokee Nation had made giant strides, moving from near termination with the Curtis Act to a fully functioning government with all branches active and operating approximately 150 programs with two thousand employees on an annual budget of 320 million dollars. The economic impact of the Cherokee Nation on the state of Oklahoma was more than five hundred million dollars annually.

Currently the Cherokee Nation has 240,000 registered tribal members. Many of them live in the one hundred identified Cherokee communities in northeast Oklahoma, but there are organized Cherokee communities around the country in Washington and Oregon, in California, in New Mexico, Kansas, and Texas. There is even a Cherokee community in Long Island, New York. At a time when much attention is being paid to the loss of Native languages, the Cherokee Nation is proud to boast of somewhere around sixty-eight hundred Cherokee speakers. Even so, Cherokee language programs are offering language courses at various locations around the Cherokee Nation and even in some of the far-flung communities. The Cherokee Nation is strong and vital, and currently it is looking forward with hope to a future of promise.

Even so, history repeats itself. Federal policy changes. Public opinion shifts. The lessons of history instruct on how to respond to challenges and to future attacks. The Cherokee people must always remain alert and vigilant.

SOURCE LIST AND SUGGESTIONS FOR FURTHER READING

Cherokee Advocate. August 1999. (This issue includes coverage of the 1999 inauguration.)

GLOSSARY

Carter Foundation. Foundation established by former U.S. President Jimmy Carter, which, among other things, serves as a watchdog organization over elections where irregularities are feared or anticipated. The 1999 Cherokee Nation election was the first time the Carter Foundation had taken on this task within the boundaries of the United States.

APPENDICES

Principal Chiefs of the Cherokee Nation

Wrosetasetow, 1721–1735. It has also been suggested that this man was sometimes known as Outacite and as Mankiller. He was not, of course, actually a Principal Chief. He was selected as a sort of trade commissioner
to deal with the British colonies. It was an early step toward the position
of Principal Chief and toward central government.

Ama-edohi, 1736–1741. Known in the histories as "Moytoy." In spite of British
claims and the concurrence of many historians that "Moytoy" had been
made "emperor," he was most likely no more nor less than
Wrosetasetow had been, a trade commissioner.

Ammouskossittee, 1741–1753. The son of Ama-edohi, Ammouskossittee was
"appointed" by the British to replace his father after his father's death.
This "trade commissioner" position was evolving into a position as
headman of the Cherokee Nation, but Ammouskossittee was apparently
ineffective, and the Cherokees did not accept him as their leader.
Therefore, his uncle, Guhna-gadoga (known to the British as Old Hop),
became the real power behind the position.

Guhna-gadoga, 1753–1760. Having been the real power during the term of his
nephew, "Old Hop," upon the death of Ammouskossittee, simply moved
into the vacated slot.

Ukah Ulah, 1760–1761. This son of Guhna-gadoga succeeded his father.

Ada-gal'kala, 1762–1778. Recorded by the historians as Attacullaculla, Ada-
gal'kala was known to the British as the Little Carpenter. His reputation
as a diplomat was second to none, but his motives were sometimes

suspect. Having been one of the most influential Cherokees for some time, he saw his chance following the death of Uka Ulah and, with the help of British Superintendent of Southern Indian Affairs John Stuart (Bushyhead), moved in. He referred to himself as the "president" of the Cherokee Nation. It is clear that the position has taken on a new status by this time.

Agan'stat', 1778–1785. In the books known as Oconostota, he was alternately a friend and ally and a rival of his predecessor. He was also a respected War Chief, and along with Ada-gal'kala, had long been one of the most respected men in the Cherokee Nation.

Tassel, 1785–1788. Tassel was treacherously killed by the Americans while under a flag of truce.

Little Turkey, 1788–1804.

Blackfox, 1805–1811. He was removed from office for presenting a removal plan to the U.S. government.

Pathkiller, 1811–1827.

William Hicks, 1827. A mixed-blood and a Moravian convert, Hicks was elected at the first national convention. In our contemporary sense of an elected chief executive, Hicks might be considered the first actual Principal Chief.

John Ross, 1828–1866. Considered by most historians as the greatest of all Cherokee chiefs, Ross presided over the Cherokee government during some of its darkest moments and most difficult times, from the Trail of Tears through the U.S. Civil War, for a period of thirty-eight years, the longest term ever for a Principal Chief. Only his death brought an end to his administration.

William Potter Ross, 1866–1867. W. P. Ross, nephew of Chief John Ross, was appointed by the Council of the Cherokee Nation to fill out the unexpired term of his uncle upon the death of the old chief. When the term expired, Ross failed to win the next election.

Lewis Downing, 1867–1872. Downing was a full-blood and a Baptist preacher. He had moved to the West over the Trail of Tears. Like many other mostly full-blood Cherokees, he served in both the Union and Confederate armies during the Civil War. As Principal Chief, Downing served one full term, won reelection, and died in office.

William Potter Ross, 1872–1875. Downing having died in office, the Council again appointed W. P. Ross to fill out the unexpired term. So Ross, twice Principal Chief of the Cherokee Nation, was never elected to that office.

Charles Thompson (Oochelata), 1875–1879. A half-blood Cherokee, Thompson was a Baptist preacher. Like Downing, he had served in both armies during the Civil War. His main concern as Chief was the intrusion of lawless whites into the Cherokee Nation.

Dennis Wolf Bushyhead, 1879–1888. Bushyhead was three-quarters Cherokee. He made a trip to California with other gold seekers in 1849, but returned to the Cherokee Nation to become involved in politics.

Joel Bryan Mayes, 1888–1891. A mixed-blood, a Methodist, a Mason, and a former Confederate soldier, Mayes died in office. A federal court for Indian Territory was established in Muskogee during his administration. He doubled the amount of money the Cherokee Nation received for the lease of the Cherokee Strip.

Thomas Mitchell Buffington, 1891. Chief Mayes having died in office, the Council appointed Buffington to fill out the term.

Colonel Johnson Harris, 1891–1895. During Harris's term the activities of the Dawes Commission began.

Samuel Houston Mayes, 1895–1899. The brother of former Chief Joel Bryan Mayes, he too was a former Confederate soldier, and he had served as Sheriff of Cooweescoowee District.

Thomas Mitchell Buffington, 1899–1903. Buffington won this, his second term in office, and became the second man to fill the office in two nonconsecutive terms. During this, his only full term and his only elected term, most of his time was taken up with the Dawes Commission.

William Charles Rogers, 1903–1917. Rogers, a former Confederate soldier, was the last elected Chief before Oklahoma statehood. Two years after his election, he was impeached and removed from office by the Council for cooperating too eagerly with the United States on the dismantling of the Cherokee Nation. The Council appointed Frank Boudinot to fill out Rogers's term, but the United States stepped in to reinstate Rogers, thus making him the first presidentially appointed chief. This practice would continue.

A. B. Cunningham, November 8–25, 1919. Presidentially appointed.

Ed M. Frye, June 23, 1923. Presidentially appointed.

Richard B. Choate, October 25, 1925. Presidentially appointed.

Charles J. Hunt, December 27, 1928. Presidentially appointed.

Oliver Hazard Perry Brewer, Jr., May 26, 1931. Presidentially appointed.

William Wirt Hastings, January 22, 1936. Presidentially appointed. (W. W. Hastings Indian Hospital in Tahlequah is named for him.)

Jesse Bartley Milam, 1941–1949. The tide had turned in Washington, and Milam was appointed for more than a day. His appointment was also a "rubber stamp" approval of a Cherokee grass-roots election. Milam worked hard at revitalizing the Cherokee Nation.

William Wayne Keeler, 1949–1975. Keeler was appointed by the president of the United States following the death of Chief Milam. He continued many of Milam's programs (and managed to get credit for them). A controversial figure, Keeler was a part-time Chief who was also Chief Executive Officer (CEO) of Phillips Petroleum Corporation. When the president "returned elections to the Cherokees," Keeler won the office handsomely and served one term as an elected chief.

Ross O. Swimmer, 1975–1985. When both Phillips and Keeler personally were found guilty of having made illegal contributions to Nixon's campaign, Keeler, embarrassed, decided not to run for reelection. His hand-picked successor was Ross Swimmer. Swimmer served two and a half terms, resigning to accept an appointment as head of the Bureau of Indian Affairs.

Wilma P. Mankiller, 1985–1995. Wilma Mankiller had been Swimmer's Deputy Principal Chief, so she automatically became Chief upon Swimmer's resignation. Thereafter she won two elections, so she served two and one half terms, as had Swimmer. During the Mankiller administration, the Cherokee Nation continued to grow and prosper, and Chief Mankiller became an international celebrity, but there was still much controversy at home.

Joe Byrd, 1995–1999. Joe Byrd was not elected. His name was on a runoff ballot with that of George Bearpaw, and the Judicial Appeals Tribunal ordered that no votes for Bearpaw would count. Byrd became Chief by default, and his administration was marked by extreme controversy and unrest.

Chad Smith (Corntassel), 1999– . Chad Smith defeated Byrd to become Principal Chief of the Cherokee Nation following a vigorous campaign. In 2003, he was reelected.

Chiefs of the Western Cherokees

Bowls, 1794–1813. Bowls led a group of Chickamaugas out of the old Cherokee country to settle in Missouri until 1811, when the great earthquake of that year drove them out. They resettled in what is now western Arkansas where they became embroiled in a long and bitter war with the Osages. They established themselves as a Nation separate from the Cherokee Nation and, under the name of the Western Cherokees, were treated with as such by the United States.

Degadoga, 1813–1818. Degadoga was initially War Chief of the Western Cherokees. He advocated the complete extermination of the Osages until he became aware of the U.S. policy to move all Indians to homes west of the Mississippi River. From then on, he worked to unite all Indian tribes and

indeed move all tribes west of the Mississippi River. But he also meant to
keep all whites east of the river. He was engaged in this effort when he died.

Tahlonteskee, 1818–1819. He died in office.

John Jolly, 1819–1838. Jolly was the brother of Tahlonteskee. He was also the
adopted father of Sam Houston. He was chief of the Western Cherokees
when the members of the Cherokee Nation began arriving in the West
following the Trail of Tears.

John Rogers, 1838–1839.

John Brown, 1839 only. He was deposed.

John Looney, 1839. The last chief of the Western Cherokees. While he was
chief, the Western Cherokees were reabsorbed into the larger
Cherokee Nation.

Chiefs of the Texas Cherokees

Chief Bowls, angry at being told once again by the United States to move,
moved with some followers clear south into Texas. They were recognized by the revolutionary government of Texas, but after the Texans
had won their independence from Mexico, with the help of the
Cherokees, the new republic refused to honor the treaty they had
signed, and the Cherokees were driven out of Texas. Bowls, in his eight-
ies, was killed on a Texas battlefield. The survivors scattered, some moving back north to rejoin the Cherokee Nation.

Richard Fields was chief for a time, but he was killed for his part in the ill-
fated Fredonia Rebellion, and Bowls became chief again.

The Confederate Cherokee Nation
and Chief Stand Watie

During the American Civil War, **Stand Watie**, already a general in the
Confederate Army, was elected Principal Chief of the Confederate
Cherokee Nation.

Chiefs of the Eastern Band of Cherokee Indians

Yonaguska, 1838–1839. (Mooney says that after Yonaguska's death, the Eastern Cherokees "knew no other chief than [Colonel William Holland] Thomas until his retirement from active life" in 1870. Colonel Thomas was a white man who had been adopted by Yonaguska.)

Flying Squirrel (Saunooke, Salonita, Kalahu), 1870–1875.

Lloyd Welch, 1875–1880.

Nimrod Jarret Smith (Tsaladihi), 1880–1891.

Stillwell Saunook, 1891–1895.

Andy Standing Deer, 1895–1899.

Jesse Reed, 1899–1903.

Bird Saloneeta (Young Squirrel), 1903–1907.

John Goins Welch, 1907–1911.

Joe Saunook, 1911–1915.

David Blythe, 1915–1919.

Joe Saunook, 1919–1923.

Sampson Owl, 1923–1927.

John Tahquette, 1927–1931.

Jarret Blythe, 1931–1947.

Henry Bradley, 1947–1951.

Osley Bird Saunooke, 1951–1955. Saunooke was also world superheavyweight wrestling champion from 1937 to1951.)

Jarret Blythe, 1955–1959.

Osley Bird Saunooke, 1959–1963.

Jarret Blythe, 1963–1967.

Walter S. Jackson, 1967–1971.

Noah Powell, 1971–1973.

John A. Crowe, 1973–1983.

Robert S. Youngdeer, 1983–1987.

Jonathan L. Taylor, 1987–1995. (The Council of the Eastern Band impeached Taylor and removed him from office.)

Joyce Dugan, 1995–1999.

Leon Jones, 1999–2003

Michell Hicks, 2003– .

◆

Chiefs of the United Keetoowah Band of Cherokee Indians

Congress recognized the UKB in 1946; Constitution, By-Laws and Corporate Charter ratified in 1950.

Jim Pickup, 1946–1954.

Jeff Tindle, 1954–1958.

Jim Pickup, 1958–1968.

Bill Glory, 1968–1979.

Jim Gordon, 1979–1984.

John Hair, 1984–1991.

John Ross, 1991–1998.

Jim Henson, 1998–2001.

Dallas Proctor, 2001–2005.

George Wickliffe, 2005– .

Cherokee Nation Treaties

Chronology

1. Treaty of 1721 with South Carolina. Beginning of treaty relationships between Cherokees and whites. Land ceded, 1,678,720 acres to South Carolina.

2. Treaty of 1730 with North Carolina.

3. Treaty of November 24, 1755, with South Carolina. Land ceded, 5,526,400 acres to South Carolina.

4. Treaty of 1761 with South Carolina.

5. Treaty of October 14, 1768, with British Superintendent of Indian Affairs. Land ceded, 544,000 acres to Virginia.

6. Treaty of October 18, 1770, at Lochabar, South Carolina. Land ceded, 5,888,000 acres to Virginia, West Virginia, Tennessee, and Kentucky.

7. Treaty of 1772 with Virginia. Land ceded, 6,986,800 acres to Kentucky, West Virginia, and Virginia.

8. Treaty of June 1, 1773, with British Superintendent of Indian Affairs. Land ceded, 672,000 acres to Georgia.

9. Treaty of March 17, 1775, with Richard Henderson et al. Land ceded, 17,312,000 acres to Kentucky, Virginia, and Tennessee. (Actually the land was sold to Henderson and Hart's Transylvania Company, and although the transaction was illegal, the United States later held the Cherokees to it.)

10. Treaty of May 20, 1777, with South Carolina and Georgia. Land ceded, 1,312,640 acres to South Carolina.

11. Treaty of July 20, 1777, with Virginia and North Carolina. Land ceded, 1,126,400 acres to North Carolina and Tennessee.

12. Treaty of May 31, 1783, with Georgia. Land ceded, 1,056,000 acres to Georgia.

13. Treaty of November 28, 1785, with the United States (Treaty of Hopewell.) From here on there will be no more treaties with individual states. Land ceded, 4,083,840 acres to North Carolina, Tennessee, and Kentucky.

14. Treaty of July 2, 1791 (Treaty of Holston). Land ceded, 2,660,480 acres to Tennessee and North Carolina.

15. Treaty of February 17, 1792.

16. Treaty of June 26, 1794 (Second Treaty of Holston).

17. Treaty of October 2, 1798 (Third Treaty of Holston). Land ceded, 984,960 acres to Tennessee and North Carolina.

18. Treaty of October 24, 1804 (Treaty of Tellico). Land ceded, 86,400 acres to Georgia.

19. Treaty of October 25, 1805 (Second Treaty of Tellico). Land ceded, 5,195,520 acres to Kentucky and Tennessee.

20. Treaty of October 27. 1805 (Third Treaty of Tellico). Land ceded, 800 acres to Tennessee.

21. Treaty of January 7, 1806 (Treaty of Washington). Land ceded, 4,397,440 acres to Tennessee and Alabama.

22. Treaty of September 11, 1807.

23. Treaty of March 22, 1816 (Treaty of Washington). Land ceded, 94,720 acres to South Carolina.

24. Treaty of March 22, 1816 (Treaty of Washington).

25. Treaty of September 14, 1816 (Treaty of Chickasaw Council House). Land ceded, 2,197,120 acres to Alabama and Mississippi.

26. Treaty of July 8, 1817 (Treaty of Cherokee Agency). Land ceded, 651,520 acres to Georgia and Tennessee.

27. Treaty of February 27, 1819 (Treaty of Washington). Land ceded, 3,802,240 acres to Georgia, Alabama, Tennessee, and North Carolina.

28. Treaty of December 29, 1835 (Treaty of New Echota, the Removal Treaty). Land ceded, 7,882,240 acres to Tennessee, Georgia, Alabama, and North Carolina.

29. Treaty of August 6, 1846 (Treaty of Washington).

30. Treaty of July 19, 1866 (Treaty of Washington). Land ceded, 1,233,920 acres to Kansas.

31. Articles of Agreement between the Cherokee Nation and the Delaware Tribe, April 8, 1867. (Although this is not, technically, a treaty between the Cherokee Nation and the United States, it was instigated by the

United States as a way of relocating these Delawares.)

32. Treaty of April 27, 1868 (Treaty of Washington).

33. Agreement between the Shawnee Tribe and the Cherokee Nation, June 7, 1869. (See comment on no. 31, above.)

34. Agreement with the Cherokee Nation, December 18, 1891 (at Tahlequah). As the U.S. Congress had ordered an end to treaty making with Indian tribes, the government began entering into "agreements" with them instead. The only possible explanation is that Congress took a hard look at the definition of a treaty as an agreement between sovereign nations and decided to further undermine the sovereignty of Indian nations by means of semantics.

35. Agreement with the Cherokee Nation, April 1, 1900.

Western Cherokee Treaties

Treaty of May 6, 1828 (Washington Treaty). Land ceded, 3,020,800 acres to Arkansas.

Treaty of February 14, 1833 (Fort Gibson Treaty).

INDEX

Abingdon, Virginia: 60
Abram of Chilhowie: 60, 64, 74
Ada gal'kala: 26, 30, 36, 40, 46–47, 49, 53–55, 57–59; Attakullakulla: 26
Adair, John: 7, 36, 39, 41, 54
Adair County, Oklahoma: 208, 214
Adams, John Quincy: 150
Agan'stat': 37, 40, 42, 47, 49, 52, 54, 57–59, 64–66, 73; Oconostota: 36, 38
Agent, Dan: 232
Ahuludegi: *See* John Jolly
Akooh: 81
Alabama: 6, 18, 25, 36, 67, 81, 83, 91, 100, 104, 141
Alabama Indians: 140, 144
Alarka: 150
Alcatraz Island: 216, 218
Algonquian Indians: language, 5, 13
American Business College: 207
American Board of Commissioners for Foreign Missions (ABC): 100, 137, 170
American Indian Renaissance: 215
American Indian Religious Freedom Act: 221

American Revolution: 66, 68, 71, 73, 85
Ancoo: 74
Anderson, Michael: 233
Ani-Keetoowahgi: 7, 13
Ani-Kutani: 14, 29
Ani-yunwi-ya: 7, 14
Appomattoc Indians: 20
Appomattox, Virginia: 177
Aquorra: 150
Arkansas: 18, 89, 97–100, 104, 131, 137–38, 157, 161–62, 169, 173–76, 185, 187
Arkansas Cherokee Indians: 159
Arkansas River: 88, 97, 99, 105, 137–38, 169, 217
Arthur, Gabriel: 21–22, 25
Asia: 1–2
Augusta, Georgia: 54, 67
Autonomous: 14
Ayunini: 14

Babbitt, Bruce: 239
Badger: 67, 76
Bakersfield, California: 204
Bartlesville, Oklahoma: 213
Bay of Santa Elena, South Carolina: 19

Beard, John: 77
Bearpaw, George: 225–27
Bearpaw, Thomas: 209
Beasley, Samuel: 90
Beauregard, P. G. T.: 173
Beck, Polly: 186–87
Beck's Mill: 186
Bell, Amanda: 211
Bench. *See* Bob Benge
Benge, Bob (the Bench): 67, 70, 75–78, 157
Bench, James Willis: 209
Benge, John: 67, 155
Bennett, Helen: 221
Bering Strait: 1–3, 14
Big Mush: 140
Big Warrior: 88
Biloxi Indians: 140, 144
Birdwell, Dwight: 229–30
Blackburn, Gideon: 82
Blackfox: 85, 138
Blalock, Diane: 229–30, 232, 236
Bloody Fellow: 67, 76, 81
Blount, William: 75, 77, 79
Blue Circle: 178
Boat: 96
Bonepolisher: 84
Boston, Massachusetts: 136, 168
Boudinot, Elias: 104, 105, 134, 136, 140–41, 160–61, 173, 180, 184–85
Boudinot, Frank: 198
Bowl: 67, 70, 77–78, 88, 105, 138–40, 145
Bowles, John: 159–61
Bradley, Lt. Earl: 209
Brainerd Mission: 100
Brewer, Oliver H. P.: 204, 211
Brewer, Perry: 202
Brown, Catherine: 104
Brown, James: 156
Brown, John: 163
Brown, Lt. Marian: 209

Brown, Richard: 96
Browne, Col. Thomas: 67
Brush Creek. *See* Nighthawk Keetoowah Society
Bryant, Jess: 235–36; Bryant's Donut Delight, 235
Bull Run, Battle of: 174
Bushyhead, Isaac: 162
Bushyhead, Jesse: 155
Butler, Elizur: 134, 154
Buttrick, Rev. D. S.: 100, 153–154
Byhan, Gottlieb: 82
Byrd, Joe: 226–27, 229–30, 232–33, 239, 241

Cabin Creek: 177
Calhoun: 96
California: 2, 169, 204, 218, 221; Southern, 2
Cameron, Alexander: 54, 58–59, 64–65
Camp Gruber: 208, 211
Campbell, Col. Arthur: 67
Canada: 83, 85
Canadian District: 167, 184, 211
Canary Creek: 139
Canby, William: 216
Captain Dutch: 104, 137–39, 163, 165; Tanchee, 107
Carter Foundation: 240, 242
Carter's Valley: 60–61
Catawba: 26, 30, 52
Cavett's Station: 77
Cayuga Indians: 5, 11
Central Africa: 237
Central America: 6
Charlestown, South Carolina: 26–29, 33, 41, 47–49, 52–53, 173
Chatahoochie River: 64
Chatooga: 104
Cheakoneske (Otter Lifter): 76

Cheeoih: 150, 152

Chelsea, Kansas: 205

Cherokee: 14, 217; and alliance with Great Britain, 29, 33; and Christianity, 42; and clan system, 6–7, 37; and Dawes Act, 193–99; Elders Council, 235, 237; and European alliances, 33–37, 39–42, 45–50, 54, 60, 63; and "French and Indian War", 45–50; fur trade, 40–41; government, 106; language, 5, 25, 168, 207, 242; migration legend, 1; Masonic lodge, 168; Medals of Freedom, 241; Mounted Rifles, 175; National Party, 159; Nighthawk Keetoowah. *See* Nighthawk Keetoowah; population, 184; and railroads, 183; removal, 132–35, 141–43, 146–57; and smallpox, 39–40, 43, 47, 49; treaties, 55–57, 73–82, 96, 99, 134, 137–43, 146–51, 163, 179–82; war with Osage Indians, 137; warfare, 51–52

The Cherokee Advocate: 168, 184, 197, 221, 232

Cherokee Baptist Association: 233, 237

Cherokee Bilingual Education Program: 219

Cherokee County, Oklahoma: 145–46, 203, 208, 224, 230, 236

Cherokee County Sheriff's Department: 233

Cherokee Female Seminary: 188, 207, 215

Cherokee Heritage Center: 215, 219, 225

Cherokee Livestock Association: 189

Cherokee Nation: 27, 75–76, 84, 89, 95–100, 103, 132–34, 142, 157–64, 169–70, 176, 179, 189, 196–97, 207, 210, 213–15, 220–23, 242; Constitution, 231; Council of, 82–84, 96–99, 106, 131–34, 141–43, 160–63, 176, 181–85, 188, 198, 226; districts, 167; Executive Committee, 211, 213; Executive Council, 203–4, 221; Grand Council, 161; History Convention, 225; Industries, 225; Judicial Appeals Tribunal, 226, 230, 232–33; Justice Department, 224; Marshal Service, 230, 233–34, 240–41; National Committee, 140; National Council, 203–4; Supreme Court of, 105; Tax Commission, 224

The Cherokee Nation News: 215

Cherokee Nation v. Georgia: 134

The Cherokee Nation News: 5, 14, 221

Cherokee Seminaries Students Association: 210–11

Cherokee Outlet: 187, 189

The Cherokee Phoenix: 105, 140

Cherokee Strip: 184

Cherokee Strip Livestock Association: 187

Cherokee Temperance Society: 168

Cheowa River: 26

Chesapeake Indians: 20

Chester, Elisha: 136

Chetopa, Kansas: 184

Chewie, John: 214–15

Cheucunsenee: 96

Chickahominy Indians: 20

Chickamauga Cherokees: 66–70, 73, 76–77, 82–84, 157

Chickamauga Creek: 66, 70

Chickasawtchee: 96

Chickasaw Indians: 14, 26, 52, 59, 68, 73, 95, 134, 174, 199, 201, 217
Chickasaw Nation: 167, 176, 183
Chicken, George: 27
Chilhowie: 61
Chisholm, Jesse: 168
Choate, Richard B.: 203
Choctaw Indians: 14, 36, 58–59, 68, 73, 90, 134, 139, 174, 199, 217; language, 168
Choctaw Nation: 167, 173, 176, 183
Choowalooka: 156
Chota: 21–22, 26, 30, 45–46, 58, 60, 73; Echota: 26, 107
Christie, Ned: 188–189
Chuckluck, Bridge: 233, 236
Chuculate, Jim: 209
Chulioa: 96
Cilley, Jonathan: 151
Civilian Conservation Corps (CCC). See United States: Civilian Conservation Corps
Clark, Adm. Joseph James: 209
Clarke, Mary Whatley: 79, 139
Clay, Henry: 148
Clermont's Town: 104
Clogittah: 33, 37
Cocke, Maj. Gen. John: 90
Cochran, Capt. Joseph Woody: 209
Cochran, Wendell: 232
Collanah: 33, 38
Collier, John: 204, 209, 216
Commission to the Five Civilized Tribes. See Dawes Commission
Conasauga: 104
Confederate Cherokee. See Pin Indians
Confederate Indian Brigade: 173–74
Confederate States of America: 173–77, 181

Conley, Evelyn Snell: 154
Conley, Robert T.: 177
Conrad, Hair: 155
Coodey, Dan: 211
Coodey, William Shorey: 136, 155, 163
Cooper, William: 29
Coosa River: 36
Coosawattee: 104
Cooweescoowee: 211
Cooweescoowee District: 211
Cornstalk: 59
Cornwall, Connecticut: 104
Coushatta Indians. See Texas Cherokee
Coweta: 90
Cowskin Prairie: 176, 178
Coyatee: 77
Creek Path: 104
Creek Indians: 15, 36, 46, 51, 59, 68, 73, 88–96, 132–34, 174, 196, 199, 217, 221; language, 168
Creek Nation: 96, 105, 167, 173, 184–85, 211, 220
Creek War: 87, 95, 104–5, 142
Crittenden, Franklin B.: 209
Crockett, David: 66, 91, 133
Cumberland River Valley: 26, 30
Comfort, Sgt. William: 209
Cuming, Alexander (Sir): 28–29, 33, 37, 53
Cunne Shote: 56
Cunningham, A. B.: 203
Curtis Act: 197, 223, 241

Daniel, Moses; 156
Davis, Jefferson: 173, 177
Dawes Act: 193–99
Dawes Commission: 193–99, 202; Commission to the Five Civilized Tribes, 195
Dawes, Henry: 193–195, 219

Dawes Roll: 215, 217
Dayunisi: 3, 15
Deer, Ada: 233
Degadoga: 104, 107, 137–38
Delaware County, Oklahoma: 203, 208, 211
Delaware District: 167, 186, 211
Delaware Indians: 6, 15, 59, 139, 184; language, 13; Lenni Lenape, 5, 15
Deloria, Vine, Jr.: *Custer Died for your Sins: An Indian Manifesto*, 216; *Red Earth, White Lies*: 2
Demere, Capt. Raymond: 46
Demere, Capt. Paul: 49
DeRosier, Arthur H., Jr.: 90, 95
De Soto, Hernando: 17–20
District of Columbia: 220, 223
Doublehead: 67, 76–78, 83–85, 142, 173
Dougherty, Cornelius: 22, 41
Dover: 33
Downing, Lewis: 179, 184, 187
Downing, Sequoyah: 209
Downing Party: 184, 191
Dragging Canoe: 57–61, 63–78, 87, 101, 157, 189
Drew, John: 156, 174–75
Dunlap, General: 148
Dutch, Captain: 161
Dutch's Creek: 161, 165
Dwight Mission: 137, 139

Eagle, Garland: 230–31
Eastern Band of Cherokees: 221
Eastern Cherokee Council: 203
Eaton, John: 136
Echoee: 48
Economic Opportunity Act: 215
Edwards, Benjamin: 140

Edwards, Hayden: 140
Elkhorn Tavern, Battle of. *See* Battle of Pea Ridge
Emerson, Ralph Waldo: 148
Emory, Susannah: 49
Etowah: 77
Euchella: 150, 152
Evans, E. Raymond: 59, 63, 67–68, 74, 77, 153
Everett, Edward: 148

Falling, Noah: 209
Fauquier, Francis: 54
Fields, Quanah: 209
Fields, Richard: 140, 163
Five Civilized Tribes: 189, 194–95, 201
Five County Cherokee Movement: 215–16, 218
Five Lower Towns: 67
Flint District: 163, 167, 211
Florida: 18, 27, 59, 64, 73
Floyd, Gen. John: 90–91
Foreman, James: 161
Foreman, Stephen: 163
Fort Dobbs: 46
Fort Gibson: 137, 139, 142, 162, 169–76
Fort Henry: 21–22, 26
Fort Jackson: 95
Fort Laramie Treaty: 216
Fort Loudon: 46–49, 52, 69
Fort Mims: 90
Fort Prince George: 46–49, 52–53
Fort Smith: 137, 169, 179, 185–88
Fort Sumter: 173
Fort Toulouse: 36, 40
Fort Wayne: 173, 178
Fraley, Meredith: 240
France: 20, 27–28, 34–46, 52, 68, 83
Franklin, (Cherokee state of): 74–75
Fredonia, Republic of: 140, 144
French and Indian War: 45–50, 54

French, Laurence: 150

GI Bill: 210
Galun lati: 3
General Allotment Act. *See* Dawes Act
Georgia: 6, 18, 25–27, 36, 40, 54–60,
         64–67, 74, 81–83, 90, 96,
         99–100, 105–6, 132–34, 141,
         146–48, 170, 189; anti-
         Cherokee laws, 133
Georgia Compact (1802): 83, 131
Germany: 37
Gettysburg, Battle of: 176
Ghigau: 61
Gilmer, Gov. George R.: 148
Gist, Nathaniel: 45, 54, 66
Glass: 67, 81, 96, 99
Goingsnake: 155, 167
Goingsnake District: 211
Grant, James: 52
Grant, Ludovic: 41
Grant, Ulysses S.: 177
Graves, Edward: 54
Graves, Thomas: 138
Graves, William J.: 151
Great Britain: 28, 33–36, 40–48, 57,
         60, 68, 73, 85; Army, 87; War of
         1812, 90
Great Buzzard: 3
Great Depression: 204
Green Leaf Hills: 208, 211
Griffin, Lt. Richard: 209
Gritts, Levi: 203, 210
Guadalajara, Mexico: 161, 165
Gulf of Mexico: 83
Gul'kalaski. *See* Junaluska
Guthrie, Oklahoma: 202

Hagerstrand, Col. Martin: 209, 215, 219
Hair, Jim: 209
Hanging Maw: 73, 77–79

Hanks, William, Jr.: 209
Harjo v. Kleppe: 220, 223
Harris, Bird: 196
Harrison, William Henry: 189
Hart, Nathaniel: 57
Hastings, W. W.: 202, 204
Hazard, Oliver: 202
Henderson, Richard: 55, 57–59
Hendrix, Janey B.: 196, 202
Henry, Gov. Patrick: 67
Hicks, Charles: 85, 131–32
Hicks, George: 156
Hicks, E. D.: 193
Hicks, Elijah: 131, 140, 155, 162
Hicks, William: 136
Hildebrand, Peter: 156
Hildebrand's Mill: 186
Hill, Sarah: 41
Hindman, Thomas: 176
Hiwassee: 84
Hiwassee River: 26, 96, 154
HMS Fox: 33
Hogner, Lt. Elsie: 209
Holston: 56, 60
Holston River: 75
Holy Ground, Battle of the. *See* War
         of 1812
Honey Springs, Battle of: 176
Hoover Commission: 213
Hopewell, South Carolina: 74
Hornbuckle, Jim: 150
Hornett, James: 209
Horseshoe Bend, Battle of. *See* War
         of 1812
Houston, Sam: 91, 99–101, 139–40,
         145–46, 160–61
Hubbard, David: 174
Hummingbird, Bill: 209
Hunter, John Dunn: 140

Illinois: 58, 156

Illinois District: 167, 196, 211

Illinois River: 137, 189

Indian Civil Rights Act: 215

Indian Claims Court: 211, 215

Indian Health Service (IHS): 220, 222

Indian John: 21–22

Indian Reorganization Act (IRA): 204

Indian Self–Determination and
    Education Assistance Act:
    220, 222

Indian Territory: 168, 175, 181, 186–89,
    194–99, 201

International Council of American
    Indian Nations: 225

International Indian Council: 225

Iroquois Indians: 5–6

Iroquois Confederacy: 11, 15

Iroquois League: 54

Itsadi: 107

Jack, Samuel: 64

Jackson, Andrew: 83, 96–99, 132–33,
    136, 146–48, 170; and War of
    1812, 90–93

James River: 21

Jamestown, Virginia: 20–23

Jefferson, Thomas: 83–85

Johnson, Andrew: 179

Johnson, N. B.: 210

Johnson, William (Sir): 54

Jolly, John: 83, 99, 101, 137, 139

Jones, Evan: 104, 174

Jones, John: 174, 184

Junaluska: 91, 93

Justice, Dick: 96

Kaneeda: 104

Kansas: 169, 176, 180–81, 184, 241

Kansas City, Kansas: 211

Keeler Complex: 219

Keeler, W.W.: 211, 214–20, 226

Keen, Ralph: 215, 226, 229–30

Keetoowah Society. *See* Nighthawk
    Keetoowah Society

Kennedy, John, F.: 214

Kentucky: 6, 25, 57, 100

Keowee: 25, 28, 30, 46

Kesterson, James: 186–87

Kettagustah: 33

Kee-too-wah Society, Inc: 203–4

Ketcher, John A.: 223

Kickapoo Tribe: 139

King George II: 29, 34, 40, 53

King George III: 53

Kingfisher: 68

Kingfisher, James: 209

Kingsport, Tennessee: 104

Kituwah dialect: 25, 30

Knights of the Golden Circle: 173, 178

Knox, Henry: 75

Knoxville, Tennessee: 77

Knowles, Nathaniel: 65

Kuwa'hi: 8, 15

Lake Chapala: 161, 165

Lake Mohonk Conference: 193

Lamar, Mirabeau B.: 160

Lee, Gen. Charles: 58

Lee, Robert E.: 177

Lewis, Maj. Andrew: 46

Lewis, Meriwether: 89

Lincoln, Abraham: 173, 176

Little Owl: 63, 67, 69

Little Rock, Arkansas: 157

Little Tennessee River: 21, 25, 30, 46,
    58, 74, 150

London, England: 33, 53

Long, Alexander: 1, 17, 105

Long Island, New York: 67, 242

Lookout Town: 67

Louisiana: 90

Louisiana Purchase: 83

Lovely, William L.: 100
Lovely's Purchase: 138, 142
Lower Towns: 25, 28–30, 46–48, 52,
    64–66, 84, 90, 96–97, 174
Lowrey, George: 54, 131–32, 154
Lowry, Col. John: 96
Lumpkin, Gov. Wilson: 141, 148

Mahican Indians: language, 13
Maine: 148
Malaquo: 58, 62; Big Island Town: 58
Malone, Henry Thompson: 85
Mankiller, Richard: 236
Mankiller, Wilma: 214–16, 221–27,
    236–37, 240
Manpower Development and
    Training Act: 214
Maples, Dan: 187–88
Marshal, John: 136
Martin, John: 136
Martin, Joseph: 66
Massachuset Indians: language, 13
Massachusetts: 193
Mathison, Edwin: 209
Maw, Thomas: 138
Mayes, Samuel Houston: 197
Mayes County: 203, 208
McAlister, Barbara: 233
McCoy, Alexander: 131
McCulloch, Gen. Ben: 174–75
McDonald, John: 54, 66–68
McIntosh, William: 90
Meigs, Return J.: 84, 163
Menawa: 90–91, 93
Meriam, Lewis: 206
Meriam Report: 204, 206
Merideth, Howard L.: 203, 205, 207–8
Mexico: 6, 83, 140, 145, 161–62, 196,
    203; Army, 140, 160
Mexico City, Mexico: 140, 163
Middlestriker: 67, 76

Middle Towns: 25, 28–29, 31, 48, 52,
    64–65, 77, 82
Milam, Jesse Bartley: 205, 207–15, 226
Miro, Don Esteban: 73
Mississippi: 18, 90
Mississippi River: 83, 88, 96–99, 132,
    155, 168, 193
Missouri: 78, 88, 169, 174, 211
Missouri, Kansas, and Texas
    Railroad: 184
Mobile, Alabama: 90
Mohawk Indians: 5, 11, 59
Monroe, James: 131
Montgomery, Lt. Jack: 209
Moore, James: 22
Moore, Samuel: 64
Morris, George: 138
Morrison, Captain: 48
Moulton, Gary E.: 157
Mound Builders: 17
Mount Wesley: 104
Moytoy: 28–31, 33, 36–37, 41; Ama-
    edohi: 28
Murrell, George: 182
Muscle Shoals: 74–75, 77
Muskogee (Creek) Nation v. Donald
    Hodel, Secretary, U.S.
    Department of Interior: 223
Muskogee, Oklahoma: 185, 193
Muskogee Indians: language: 5, 15

Nacogdoches, Mississippi: 139
Narragansett Indians: language: 13
Nashville, Tennessee: 68, 79
National Congress of American
    Indians (NCAI): 210–11
Natchez Indians: 196
Neanderthal Man: 2, 15
Needham, James: 21
Neeley's Grove: 104
Neosho River: 171

Neutral Land: 184
New Echota: 106–7, 131, 136, 141, 149
New Madrid, Mississippi: 88
New Mexico: 241
New York: 49, 105
New York City, New York: 239
Nickajack: 67, 71, 79
Nighthawk Keetoowah Society: 16,
 174, 184, 188, 197–203, 210;
 Brush Creek, 203; Yellow
 Locust Fire, 203
Nikwasi: 28, 52
Nipmuc Indians: language, 13
Nixon, Richard: 216, 220
Nolichucky River: 60
North America: 1–2, 6
North Carolina: 3, 6, 19, 25–26, 47,
 54–55, 64–66, 73–75, 81, 100,
 142, 150, 159, 173, 177, 187, 189

Oconeechee Indians: 21–23
Oconostota: 48
Ohio River: 154–55
Ohio Valley: 67
Oklahoma: 18, 100, 137–38, 146, 155,
 188–89, 201–5, 211, 214–17,
 224, 241
Oklahoma City: 211, 220
Oklahoma Indian General Welfare
 Act (OIGWA): 204–5,
 210–11, 223
Oklahoma, University of: 207
Old Field: 156
Old Settlers: 159–63
Old Tassel: 73
Oneida Indians: 5, 11
Onondaga Indians: 5, 11
Ontario, Canada: 90
Oowatie, Buck. See Elias Boudinot
Opothleyahola: 173, 178
Oregon: 204, 241

Original Cherokee Community
 Organization (OCCO): 216, 218
Osage Indians: 142, 171
Osage Nation: 99–100, 104, 138–39
Ostenaco: 45–46, 50, 52–53
Ottawa Indians: 62
Oukah–Ulah: 33
Oukanekah: 34–35, 38; Ada
 Gal'kala: 33
Ounankannowie: 33, 38
Overhill Cherokees: 78
Overhill Towns: 24, 26–31, 46, 58,
 64–67, 73–74
Owen, Robert Latham: 202
Owens, Susanna: 209

Pamunkey Indians: 20–21,23
Pardo, Juan: 19
Park Hill, Oklahoma: 163, 168–69,
 175–76, 179, 207, 225
Paris, Ben: 209
Paris, France: 68
Parsons, Francis: 53
Pathkiller: 96, 132
Pea Ridge, Battle of: 175
Peak, William: 211
Pearis, Richard: 54, 58
Pegg, Thomas: 181
Pequot Indians: language, 13
Petersburg, Virginia; 21
Philadelphia, Pennsylvania: 76, 105,
 176, 179
Phillips Petroleum Corporation:
 213–15, 219–20
Pike, Albert Sidney: 173, 175
Pin Indians: 174–75, 178, 180–84
Pinckney, Maj. Gen. Thomas: 90
Pocohontas: 20, 69
Poinsett, Joel R.: 154
Polk, James K.: 163
Pope County, Arkansas: 137

Potomac Indians: 20
Pouting Pigeon: 53
Powhatan Confederacy: 20, 23
Powhatan Indians: 21, 23
Princeton University: 183
Proctor, Johnson: 187
Proctor, Zeke: 186–87
Prophet. *See* Tenskwatawa
Pumpkin Boy: 67
Pushmataha: 90

Quinton, Bennie: 209

Ragsdale, Pat: 230, 233, 234–35, 240
Raven of Chota: 60, 64
Reagan, Ronald: 221
Red Clay, Tennessee: 136, 221
Red Crawfish (Tsiska gili): 4
Red Eagle (William Weatherford):
    87, 90
Red River: 138–39, 169
Red Sticks: 89–94, 96, 132
Red Stick War: 91–93, 95–96
Redbird Smith: 193, 197–98, 202–3, 226
Redbird Smith Movement: 196–99
Reece, Charles (Whale): 92
Reno, Janet: 239
Reynolds, Joshua (Sir): 53
Rider, Suel: 163
Ridge, John: 136, 139, 141, 160
Ridge, (Major): 84, 87–92, 96, 104, 131,
    141, 143, 147, 160
Rodgers, William: 136
Rogers, Clem: 202
Rogers, James: 141
Rogers, John: 138
Rogers, Will: 202, 219
Rogers, William C.: 198–99, 202–3
Rogers County: 209
Rolfe, John: 20
Roosevelt, Franklin: 204

Roosevelt, Theodore: 202
Ross, Andrew: 136, 141
Ross, John: 91, 96, 104, 131–34, 141,
    146–51, 154–62, 169–71, 174–86,
    211, 225; death of, 182
Ross v. Neff: 224
Ross Party: 162, 184
Ross, William Potter: 183, 185, 194
Royce, Charles C.: 55
Running Water: 67, 77–79
Rutherford, Gen. Griffith: 64

Sacajawea: 69
Saline District: 167, 211
Sallisaw: 220, 223
Sander, Soldier: 209
Santa Elena: 19, 23
San Felipe: 19
San Francisco Bay: 218
Sara Indians: 19, 23; Cheraw: 19
Saunders, Alex: 84
Savannah River: 25, 31, 46
Savanooka: 57
Saxony: 36, 38
Scott, Barbara Starr: 229
Scott, William: 77–78
Scott, Gen. Winfield: 148–50, 154
Seekaboo: 88–89, 93
Seminole Indians: 134, 199, 217
Seminole Nation: 167
Seneca Indians: 5, 11
Seneca, Missouri: 184
Sequoyah: 91, 93, 138, 161–62;
    Cherokee syllabary, 105
Sequoyah County, Oklahoma: 139,
    208, 234, 236
Sequoyah District: 211
Sequoyah, State of: 201
Seven Clan Society: 210
Sevier, John: 67, 73–74, 77
Seward, William H.: 174–75

Shabbona: 69

Shade, Hastings: 240

Shawnee Indians: 16, 22, 26, 45–46, 59, 67–68, 85, 139, 184

Shelby, Col. Evan: 67

Shiloh, Battle of: 175

Shorey, William: 49, 53

Sioux Indians: Language: 5

Situwakee: 155

Sixkiller, J. B.: 211

Sixkiller, Lt. William: 209

Skin Bayou District: 167

Sky Vault: 7

Smith, Ben: 211

Smith, Chad: 224, 226–34, 240–41

Smith, John: 139

Smoky Mountains: 89

Sour Mush: 96

South Carolina: 6, 19, 21–29, 34, 36, 39–40, 47–48, 54–55, 58, 64–67, 73–74, 96, 100, 173

Southern Cherokee: 179, 184

South Dakota: 216

Southern Rights Party: 173, 178

Spain: 17–18, 20, 22, 42, 68, 73

Spring Place: 82

St. Francis River: 89

St. Luke's Hospital: 211

Stalking Turkey: 53

Stand Watie: 136, 141, 176, 178

Standing Turkey: 53

Stansill, Hill: 211

Starr, Bean: 162

Starr, Caleb: 64

Starr, Eldee: 211

Starr, Ellis: 162–63

Starr, James: 136, 141, 146, 155, 162, 186

Starr, Tom: 162–63, 186

Starr, Washington: 163

Starr, William: 163

Steiner, Abraham: 82

Stekoih: 150, 152

Stilwell, Oklahoma: 225

Stuart, Henry: 58–60

Stuart, Capt. John: 49, 53–54, 58, 157

Sullacoie: 104

Sunday, W. H.: 211

Swimmer, Ross O.: 220–21, 223, 240

Syacust Ukah: 56

Sycamore Shoals: 56, 58, 62, 65

Tahchee. *See* Captain Dutch

Tahlequah, Oklahoma: 161–69, 174–76, 180–84, 187, 193, 211, 215–19, 225, 230–31, 235, 239

Tahlequah City Police: 233–34

The Tahlequah Daily Press: 225

Tahlequah District: 167, 211

Tahlonteskee: 83, 85–86, 99, 101, 104, 137

Tahtiowie: 33, 38

Tallapoosa: 94

Talligewi: 16

Tanase Warrior: 57

Tawakoni Indians: 139, 144

Taylor, Capt. Richard: 96, 156

Tecumseh: 85, 87–94, 196; death of, 90

Tellico: 28, 31, 36, 41, 79, 165

Tellico River: 46

Tennessee: 6, 18, 25–26, 54–57, 66–67, 81, 90–91, 96, 99–100, 131–33, 141–42, 148, 173–77

Tennessee River: 75, 77–78, 154

Tennison Hotel: 132

Tenskwatawa (the Prophet): 87, 89, 94; and Dance of the Lakes, 87

Terrapin: 57

Texas: 18, 105, 138–39, 145, 160–62, 176, 183, 197, 241

Texas Cherokee Indians: 140, 159–60, 165, 211, 213

Texas Revolution: 140

Thames, Battle of the. *See* War of 1812
Thomas, Heck: 188
Thomas, Paul: 235
Thomas, Will: 150, 177, 189
Thornton, Russell: 89
Timberlake, Henry: 53
Tinsawattee: 104
Tobacco Will: 138
Tohopeka: 91, 94
Tolbert, Paden: 189
Tonto: 69
Trail of Tears: 143–57, 160–62, 171,
    204, 221
Transylvania Company: 57–58, 59,
    62, 65, 74
Treaty of 1846: 163
Treaty of Fort Jackson: 95–96
Treaty of Holston: 75
Treaty of Hopewell: 74–75
Treaty of Long Island: 69
Treaty of New Echota: 137–43, 146, 160
Treaty of Paris: 54, 56
Treaty Party: 159–63, 178
Truman, Harry: 213
Tsali (Charlie): 149–50, 152
Tuckabatchee: 87–88, 94
Tuckasee: 57, 73, 99
Tuckasegee: 31
Tugaloo River: 25, 31, 64
Tuggle, Hiawatha: 209
Tulsa, Oklahoma: 207
Tulsa Cherokees: 203
Turnbull–Lewis, Linda: 234
Tunican Indains: language, 5
Turnip Town: 132, 136
Turtle Fields: 104
Tuscarora: 26, 31, 46
Tuskegee Tribe: 71
Tuskegee Island Town: 67

Uncas: 69

Union Agency: 185
Union Mission: 168, 171
United Foreign Mission Society of
    New York: 171
United Keetoowah Band of
    Cherokee Indians in
    Oklahoma (UKB): 210–11, 224
United States: 5, 18, 105; Army, 137,
    139, 164, 173, 209; Bureau of
    Indian Affairs, 208–10, 215,
    219–24, 231, 233–39; Bureau of
    American Ethnology, 3, 14;
    Civilian Conservation Corps,
    211; Department of Interior,
    211, 214, 220; Department of
    Justice, 233; Civil War, 173–77,
    179, 184, 186; Civilian
    Conservation Corps, 208;
    Congress, 131–33, 141–43, 151,
    194, 198, 201, 211, 215–17, 220,
    222; Revolution. *See* American
    Revolution; Route 66, 204;
    Senate, 146, 221; Supreme
    Court, 134, 136, 170, 205, 217,
    232; treaties, 73–81, 96, 99, 134,
    137–43, 146–51, 163, 170–82
Upper Towns: 25, 47–48, 84, 88, 90, 97
Ustanali: 74, 88–89, 104

Valley Town: 104
Van Buren, Martin: 148
Vann, David: 82, 162
Vann, James: 83–84
Vann, John: 58
Verdigris River: 137
Vicksburg, Battle of: 176
Victory, C.C.: 211
Viles, Philip: 226–27
Vinita, Missouri: 184
Virginia: 6, 22, 25, 27, 45–49, 53–55,
    65–67, 77, 100, 174

Walam Olum: 16

Walker, Capt. John: 96

Walker, John, Jr.: 136, 141

Wampanoag Indians: language, 13

War of 1812: 90–92; Battle of the Holy
    Ground, 91; Battle of
    Horseshoe Bend, 91–92; Battle
    of the Thames, 90

Ward, Bryan: 54, 68

Ward, Nancy: 59–60, 64, 66, 68–70, 97

Ward, Wirtner: 209

Washburn, Rev. Cephas: 137, 139

Washington: 204, 241

Washington, George: 45, 48, 66,
    75–76

Washington, D.C.: 84, 96, 132, 136, 138,
    141, 146, 163, 176, 180–81, 239

Watauga River: 54, 56, 59–60, 62, 64

Watauga settlements: 68

Watie, Stand: 161–65, 173–77, 184

Watts, John: 67, 75–79

West, Lewis: 209

Weatherford, William: 91–92, 94

Webber, Will: 67

Webbers Falls: 174, 184

Webster, Daniel: 148

Weesocks: 21–23

West Virginia: 100

Western Cherokee: 99–100, 104–5,
    137, 139, 142–43, 159–61, 163;
    Council, 203

Western Cherokee Nation: 138

Western dialect: 26

West Virginia: 6, 25

Wickliffe, Charlie: 198

Wilson, Woodrow: 203

Wheeler, Perry: 220, 223

Wheeler–Howard Act. See Indian
    Reorganization Act

White, Brig. Gen. James: 90

White Bear: 8

White House: 132

Whitepath: 155, 196; Nunna-tsunega,
    132, 136

White River: 88, 97, 99

Whitepath Rebellion: 132

Whitehall Palace: 33

Whitemankiller: 77

White's Fort: 75

Wiggan, Eleazar: 33, 35

Wilkins, Thurman: 88

Wilson's Creek, Battle of: 174

Williamsburg: 53

Williamson, Col. Andrew: 64

Willinawa: 57

Wills Town: 67

Will's Valley: 104

Wolf Hills: 60

Wool, General: 146–48

Worcester, Rev. Samuel: 134, 136,
    168–69, 171

Worcester v. Georgia: 136

World War Two: 207–11, 236

Worm: 162

Woyi, Wili: 187–89, 191

Wright, Sharon: 230

Wrosetasatow (Mankiller): 27, 31,
    41, 84

Yamassee Indians: 26, 32; Yamassee
    War: 26

Yellow Locust Fire. See Nighthawk
    Keetoowah Society

Yorktown, Battle of: 68

Younaguska: 150, 152, 159